THE GEORGE GUND FOUNDATION
IMPRINT IN AFRICAN AMERICAN STUDIES

The George Gund Foundation has endowed
this imprint to advance understanding of
the history, culture, and current issues
of African Americans.

LAWYERING FOR LIBERATION

The publisher and the University of California Press Foundation gratefully acknowledge the generous support of the George Gund Foundation Imprint in African American Studies.

LAWYERING FOR LIBERATION

Edited by AMECA REALI *and*
MARBRÉ STAHLY-BUTTS

A TOOLBOX FOR MOVEMENT LAWYERS

UNIVERSITY OF CALIFORNIA PRESS

University of California Press
Oakland, California

Library of Congress Cataloging-in-Publication Data
Names: Reali, Ameca, editor. | Stahly-Butts, Marbre, editor.
Title: Lawyering for liberation : a toolbox for movement lawyers /
    edited by Ameca Reali and Marbre Stahly-Butts
Description: Oakland, California : University of California Press, 2026. |
    Includes bibliographical references and index.
Identifiers: LCCN 2025015436 (print) | LCCN 2025015437 (ebook) |
    ISBN 9780520392359 (hardback) | ISBN 9780520392366
    (paperback) | ISBN 9780520392380 (ebook)
Subjects: LCSH: Cause lawyers—United States—Handbooks,
    manuals, etc. | Public interest lawyers—United States—Handbooks,
    manuals, etc. | Lawyers—Political activity—United States—
    Handbooks, manuals, etc. | Civil rights movements—United States. |
    African Americans—Civil rights. | Social movements—United
    States. | Black lives matter movement—United States. | Social
    justice—United States.
Classification: LCC KF299.P8 L397 2026 (print) | LCC KF299.P8
    (ebook) | DDC 303.48/40243400973—dc23/eng/20250501
LC record available at https://lccn.loc.gov/2025015436
LC ebook record available at https://lccn.loc.gov/2025015437

GPSR Authorized Representative: Easy Access System
Europe, Mustamäe tee 50, 10621 Tallinn, Estonia, gpsr
.requests@easproject.com

34 33 32 31 30 29 28 27 26 25
10 9 8 7 6 5 4 3 2 1

We dedicate this book to our ancestors. Especially the ones whose lives, and deaths, shaped us and the movements we owe our awakening to. Among them we honor the legacy and freedom dreams of KIAH DUGGINS, a Law for Black Lives fellow and the brightest of lights.

We dedicate this book to future generations. Specifically our children, two of whom were born as we wrote, edited, and poured ourselves into this book. ABEO, AMANI SEKOU, and KANANDI BELL: We do this work for you.

Contents

Preface

No one gets free alone, and as long as anyone is unfree, everyone is unfree. We can't do anything alone that's worth it. Everything that is worthwhile is done with other people.

—MARIAME KABA, *We Do This 'til We Free Us* (2021), 178

This book is brought to you by many hands. It was a collective effort, fueled by a commitment to social change and a belief in the dreams of Black radical visionaries. We wanted to include as many voices as possible because freedom work is collective work and because collaboration is at the heart of the political values that underpin Law for Black Lives (L4BL). As such, the perspectives of lawyers, organizers, and people impacted by the oppressive systems that we are fighting against fill the pages that follow.

The first part of this book, "Making Change: The What of Movement Lawyering," features two distinct voices. They are those of the primary authors and editors of this book—two Black women, Marbré Stahly-Butts and Ameca Reali. Each of us traveled a unique path to movement lawyering, and we bring our own set of experiences to the work. Our paths crossed for four formative years at Law for Black Lives, where we both worked supporting movements and lawyers during an epoch of the Black Lives Matter Movement (2019–23).

During our time at Law for Black Lives we developed much of the material that forms the foundation of *Lawyering for Liberation*. The book is especially informed by and modeled after the trainings we did for lawyers, law students, and legal advocates who were new to movement lawyering. The trainings focused on introducing people to movement lawyering and grounding them in the radical politics that inform the work of Law for Black Lives. Those trainings were almost always done in partnership with two or more facilitators and drew upon the expertise of scholars, organizers, lawyers, comrades, clients, and our own experiences doing this work.

The second part of the book, "Get in Formation: The How of Movement Lawyering," is comprised of pieces of different lengths and formats that were developed by people working on the ground. Each contribution offers unique perspectives and insights about the messy, the difficult, and the beautiful things that arise when using imperfect legal tools to help get us closer to a freer and more just world.

Our hope is that you make room for the different textures and tones in each of the contributions. Furthermore, if there is something that you take away, let it be that you don't have to do this alone. In fact, the best way to do this work is with others.

Acknowledgments

This book, like all things worth doing, was a collective effort.

First, it was a product of the vision and the commitment of the collective of lawyers and legal workers who founded Law for Black Lives (L4BL) in 2015. Under the leadership and brilliance of Purvi Shah, Alana Greer, and others, this group of lawyers was able to create a vision and a community that has given birth to so many organizations, countless projects, and certainly this book. Thank you for your commitment to collectivism and liberation.

Law for Black Lives would not have become the organization it is today, and this book would not have been possible, without the support and vision of the L4BL Founding Board. We are so grateful for how you stewarded the organization in those early years and provided invaluable lessons and support. The Founding Board included Daryl Atkinson, Iman Freeman, Anneke Dunbar-Gronke, Andrea James, Scott Roberts, Purvi Shah, Alana Greer, Amna Akbar, Marbré Stahly-Butts, and Vince Warren.

Lawyering for Liberation is a love letter to Black Liberation movements and other radical movements, past and present, that have provided beauty and possibility against all odds. Our commitment to movement lawyering is rooted in our belief in these movements and their vision. We are indebted to the organizations and organizers who have committed themselves to our collective liberation. Thank you.

This book weaves together the experiences, insights, and brilliance of more than thirty-five lawyers, legal workers, and organizers. Thank you to each contributor who shared their words and time and added their voice to this labor of love.

We also are grateful for the contributions of current Law for Black Lives staff members, including Bryce Larkins, who brilliantly helped us design some of the popular education visuals, and Elizabeth Jones and Deanie Anyangwe for their hours and hours of labor helping us with citations.

Lastly, thank you to our families and the villages around us that made the countless hours we poured into this book possible. Your belief in and patience with us are everything. Special shout-out to Gaga Geri and Papa Burvell for the lifetime of unconditional love (and the free childcare).

Together we believe that we will win!

Introduction

Nearly every successful social movement has involved lawyers. While lawyers play a variety of important roles, no social movement has won by relying solely on legal tools or lawyers. To be effective, the law must be used in concert with other tactics and in service of a clear purpose.

This book is about how the law can be used by movement lawyers to fight power and to build power. When organizers and communities are under attack from state actors or vigilantes, the law can mitigate harm, keeping people out of jail or in their homes. In moments like this, when the whole state apparatus is being weaponized against vulnerable communities, skilled lawyers can sometimes slow the machinery of an oppressive state or at least expose its cruelty. At its best the law can create space for folks to continue the liberatory work of organizing. When used to build power, the law can help protect movement wins and memorialize some of the ambitions of movements in the form of policy and precedent.

Movement lawyers (known by a variety of different names, from radical lawyers to community lawyers) are people who have chosen to use the law to build the power of social movements. Movement lawyers are important in defending, advancing, and sustaining movements. While we are not, and should not be, directing social movements, we are an essential part of the movement ecosystem. A cadre of trained, committed, and supported movement lawyers ensures our movements are better able to protect their victories and advance their aims.

After the high-profile killings of Eric Garner, Michael Brown, Sandra Bland, and other Black people in 2014 and 2015, a group of over twenty movement lawyers founded Law for Black Lives. People in cities from Ferguson to Baltimore were rising up in agony and anger. The police responded with tear gas, war tanks, harassment, and surveillance. Politicians responded with false solutions (or what we call reformist reforms) and empty platitudes. Many legacy legal organizations responded by condemning the "protestors" and giving unsolicited advice on how radical young people should conduct themselves.

The founders of Law for Black Lives believed in the visions of the mostly young, mostly Black, mostly working-class protestors and organizers. We believed that the future they were starting to articulate—one free of jails, police, and poverty that centered the power and experience of those historically marginalized, including poor people, queer people, and Black people—was worth fighting for. We believed that together we could create a radically different reality for our communities. And we knew it was their leadership, not ours, that would make that future possible.

We also knew these protestors and organizers needed lawyers. Lawyers to sue the police who were marshaling weapons of war against them. Lawyers to fortify jail support structures and coordinate mass defense when they were arrested and detained. Lawyers to dream and scheme with the evolving movement and help them translate some of their visions into specific policy demands and platforms. The founders and members of Law for Black Lives have served in these roles and many others. This book reflects the lessons we have learned in our capacity as movement lawyers with this specific iteration of a Black liberation movement.

Plenary session at the inaugural Law for Black Lives Conference in New York City, 2015. Courtesy of Center for Constitutional Rights.

Law for Black Lives was also born of the realization that movement lawyers committed to the work of liberation needed a community and a political home to sustain their energy and sharpen their politics and skills. Since the law normally maintains and legitimizes the status quo that lawyers often benefit from, movement lawyering is inherently subversive. It can be isolating. For movement lawyers to effectively support movements, they need to be trained in the politics of the movement they are seeking to support. They need a space to think through the implications of those politics on their legal tactics. A place to hone their tactical interventions. And perhaps most important, they need a place to feel valued so they can sustain the work. Law for Black Lives cultivates community and hope amid a profession that degrades lawyers and legal workers who put people above the law.

Since our founding in 2015, the need for movement lawyers has only increased. We are living in dangerous times. The election of

Donald Trump in 2016 and the normalization of his extreme politics through his reelection in 2024 are painful reminders of the tenacity and power of patriarchy and white-supremacist thought and political organizing. His second term has been a shocking consolidation of the reactionary Right, which promotes a return to a past where women could not control their bodies and when our institutions and halls of power were only open to rich white men. How close we are to a complete breakdown of democracy is evidenced by the decimation of civil society, the destabilization of educational institutions, the undermining of the courts, and the suppression of dissent of all kinds (whether from college students protesting genocide or white-shoe law firms representing the administration's political foes). And despite the continuing crisis of poverty and police violence, cities, states, and the federal government continue to pour billions of dollars into prisons, jails, the militarization of police and our borders, and global aggression, while abandoning the health, housing, and basic needs of our communities. Meanwhile, the United States Supreme Court is effectively turning back the clock on hard-won rights, from bodily autonomy to affirmative action to environmental protections. The rhetoric and actions of the Trump administration and his political allies suggest that we are over the precipice of neofascism. As if that wasn't enough, our planet is beyond its breaking point, and we are starting to see the deadly and irreversible impacts of the human-made climate crisis.

While it feels a lifetime ago, the mass protest movement of 2020 was a glimmer of hope: a reminder that there are millions of people, from diverse backgrounds and identities, who want a different world and will fight for it if given the opportunity. The protests were about racial justice, but they were also demanding the state put people over profit. People flooded the streets to demand that the government respond to the multiple crisis exposed by the pandemic, not with indifference or profiteering but with policies that leverage the immense wealth of the United States toward relief and recovery. All of a sudden, long-standing demands from the Left like debt forgiveness, rent relief, cash payments to families, universal health care, and releasing people from jails and prisons not only felt possible but obvious and necessary.

Considering the transformative possibilities of that moment, it is no surprise that the backlash has been intense and violent. To fight the forces of misogyny, fascism, and racism, we need a massive movement. A movement that is pro-democracy, pro-people, and pro-human rights. It must muster the ambitions and demands of the millions of people who marched, voted, and protested over the past decade. Such a movement, while led by those most impacted, must be flanked by a strong infrastructure of movement lawyers.

There is an urgency to this moment. The only thing left to do is fight. We need to train, support, and grow the ranks of movement lawyers. And we need to do it fast. *Lawyering for Liberation* is meant to be a resource for lawyers and legal workers who want to join this movement and utilize their legal skills to advance it. We hope that this book provides both the theoretical grounding and practical examples needed to start or sustain the journey of movement lawyers now and in the years to come.

This book is written by lawyers and legal workers whose experience and expertise are largely in lawyering with and for Black liberation and civil rights movements. However, we believe that there are many lessons that can apply to a variety of social justice movements. First, the most recent iteration of the movement for Black liberation is intersectional, meaning we embrace the Combahee River Collective's assertion that the freedom of marginalized Black people necessitates the freedom of all people. Therefore our work, though often centered in Black struggle, is deeply concerned with the freedom of all people. Second, we believe that many of the lessons we reflect on from the past decade of movement and backlash contain important harbingers for other movements. As Lani Guinier and Gerald Torres reminded us, Black people are often the "canary in the coal mines." Understanding the responses to Black repression will likely provide a useful roadmap to navigate the repression and suppression of other movements, from climate justice to pro-democracy work.

The book begins with a grounding in the politics and ideologies that animate movement lawyering for liberation. Part I explores what it means to be a movement lawyer, how we believe change happens, and the politics that we believe undergird this specific movement. These political frames help us better diagnose the problems we are facing so that we can develop solutions that grasp at the roots of those problems. We end part I with some of the dos and don'ts of movement lawyering.

In part II we move into praxis, or the symbiotic relationship between practice and theory and how they inform and shape each other. In examining the praxis of movement lawyering, we feature the reflections of twenty movement lawyers and organizers. These chapters are organized by tactic, including rapid response/protest response (chapter 4), litigation (chapter 5), frontline defense (chapter 6), policymaking (chapter 7), and academia (chapter 8). But each chapter asks and attempts to answer the same questions: What are the limitations and the possibilities of using the law to build power with this tactic? What have you learned that will help others more skillfully and effectively support movement? The answers form a mosaic of insights and possibilities about how to approach this work.

We hope that *Lawyering for Liberation* will be a resource for young and old movement lawyers alike. It is an invitation to join, reengage, or sustain a commitment to building power and movement. However you choose to navigate this book, remember: there is a place here for you and we need you.

I *Making Change*

THE WHAT OF MOVEMENT LAWYERING

1   *Revolutions Happen in the Streets Not Courtrooms*

If you are interested in changing things in the world, it is important to think about how change happens. In general, the stories we are told about how any major social change happens focus on heroism, specifically the courageous acts of individuals. That's not to say that change does not occur in these instances, but long-term sustainable change rarely results from the efforts of a single person. Particularly in the United States, popular narratives about major shifts in our culture and society serve to reinforce American values of individualism and exceptionalism. When the individual self is thought to be of the highest value, collective work, especially freedom work, is seen as antithetical to our ethos as a country and is rarely celebrated. Historical accounts of transformational events are told in a way that makes invisible the effort and labor put in by collectives of people, formations, and organizations over time.

One place where these values dominate is in the law and the legal system. We have all seen the movie or heard the tale of a lawyer who set out to right a wrong and became a hero in and out of the courtroom. In these stories the law is seen as the most powerful tool against injustice. However, the idea of using the law as the primary tool for achieving justice or equity is fundamentally flawed because the law is designed to protect the status quo. Lawyers who use traditional lawyering models are often positioned as defenders of inequality, not champions for the common person.

The collective struggle for freedom has been a significant storyline in the histories of people all over the world. At Law for Black Lives (L4BL) we believe that all major positive shifts in culture, laws, or customs happened because a group of people came together, got organized, made demands, and took action in the interest of themselves and others. Put simply, we think change happens through organizing.

This chapter is an exploration of how and why change happens. In the words of Amílcar Cabral, "nobody has yet made a successful revolution without a revolutionary theory."[1] This means, to make any meaningful changes to the world, you must have a vision of the world you want and a plan for how to bring about the changes required to make the vision real. Having a vision and a plan is a key difference between lawyering to build the power of the people and lawyering to build the power of the law. This chapter unpacks some of the ways in which organizing and movement work have been the catalysts for social change but have been left out of the histories we are told. As a cautionary tale, we highlight the ways in which lawyers and the law have worked against social movements. Lastly, the chapter lays the foundation for a key question: What is the role of a movement lawyer at this time in history?

Theory of Change

Theory of change is a concept borrowed from organizers. Organizers often talk about their theory of change before they form coalitions or develop campaign strategies. A theory of change is simply a way to understand how change happens. In other words, what is the world you are fighting for and what do you think you need to do to get there?[2] This informs who organizers are in relationship with and what strategies and tactics they deploy. By developing a clear theory of change, we are better able to create a roadmap of how to realize our visions.

Many people who find themselves in law school are motivated by a desire to change the world in some way. However, it's not uncommon for law students and legal professionals to lack an understanding of how change happens. In law schools and in dominant public narratives, the law is positioned as the primary tool of change and lawyers as the primary architects of change.[3] The legal profession perpetuates this myth by encouraging lawyers to see themselves as the arbiters of what is just and as leaders in our broader society often without an analysis of power, race, gender, class, and their intersections within the law.

Common Theories of Change

To understand how change happens, it is helpful to study history. There are moments throughout history when significant progress has been made to protect human rights and the dignity of oppressed people. Popular narratives, especially in the United States, focus on the heroic actions of an individual or the law as a moral guidepost. However, organizers have been erased from this history, and their collective efforts have been minimized. This section explores common mythologies about how change happens and challenges the dominant narratives about how change occurred.

Lone Brave Actor

One common theory of change is the lone person acting courageously in the face of an extreme challenge. Their frustrations lead to action that causes widespread societal change for all. The story of Rosa Parks and the Montgomery Bus Boycotts is one example of this

Interviews with Lawyers

AMNA A. AKBAR

What is your theory of change?
A theory of change needs a criticism of the world as it is, a horizon in view for the world we hope to live in, and a praxis or practice to bridge the two. These must be fluid and dynamic. In other words, a theory of change must be a working theory—a criticism, horizon, and praxis that respond to the struggles we are engaged in and what we are learning from those struggles and our study of past struggles and struggles around the world. What strategies and tactics are working? How and why are they working? Which ones are not and why not? All of this, we must do together, collectively, with as many people as possible, and with humility, a sense of purpose, tradition—even discipline.

On the Left, there are a range of theories and practices of social change, but at the heart of left theories of social change is a recognition of the power of the people and a commitment to building *popular power*, building the collective power of people subordinated by the long tentacles of capitalism, colonialism, and racism.

A decade ago, one of the hardest lessons for me to learn was the idea that being movement-oriented required moving beyond my area of legal expertise. That it didn't matter very much what I knew as a lawyer or as an academic. Instead, I need to pay attention to people's militancy, social and collective unrest and energy, where people are agitated and moving together in one way or another. From there I could learn what I needed to learn to support those struggles. Always we need to be asking how to deploy our skills, aptitudes, and relationships—our care—in support of social organization of Black, Brown, and working-class and poor people against the status quo and toward something new.

Why is a theory of change important for movement lawyers?
A theory of change helps us understand what we are doing and why.

We have seen incredible organizing, campaigns, and people's riots and rebellions on the streets since Occupy in 2011. Ferguson in 2014. Baltimore in 2015. Standing Rock in 2016. Minneapolis in 2020. The Palestinian solidarity student encampments of spring 2024. Historic strikes among teachers, nurses, writers, dockworkers, and autoworkers. A lot of organizing and activism made those moments of social insurgency possible: building capacity and shifting popular consciousness around state and imperial violence and exploitation. Unbearable injustice, racism, violence, expropriation, exploitation, and premature death produced this long cycle of struggle. There is a lot to learn from this period about the mechanics of racism, capitalism, and colonialism; how vulnerable to challenge they are, and how obdurate and adaptable they are. This raises serious questions about what movements, and in turn, what lawyers should be doing.

Right now, we are arguably still living in a time of flourishing left politics: we have lots of podcasts, books, and zines about capitalism, racial capitalism, and heteropatriarchy, Marxism, communism, socialism, prison abolition, anarchism, abolition democracy, and more. Our critiques and our horizons are as sharp as they have been during my lifetime. Don't get me wrong: we have room to grow, loads to learn from each other, from careful study of the world around us, and from past freedom struggles and their intellectual traditions.

But where we have the most work to do is on the organizing popular power front. The Left is struggling to build organizations that are democratic and rooted in a base and running and winning strategic campaigns that respond to people's needs. That puts us at a real disadvantage when we face off with capital, police and prosecutors, and the right wing, who respond to the crises of capitalism and colonialism in perverse ways that double down on preserving the status quo, even making things worse.

A primary footprint of the past decade of racial justice protests and uprising is within the nonprofit structure. There are real limits to a social movement and social change projects where campaigns and projects are largely rooted in 501(c)(3).

How should a theory of change impact movement lawyers' work?
The ecosystem for movement lawyering has changed in the past ten years in ways that reflect differing theories of social change and the need for more capacity and experimentation with what legal support looks like. The older professional and membership-based movement lawyering shops like the National Lawyers Guild and the National Conference

for Black Lawyers have had revivals to varying degrees. Organizations forged within the crucible of twentieth-century struggles like the People's Law Office and the Center for Constitutional Rights (CCR) continue to play important roles. There are a whole host of new organizations—Law for Black Lives (L4BL), the Detroit Justice Center, the Amistad Law Project, the Community Justice Project, the Abolitionist Law Center, the Movement Law Lab, the Baltimore Action Legal Team (BALT)—and some more medium-term, like the Advancement Project and the Sylvia Rivera Law Project. These organizations do mass defense, bring civil rights lawsuits, provide political education and training, and write reports and provide support for all sorts of policy support. They work on housing justice and racial justice; they are embedded within abolitionist, feminist, and anticapitalism struggles; they support community organizing and movement building.

Some of these formations were born out of particular episodes of struggle and the recognition of the need for legal support against carceral power: for example, the Water Protectors Legal Collective that was born out of the #NoDAPL Standing Rock encampment from 2016. Lawyers at some legal aid and legal services chapters, as well as law school clinics, work with movement-based organizations and community-based groups in various law and organizing projects. You have organizations doing essential legal work without necessarily relying on lawyers like community bail funds and participatory defense hubs.

This list is not complete. I know less, for example, about the legal flanks for labor and worker organizing. We need to map this together. As we move forward, we have to figure out how best to support the building of people power, how to grow our movements, how to offer our skills and our whole selves to these long freedom struggles we are so lucky to be a part of. We have to figure out where legal support is needed and assess critically where we are showing up and how, where what we are doing is working, and where we are hitting walls. We must take failure as a place from which to learn and to move differently.

One of the things we've seen across the country is how quickly the state will criminalize movements. That signals our power and our vulnerability. While we have gotten more organized with legal observing and jail support in many parts of the country, we are still relatively disorganized in providing criminal defense or legal services or advice at the point when the cops are knocking on doors and police are prosecuting people. This is a real and persistent challenge, and we have yet to meet that need as lawyers, legal workers, and law students. We have to figure out how to grow our ranks as people with legal skills committed to democratizing and distributing their deployment.

Organizers from Atlanta's Stop Cop City struggle talk about the need to respect "multiple grammars of struggle." People with different theories of change, who deploy distinct strategies and tactics, must understand that they need each other. As lawyers and legal workers, we must develop our capacity to support the multiple grammars of struggle necessary to meet the challenges of a planet and the form of the nation-state in crisis. The stakes couldn't be grander, but we have to build from a sober assessment of where we are.

theory of change. As it has been told, Ms. Parks, a seamstress, was tired after a long day at work and was riding the bus home. A white passenger wanted her seat and she in her exhaustion refused, knowing the consequences. Police were called and she was arrested, which led to the Montgomery Bus Boycotts and eventually the desegregation of public transit in Alabama and the country. But Black resistance to discrimination in public transit was happening long before Rosa Parks refused to get up. In fact, over one hundred years before Parks, New York City's rail service was desegregated after the 1854 arrest and trial of Black school teacher Elizabeth Jennings.[4] Around the same time Frederick Douglass was kicked off a segregated train car after attempting to integrate it.

Before Parks refused to give up her seat, tension had been building because of resistance to segregation all over the South. Organizers across the region were beginning to develop innovative strategies to address segregation. Black riders on public transit were required to sit in a section at the back of the bus that was designated for them. However, if they sat in the front or the middle of the bus and a white passenger was standing, they could be asked to get up. Black riders were subject to humiliation, disrespect, and removal from the drivers and other riders. Drivers and employees of the bus company often struck Black passengers. In fact, Parks and the driver of the bus had several previous altercations during which he threatened to physically harm her.[5]

Three women in Montgomery had been arrested for refusing to give up their seats on a bus before Parks. Claudette Colvin was a fifteen-year-old student who was riding the bus with classmates after school. She was asked to give up her seat but refused, even though her classmates moved and there were empty seats available. When the white passenger refused to sit next to Colvin, she was arrested. Despite the potential danger, Colvin intended to resist and to provoke a confrontation. Her arrest caused Martin Luther King Jr. to join the discussions among Black residents about boycotting.[6] These incidents did not happen in isolation; instead they escalated efforts that had already been under way to challenge Jim Crow segregation. One thing that made Parks's arrest a tipping point was that there was a movement of organizations and individuals behind her who had been preparing for that moment. This included local churches as well as Black political organizations and professional groups.

Rosa Parks was not just a tired old lady. She was an organizer. She was an active and engaged member of her community and had been aware of some of the arrests on buses in Montgomery. She was a member of the local NAACP chapter along with Claudette Colvin. The NAACP in Montgomery had been involved in efforts to end segregation, and they supported the bus boycotts. They used Highlander Folk School as a training ground for civil rights activists and a meeting space for organizers of the movement. Parks attended training at Highlander just months before she was arrested on the bus.[7] Interestingly, a lot of her organizing focused on the rampant sexual assault of Black women and the fraudulent accusations of rape and sexual assault charges directed at Black men, like the Scottsboro Nine or Emmett Till, which Parks viewed as symptomatic of white patriarchy and anti-Blackness.[8]

When the boycotts finally began, they lasted for thirteen months. About two months into the boycotts, four women who had been treated similarly to Parks—Colvin and Aurelia Browder, Mary Louise Smith, and Susie McDonald—filed a lawsuit challenging segregation on public transit.[9] While the legal battle moved through the courts, the boycotts continued to put pressure on the transit system and local officials. Local people and organizations built a deep organizing and mutual aid infrastructure to sustain the direct action. This infrastructure was an organizing triumph. Hundreds volunteered and various measures were put in place to make sure that the boycott could be sustained. People started carpools, taxi drivers lowered taxi fares, and others walked. Some organizations decided to take on desegregation by engaging in political education, tactical training, and strategic interventions. Even though the courts eventually ruled in favor of desegregating buses, organizers continued their efforts until it was implemented in Montgomery.[10]

The Montgomery Bus Boycotts weren't about one tired woman. There was an entire community of people, some who were trained and organized to push back against segregation that resulted in the buses being desegregated.[11] When we rely on theories of change that are individualized, we erase the work and ideas of groups of everyday people. Often this means erasing the labor of women and people who are not in positions of authority. When we disregard the brilliance of people and movements whose love for others has enabled us to get closer to a more just world, we deny their power and capacity to bring about change.

Charismatic Leader

Another common theory of change is that of the charismatic leader. This theory relies on the idea that one single person can make a lasting and widespread impact, even inside of systems that are carefully designed to oppress and control people. This leader is often seen as having exceptional skills that the common person does not possess. This person is magnetic, drawing people in and convincing powerful people to bend to the will of those who are oppressed. Not coincidentally, this person is often a man, almost always cisgender, and rarely queer.

Nelson Mandela is a great example of this theory of change. He has been portrayed by some as the man who single-handedly ended apartheid. However, he was part of an international movement led by South Africans that had been waged over decades to bring about a democratic South Africa. And while Mandela spent decades in prison for his anti-apartheid work, thousands of people created the conditions for his release and ultimately his successful leadership.[12]

Apartheid was a system of racial segregation and oppression that was codified into law in 1950 by the Afrikaners who had come into power through an election that banned Black South Africans. Apartheid was preceded by hundreds of years of colonial occupation, land dispossessions, and economic and social exclusion of Black South Africans. Characterized by violence and acts of repression by the government, this period was also filled with acts of resistance by Black South Africans and their allies. The African National Congress (ANC), founded in the early 1900s, played a significant role in the fight to end apartheid. Mandela was a young lawyer working in Johannesburg when he joined the ANC in 1943. He eventually led the armed wing of ANC, or the uMkhonto we Sizwe ("Spear of the Nation"), which formed in 1961. Mandela's activities as a leader in the ANC were what eventually led to his arrest and incarceration for decades.[13]

A series of actions taken by Mandela, his comrades in the ANC and the Pan African Congress, as well as a national and international movement put pressure on the government to end apartheid. In the

Black township of Sharpeville, for example, actions were organized to protest the passbook requirements. Anyone who was not white was required to carry one and supply it on demand to police or risk being arrested and jailed. In 1960, when twenty thousand people marched to a police station in Sharpeville without their passbooks, the police responded with machine guns. Almost two hundred people were injured and eleven thousand were arrested. Most of the dead were women and children. This brought international attention to the fight against apartheid.

The Sharpeville incident is illustrative of the size and power of the movement to end apartheid.[14] The movement utilized many different tactics and required support from a broad base of people both in the country and across the world to sustain. These tactics included boycotts, sanctions, and cultural organizing, among others. Laborers and students can be credited with organizing some of the most effective actions in the fight. Recognizing that the apartheid economy relied heavily on Black laborers, in 1973 nearly thirty thousand workers walked off their jobs and went on strike in Durban. That inspired the 1976 efforts by students to boycott the newly passed law that required Black schools to teach all subjects in Afrikaans and English in equal amounts. Over ten thousand students, led by the Soweto Students Representative Council's Action Committee, left school and took to the streets. Police responded by unleashing dogs and shooting. This protest put additional pressure on the international community to act to end apartheid.[15]

The struggle to end apartheid was one that took place in streets across South Africa and in solidarity across the world. While Mandela's skills led him to be a successful leader in the movement, his actions alone did not bring the end of the Afrikaans government. Furthermore, the end of apartheid did not bring about a material change in conditions for Black South Africans. Nelson Mandela personifies the reality that movements create the path for powerful and charismatic leaders to step up. However, leaders do not make movements.[16] When we center only those who are charismatic, we are in opposition to the idea that all people can and should play a role in their own liberation.

Legal Victories

One very popular theory of change is that of legal victories. This is the idea that substantial societal change can be brought about by engaging in and winning litigation. There is perhaps no better example of this theory of change than school desegregation—specifically, the decision in *Brown v. Board of Education of Topeka*.[17] In 1954 the Court held in *Brown* that the separate-but-equal standard that was established in an 1896 case, *Plessy v. Ferguson*, was not constitutional and that separate facilities in public schools violated the constitutional rights of children.[18]

Students across the United States, particularly in public schools, are taught in history classes and law school seminars that *Brown* and its successor *Brown II* were the impetus for school integration. Over the years school desegregation, the *Brown* decisions, and all the work done by NAACP in an effort to desegregate schools has become associated with educational equity and advancement for Black students and students of color.[19] However, schools today are largely still segregated. White parents still wage battles to keep Black students out of majority-white schools. So why were these landmark Supreme Court decisions not successful in integrating schools and society?[20]

First, it was primarily a legal strategy to end segregation broadly. The NAACP chose to focus on challenging segregation in schools because of the obvious and stark differences in facilities, materials, and teacher pay. It was also seen as an egregious kind of racial discrimination because it was being aimed at children and their education. There had previously been cases brought by parents across the country in South Carolina, Virginia, Delaware, and Washington, DC. In these cases students had been denied access to school facilities near them or to school facilities that had been funded adequately because of their race. The NAACP's solution to this was to file a series of lawsuits with the primary goal of establishing legal precedent that would set the stage for nationwide desegregation. When recalcitrant school boards and angry parents refused to comply with *Brown*, the NAACP sought an order from the Supreme Court to hurry things along. In 1955 the Supreme Court in *Brown II* did not grant the request, instead only requiring that desegregation proceed with "all deliberate speed."[21]

Armed with the Supreme Court's ruling in *Brown II*, the NAACP started the job of implementing their plan by engaging local lawyers to litigate parents' grievances. Soon it became apparent that there were unforeseen consequences resulting from the focus on legal victories. Children who integrated schools at the time suffered humiliation and violence, at the hands of parents, students, and some teachers. School expulsions and disciplinary action against Black students in integrated schools were high—a phenomenon that continues today.[22] Even though children had been previously denied admission to schools near their homes because of their race, students under the *Brown* ruling were sometimes bussed into schools miles away or into school settings that were worse for them than the schools they attended prior to enforced desegregation.

Most important, some parents in places like Boston and Atlanta noticed that their children's access to quality education had not improved. Even after all the litigation, better educational outcomes for Black students were elusive. Parents in Boston penned a letter to the federal judge overseeing their cases which demanded that student performance and educational quality be placed in school desegregation plans. The letter was signed by parents and Black leaders in the community.[23] In Atlanta, parents and community members decided that integration of their school by bussing was not as important as improving the schools that their children were already enrolled in. They asked that the Atlanta plan include less bussing and more mandates for the school district to hire Black teachers and administrators. The local school board, the community, parents, and even the local NAACP chapter president endorsed the new plan, but the national organization opposed it.

Lawyers, singularly focused on enforcing the legal victory of desegregation, disregarded the wishes of communities and parents and their desires for their children's future. Even when their legal solutions were causing young people and their families to endure very difficult conditions and educational outcomes were stagnant, lawyers stuck to the plan. Desegregation was not the same as a quality education for some families, and lawyers ignored that, even after parents vocalized it. What was legal in the context of the *Brown* decisions was not the justice that some parents were seeking when they opted into school desegregation lawsuits. Placing all trust in a system that is not built to deliver just outcomes is one of the primary issues with this theory of change. The nature of litigation is such that it is easy for people and movements to get lost or made secondary to legal processes. Moreover, litigation is not a self-actualizing engine of change. Changes require organized movements and political will to enforce.

The Theory of Movement Lawyering

Even though lawyers have been working with radical social movements for as long as people have been organizing themselves and building power, there isn't one universally agreed-upon definition of movement lawyering. It has been referred to by many different names over time. That may be because movement lawyering as a praxis has evolved as well, in part as a response to the critiques of other ways of lawyering and in part a recognition that lawyers can

Interviews with Lawyers

OMAVI SHAKUR

What is your theory of change?
This offering is but one of many theories of change that complement, inform, and challenge each other. It evolves with each movement convening, conversation with my niece, and subway ride. Put plainly, it is not to be read as definitive. It flows from a single voice in a chorus chanting down Babylon. South African freedom fighter Steve Biko encouraged Black people to be conscious of the forces they fight against, the future they fight for, and strategies needed to realize this liberated future. I have engaged in this analysis in community, along a dirt road in Arkansas, in the jails of New Orleans, and in a tenement in East Flatbush. My experience has taught me that by learning, strategizing, and organizing alongside and amid vulnerable communities, movement lawyers can help marginalized people realize transformative shifts in consciousness and power.

Elites currently horde power, privilege, and prestige. Their ability to do so largely derives from the displacement and slaughter of Indigenous peoples and the enslavement and subordination of Black people. It also derives from the vindictive neglect of women, disabled people, migrants, nonbinary people, and labor. The white social dominance fueled by these harms is sustained by violence, such as punitive policing, incarceration, and militarism at home and throughout the Global South. Amid this oppression, we—oppressed peoples—are envisioning and realizing a healthy, healing, nonhierarchical society. One in which collectives work together to reduce future harms, provide reparation to those affected by past and present harms, and create an empowering environment designed for all to thrive. As we fight for this just society, vulnerable communities must have protection from violence and despair, harms must be reduced and repaired, and nurturing spaces must be created.

In community, we must devise and carry out cunning strategies that have scientific, spiritual, and artistic dimensions. Recognizing that "dogmatism and tribalism are the twin enemies of revolution," our energy is better spent discerning relationships of oppression than debating over hierarchies of oppression. All the while, we should never entertain the thought of losing.

Why is a theory of change important for movement lawyers?
A theory of change should help the movement lawyer maintain perspective while navigating various legal systems. Litigation and other legal tools may help more community members live to see a just society than would otherwise. Legal tools may also increase the agency of vulnerable community members navigating various legal systems. Thus legal skills should be made available to formations struggling for liberation.

How should a theory of change impact movement lawyers' work?
My theory of change has been my anchor when a judge yells at me for preserving an issue for appeal during a jury trial. It has guided me to negotiate for settlement terms that reflect the desires of impacted communities. It has meant agreeing to take my client's case to trial against the advice of my trial chief (and winning) and not forcing another client to go to trial to get more attorney's fees.

A movement lawyer's theory of change should also impel them to leverage their privilege on behalf of the vulnerable and to take their advocacy out of the courtroom. For example, mine led me to translate formerly incarcerated people's demands for food stamp and welfare benefits into legislation. The interest of clients and vulnerable communities predominate. Properly wielded, legal skills may also help raise people's awareness about the harm-inducing dimensions of white supremacist, capitalist, imperialist, heteronormative patriarchy. Such an awareness undermines the logic undergirding—and sharpens subalterns' critiques of—the prevailing unjust order.

play a meaningful role in lasting social change but not primarily as the leaders.

Movement lawyering as an approach is rooted in a theory of change that centers collective action and building power.[24] It is a way of using legal skills and training to support and advance social movements, defined as the building and exercise of collective power, led by the most directly impacted, to achieve transformative change.[25] To that end, movement lawyering is about the relationship between the law and social change.[26] The primary role of a lawyer or legal worker inside of any community-led effort is twofold: to fight power and to build power. Fighting power is helping communities and organizers identify and break down centers of oppressive power. Building power is helping them get closer to enacting and sustaining change often through stronger organizations.[27] For L4BL, much of what has informed our understanding of how lasting change happens is the recognition that many successful struggles for freedom were not won in courtrooms.

Subsequent chapters of this book include a lot of tips, ideas, and perspectives about how to be a movement lawyer, and in some instances, how not to be. What is important to emphasize about movement lawyering and the theory of change that undergirds it are the following: Legal education and conventional lawyering teach us that power rests in legal institutions and with legal practitioners. Movement lawyering is the practice of not only sharing power but also a commitment to helping to build power with and for marginalized and oppressed groups in favor of a just outcome.[28] Traditional lawyering is practiced without regard for the power everyday people have in participating in their own liberation and movements for the liberation of others. Movement lawyering seeks to protect and expand that power. As movement lawyers, we commit to sharing power with movements, often taking direction from movement leaders and organizers. That does not mean that movement lawyers are passively involved in struggles for freedom. Movement lawyers are just as interested in the outcome and use our skill and legal training to assist and advance movement goals. Solidarity is a necessary prerequisite to movement lawyering.

A commitment to self-reflection is also critical. Because lawyers who choose this path are simultaneously engaged both in unlearning and building new skills and techniques, we must be constantly reflecting and asking for feedback. This is a characteristic of movement lawyering, especially for those who aim at pushing back against oppressive systems.

. • .

People organized, acting together, have been the primary force for measurable and lasting social change. There are countless documented and undocumented examples to support that assertion. L4BL is committed to working with groups that have a vision for change that expands beyond what is legal and in favor of what is just. Throughout history, lawyers have done more harm to movements than good, all the while being romanticized as heroes. The kind of lawyers we need are those who are ready to shift power, to work creatively and collectively with organizers. It is not a status to be achieved but rather a set of practices and politics that you refine as you use them and as the political landscape and material conditions of people fluctuate and change.[29] In chapter 2 you will learn more about the political values and lenses that we apply to the work of movement lawyering and how that shapes the work.

Learn Something from This

- The theory of change embraced by movement lawyers is that sustainable change happens through shifting power to communities most impacted, which is best accomplished through organizing.
- Being clear on your theory of change, including understanding your vision for the world and how you get there, is essential in the work of a movement lawyer.
- When analyzing the stories we are told about how change occurs, we should interrogate those that place a high value on individual effort over collective action.

- Having an analysis of power and how it can be shifted and built among marginalized people will help you better understand your role as a movement lawyer.
- Even though it can be used to mitigate harm or advance movement goals, the law is a tool of social control. If we align ourselves with movement, we must work to understand our role in this system of control. We must always be thinking about how this privilege shows up in our work.

Resources

- The Ayni Institute, a movement training organization, has a series of virtual trainings focused on different approaches to social change and what they call the movement ecosystem. You can check out their resources at their website and on their YouTube channel. We specifically suggest you watch Part 4 of their "Intro to Movement Strategy" on theories of change: www.youtube.com/watch?v=eLF2_K70SyE.
- Jennifer Gordon's law review article on the role of movement lawyers in the United Farm Workers organization is a helpful grounding on how a theory of change focused on building the power of directly impacted people can mold a legal strategy. Check out her 2005 article in volume 8 of the *Pennsylvania Journal of Labor and Employment Law*: "Law, Lawyers, and Labor: The United Farm Workers' Legal Strategy in the 1960s and 1970s and the Role of Law in Union Organizing Today."

Reflection

How do you think change happens? Think of one or two historical examples that affirm or illustrate your theory of change.

Notes

1. Amílcar Cabral, *Tell No Lies, Claim No Easy Victories* (Inkani Books, 2022).

2. Center for Theory of Change, www.theoryofchange.org/what-is-theory -of-change/toc-background, accessed April 19, 2022.

3. Luz E. Herrera and Louise G. Trubek, "The Emerging Legal Architecture for Social Justice," 44 *N.Y.U. Rev. L. & Soc. Change* 355 (2020), https://scholarship .law.tamu.edu/facscholar/1427.

4. Olivia B. Waxman, "'I Was Not Going to Stand.' Rosa Parks Predecessors Recall Their History-Making Acts of Resistance," *Time*, March 2, 2020, https:// time.com/5786220/claudette-colvin-mary-louise-smith.

5. Jeanne Theoharis, "Rosa Parks: 'I Had Been Pushed as Far as I Could Stand,'" *Salon*, February 3, 2013, www.salon.com/2013/02/03/rosa_parks_i_had _been_pushed_as_far_as_i_could_stand.

6. Waxman, *supra* note 4.

7. Theoharis, *supra* note 5.

8. Angela Y. Davis, Gina Dent, Erica R. Meiners, and Beth E. Richie, *Abolition. Feminism. Now* (Haymarket, 2022), 34.

9. Browder v. Gayle, 142 F. Supp 707 (M.D. Ala. 1956), aff'd 352 U.S. 903 (1956).

10. The Martin Luther King, Jr. Research and Education Institute, "Browder v. Gayle, 352 U.S. 903," https://kinginstitute.stanford.edu/browder-v-gayle -352-us-903, accessed August 29, 2024.

11. Theoharis, *supra* note 5.

12. "Unit 5. Reigniting the Struggle: The 1970s through the Release of Mandela," Michigan State University African Studies Center, https://overcomingapartheid .msu.edu/unit.php?kid=163-571-7&page=2, accessed July 12, 2023.

13. "Apartheid," History.com, October 7, 2010, www.history.com/topics /africa/apartheid.

14. Becky Little, "Key Steps That Led to the End of Apartheid," History.com, November 20, 2020, www.history.com/news/end-apartheid-steps?li_source= LI&li_medium=m2m-rcw-history.

15. Lester R. Kurtz, "The Anti-Apartheid Struggle in South Africa (1912–1992)," International Center on Nonviolent Conflict, June 2010, www.nonviolent-conflict .org/anti-apartheid-struggle-south-africa-1912-1992, accessed April 22, 2025.

16. Jeb Larson, "4 Lessons on Organizing from the Anti-Apartheid Movement," *Teen Vogue*, June 16, 2020, www.teenvogue.com/story/anti-apartheid -movement-organizing.

17. Brown v. Board of Education, 347 U.S. 483 (1954).

18. Plessy v. Ferguson, 163 U.S. 537 (1896).

19. Derrick A. Bell Jr., "Serving Two Masters: Integration Ideals and Client Interests in School Desegregation Litigation," 85 *Yale L.J.* 470 (1976).

20. Nikole Hannah-Jones, "Choosing a School for My Daughter in a Segregated City," *New York Times Magazine*, June 9, 2016, www.nytimes.com/2016/06/12/magazine/choosing-a-school-for-my-daughter-in-a-segregated-city.html.

21. Brown v. Board of Education II, 349 U.S. 294 (1955).

22. Hawkins v. Coleman, 376 F.Supp.1330 (N.D. Tex. 1974).

23. Bell, *supra* note 19.

24. Jonathan McCully, "Join Our Workshop on Movement and Community Lawyering in London," Digital Freedom Fund, June 9, 2022, https://digitalfreedomfund.org/join-our-workshop-on-movement-and-community-lawyering-in-london. This is something we attribute to Purvi Shah, and we have long used it without any citation. For the purposes of this book, we found her quotes as saying it, which is cited here.

25. Betty Hung, "Movement Lawyering as Rebellious Lawyering: Advocating with Humility Love and Courage," 23 *Clinical L. Rev.* 663 (2017).

26. Susan Carle and Scott Cummings, "The Ethics of Movement Lawyering," 31 *Geo. J. Legal Ethics* 447, 452 (2018).

27. Vince Warren, "Movement Lawyering," online lecture (recorded video), July 11, 2023.

28. *Id.*

29. Susan Carle, "Ethics and the History of Social Movement Lawyering," *Wis. L. Rev. Forward* 12 (2018), https://digitalcommons.wcl.american.edu/facsch_lawrev/1370.

2 Beyond Your Mama's Liberation Movement

A Grounding in Our Politics

It is difficult in this moment, as communities navigate the violent anti-trans, anti-immigrant, and anti-DEI (read anti-women, anti-disabled, anti-Black) politics, to remember that over the past decade we have witnessed a rare period of sustained movement here in the United States (and globally). These movements include the 2011 Occupy Wall Street protests, the organizing led by young people for immigration reform, the Black Lives Matter movement, Standing Rock and the Indigenous People's movement, and the global solidarity movement against the war on Gaza. These movements have gone through cycles of mass protest, base building, electoral engagement, political sharpening, and of course backlash. Donald Trump's second presidency is a powerful, and scary, manifestation of the backlash to the sustained nature of social and culture change through the 2010s.[1] In many ways the intensity of the backlash discloses the revolutionary possibilities of these movements, many of which imagined a whole different world based on a reckoning with the past.

These movements developed within a neoliberal state and amid increased militarization, escalating environmental catastrophes, resurgent anti-Blackness and xenophobia, visible and widespread white nationalism and in the face of a global pandemic. Despite, or perhaps because of, this unique concoction of circumstances, the contemporary iteration of the Black freedom struggle is more visionary than any other.[2] Organizers' vision of liberation leaves nobody behind. They are indicting systems of racial hierarchy as well as those that perpetuate gender violence, environmental destruction, and poverty. They are fighting for transformation of the systems that harm us while recognizing that true transformation requires that our movements, our relationships, and we as individuals are open to transformation.

A key difference between traditional lawyering, even traditional movement lawyering, and the type of lawyering we champion is we believe effective movement lawyering requires a grounding in a set of political beliefs. Your political beliefs shape your relationships and help determine what tactics and strategies you deploy. Lawyering is never apolitical. If you are not clear about which political ideologies guide your work, you are likely complicit in legitimizing the current prevailing political ideologies including white supremacy, capitalism, and patriarchy. When we say "politics" we are not talking about your political affiliations. We do not mean whether you vote Democratic or Republican (or frankly even if you vote). We are talking about how you interpret new information. How do you understand the problems we face? What do you think causes them?

When we say "politics" at Law for Black Lives (L4BL), we are really referring to a combination of political ideologies and personal values. What the Black queer feminist organization Black Youth Project 100 (BYP100) calls your "political lens."[3] A lens is a helpful way to understand it because if you wear glasses, you see the world through a lens. Depending on the type of lens you are wearing, you see the world differently.[4] Similarly, the political lenses you adopt will help you understand the world and will help you identify the appropriate use of your legal skills. The more developed your politics, the more able you are to make accurate assessments that allow for impactful legal interventions.

As abolitionist organizer and author Mariame Kaba writes, "when we set about trying to transform society, we must remember that we ourselves also need to transform. Our imagination of what a different world can be is limited. We are deeply entangled in the very systems we are organizing to change."[5] This is especially true for lawyers because many of us depend on these systems for jobs and legitimacy. In order for us to be effective co-conspirators to liberation movements, we must commit to our own continuing transformation. Part of that journey is a disciplined commitment to engage in study and political education. At L4BL we have chosen to adopt the lenses of abolition, Black queer feminism(s), and anticapitalism.

We adopt these political ideologies because these are the politics of the organizations we were founded to lawyer on behalf of. This is not a coincidence. We seek to serve movements for Black liberation because we see ourselves as part of those movements. We do not see ourselves as tacticians inside of someone else's movement. We regard ourselves as active participants who bring a set of specific legal tools to the table. It is essential that movement lawyers find alignment with the movements they work on behalf of.

We also adopt this set of politics because we believe in the radical nature of them. When we say "radical" we are referring to the definition offered by civil rights organizer Ella Baker, who defined "radical" as "grasping at and understanding the root cause" of the systemic problems we are facing.[6]

We believe that our communities cannot be liberated if we do not account for and address white supremacy, patriarchy, and capitalism. To win real change, we must move beyond just treating symptoms and start to address the underlying and long-standing causes of the issues facing our communities. Our failure to address root causes is why we continue to see new manifestations of age-old oppressions. Slavery gives way to convict leasing, which gives way to Jim Crow, which gives way to racialized incarceration followed by racialized mass surveillance. This evolution is a result of us never addressing the way that racialized capitalism undergirds each of these phenomena. The list will go on and on unless we commit ourselves to transforming and not just tweaking the current systems and practices that govern our lives.

The politics you embrace will dictate the type of lawyer you are. The white nationalist and fascists movement has lawyers too (and unfortunately for us, they are not all as incompetent as Rudy Giuliani). Often lawyers serving white supremacist or fascist movements shroud themselves in narratives of apoliticalness or legal objectivity. However, their actions, their affiliations, and their work disclose their political commitments. This is part of why we so fervently reject the mythology of the apolitical lawyer. As Charlene Carruthers has written, "what we believe to be true matters for our movements. What we believe impacts how we move in the world, what we imagine is possible, what we choose to fight for, and what we fight against."[7]

If you are trying to lawyer in relationship with social movements, you must be rooted in a set of political beliefs and values. You don't have to believe what we believe, in fact we hope you hone and develop your own political beliefs. But you do have to be clear on what you believe. Take the time to study, sharpen, and adapt. This chapter provides a very brief overview of the politics that we root our practice in. We hope this grounding helps you better understand the contributions in part II "Get in Formation: The How of Movement Lawyering" and reiterates the importance of politics to legal practice.

However, this book is not primarily about these political ideologies. The explanations that follow are incomplete and cursory. We encourage you to engage with organizing groups, political organizations, colleagues and comrades to explore and sharpen your politics.

To get a sense of what these politics look like in action, throughout the chapter you will find excerpts of short conversations with lawyers who are incorporating these politics into their practice. At the end of the chapter we provide reading lists and resources if you are interested in learning more. We hope you engage with these ideas. But political lenses should shift and grow as we do the work. It is essential that you are in community with organizers and other lawyers and legal workers as you embark on your political education journey.

Our Politics

Prison Industrial Complex Abolition

For lawyers and legal workers, abolition of the prison industrial complex (PIC) may seem like an extreme stance. It means disavowing systems from which many of us derive much of our professional identity and privilege. And yet abolition is becoming increasingly appealing, as contributors detail in chapter 6, to many lawyers who have spent years in the belly of the beast.

Because of my own experiences as a Black woman who saw people I care about entangled in the criminal legal system, I was always skeptical of it. But I became an abolitionist in the aftermath of the failure to prosecute the killers of Michael Brown and Eric Garner as well as the failure to convict the killer of Reika Boyd. The failures of the criminal legal system to hold itself accountable made me feel hopeless. But the vision and energy of organizers made me realize that we could imagine, organize, and implement systems of care and accountability that were not based in racism, violence, and exploitation. In other words I came to the political ideology of abolition on the wave of mass movement. The organizing and agitating that characterized the summer of 2015 into the summer of 2016 made me realize a world beyond my imagination was possible, and our understanding of "justice" did not have to be limited to a violent system that was never meant to keep us safe.

Interviews with Lawyers

AL BROOKS

What does "abolition" mean to you?
Abolition is a movement to make the self-determination of oppressed people possible. It is a path we walk down, and make for ourselves, that points at the world we all deserve to live in. The meaning of "abolition" evolves constantly for me and branches out and touches countless intersecting movements. It envisions a fundamental transformation of our social order, which is beyond any single person or group's imagination. Fundamentally, abolition means building systems that support self-determination, like free and equitable education, health care, housing, and food. It also means freeing people from systems that *prevent* self-determination, like prisons, police, and other forms of systemic oppression through which we devote time and money to fighting among ourselves. Abolition is not an abstract cure-all pipe dream. Abolition involves a lot of hard, thankless, unsexy work, and leaps of faith. Abolition means each individual taking accountability for ourselves. We can build from that basis to make communities where mutual trust enables mutual support, and we can each free each other.

What are the roots of abolition?
The roots of abolition are in societies that did not have carceral states. They prove that carceral state abolition is possible because it has already happened. While no society has been perfect, when the Arawaks first encountered Columbus, they had no police and no prisons, but they did have safety and systems of mutual support. The United States had no police or prisons until the white elites began using poor white people to chase people escaping slavery and violently repressing people organizing against class inequality. The carceral state exists to pit us against each other and force us to yield accountability over ourselves and our communities to those in power. Anyone challenging these oppressive uses of political violence and incarceration has provided a root for abolition—from Jesus to Harriet Tubman, Malcolm X, the Black Panthers, and George Jackson. Slavery is an example of social subordination by one group of another. When I went to Angola Prison as a law student

in 2019, I still saw armed white men on horseback overseeing Black men picking cotton. Slavery is still legal in this country, so that abolitionist struggle continues, but it is part of the larger abolitionist struggle against social subordination.

Why are abolitionist lawyers important?
Abolitionist lawyers are important because the legal system, as currently structured, decides who is and who is not free, and gives lawyers power in those decisions. There are a lot more factors influencing these decisions than just the lawyer. Often, the die is cast before a lawyer does anything, by politicians, judicial biases, or the inability of legal advocacy to fix systems designed to fail people. And genuine social change is the product of mass movements of people, not just lawyers. However, abolitionist lawyers can make huge changes in pushing back against the state's ability to oppress people. In my work in capital appeals, I have seen countless Black people sentenced to die in prison almost entirely because there weren't effective lawyers there to represent them. I have also seen lawyers help free people and become meaningful members of larger movements for genuine change.

What does abolitionist lawyering look like?
Abolitionist lawyering looks like advocating to stop the powerful from harming people and transferring power from those with it to those without it. For me, this looks like trying to fight ongoing torture against people incarcerated in solitary confinement. It means giving trans incarcerated people agency over their health care and housing. Abolitionist lawyers should not decide what peoples' lives look like; we should help people access the power to decide for themselves.

At L4BL we borrow a lot of our abolitionist lessons from such organizations as Critical Resistance, Project Nia, and Interrupting Criminalization as well as thinkers and organizers like Ruth Wilson Gilmore, Derecka Purnell, Andrea Ritchie, Angela Davis, Rachel Herzing, and Mariame Kaba. Much of what follows comes from their work. "Abolition" literally just means the act of ending or stopping something. But in the context of our work and organizing, it also means creating something new. Abolition is as much about what we dismantle as what we build. As Mariame Kaba writes, "PIC abolition is a political vision, a structural analysis of oppression, and a practical organizing strategy."[8]

The political vision of PIC abolition consists of a world where imprisonment, surveillance, and policing are unnecessary, and where other forms of state violence (including things like taking away people's kids or banning people from public support or benefits) are not used as forms of punishment. It is a vision where we work together to ensure that people's needs are met, and when harm does occur, it is addressed through community processes that prioritize ending that harm and creating conditions for accountability and repair.

The structural analysis of oppression that abolition offers is premised on the well-established (but often rejected out of hand) reality that these institutions that claim to keep us safe and prevent harm actually create more harm than they deter. Prisons, jails, police, the family regulation system (aka family protective services or child welfare agencies), and immigration detention centers do not keep us safe. There is no evidence that these institutions prevent crimes, and you only have to look to their origins to see that they have never been about safety—they are about control and maintenance of racialized and class-based power structures.[9] Instead of safety, these systems perpetuate violence and inequality.

Abolition values and prioritizes safety. It believes that safety comes from strong and thriving communities that develop practices for accountability and harm reduction. Abolition as a practical organizing strategy is visible throughout the country as groups work to create mutual aid networks, sharpen their transformative justice skills, reduce the footprint of police and prisons, and constantly question the logic, efficacy, and legitimacy of jails, prisons, and violence as solutions to harm. Many of those responsible for the organizing that brought PIC abolition to the forefront are Black women and queer folks. As Angela Davis writes, "abolitionist traditions have relied on feminist analysis and organizing from their inceptions and the version of feminism that we embrace is also not possible without an abolitionist imagination."[10] Some of the key takeaways of PIC abolition include:

- The criminal legal system, including policing, is not broken. It is rooted in slave patrols in the South and the suppression of labor strikes in the North.[11] It is doing exactly what it was created to do—it is protecting the wealth and privilege of the rich.
- Abolition evolves with social conditions, but it has a set of core principles that include the elimination of police, imprisonment, and surveillance.
- Abolition seeks not only the end of prisons and police but, to paraphrase Angela Davis, it seeks a world where these institutions are unnecessary.
- Abolition is as much about what we destroy as what we build. Abolitionists are constantly experimenting with better ways to address harm when it occurs and have built extensive mutual aid networks.
- Abolition will not happen overnight, so we engage in organizing strategies that chip away at the legitimacy, footprint, and funding of the PIC.
- Abolition embraces the imperative of organizing with and taking leadership from directly impacted individuals and communities. This does not mean that just because someone is in jail or prison that they have all the answers, but it does mean that we value the insights and expertise of those most impacted, and we work with them in nonhierarchical ways.

Interviews with Lawyers

MANDISA MOORE-O'NEAL

What does Black queer feminism(s) (BQF) abolition mean to you?
BQF is a lens for how to see the world, how to do my work, including as
a leader and how I support others in doing their work. Much like one
may put on eyeglasses or contact lenses to see the world more clearly
and to deeply focus on matters close and far, Black queer feminism(s)
and abolition provide me a framework to understand how power is ar-
ranged, how to dismantle oppressive systems and unaccountable power
structures, and most important, what we must construct and practice in
its place. BQF and abolition is a framework within which I can expan-
sively do my work and notice more possibilities.

What are the roots of BQF?
BQF is rooted in the experiences of Black women and those socialized
as or otherwise assigned "Black woman" across the African diaspora. I
think of the Combahee River Collective Statement as an important
starting place, particularly when it declared "Black women are inherently valuable." I also think of the works of Black feminists such as bell
hooks, Patricia Hill Collins, Toni Morrison, Toni Cade Bambara, Julie
Dash, Cathy Cohen, Dorothy Roberts, Beth Richie, Andrea Ritchie,
Charlene Carruthers, and of organizations like INCITE!, Interrupt
Criminalization are such a deep part of how I know and embody BQF.
Any Black woman and Black femme who has screamed, whispered,
written, taught, led that "you are whole" and "I am enough" and "all of
you deserves to be here" has declared again and again that picking and
choosing what oppressions to address will *not* lead to freedom has
served as deep roots to BQF.

Why are BQF lawyers important?
Someone must bear witness to the depth and breadth of what is actually
happening, not just what the social justice/civil rights lawyering system
has the capacity to name. Even when they attend the trainings and
"win" cases, there is an inability to see us as fully human past the win-
nability of a particular case, always with a watered-down fact pattern

and often a decentering of the communities we come from and a centering of themselves as the "saviors," the "legal geniuses." BQF lawyering is important because when we see the inherent value of our people—not as clients, not as steps to further our careers—but as fully human, we see past the case and see a fuller, more complete picture of the repair needed. We can much further assess the limits of the law and therefore what else we can do.

What does BQF lawyering look like?
BQF lawyering is a commitment to continuously and rigorously locating yourself and your work in the power arrangement. This means you apply a power analysis to your legal strategies that will deeply inform your arguments and pleadings. This power analysis includes an understanding of what the law (at best a tool) can accomplish and what it can't, so what are the other ways to meet the needs? It means constantly asking yourself, *How does the belief that Black women are inherently valuable show up in my work? Where are the areas of improvement?* BQF lawyering looks like taking care of your needs (including boundary-setting and accurate capacity assessment) while also decentering yourself. This is not easy or obvious work, so ultimately BQF is a commitment to a consistent practice of learning/unlearning this.

Black Queer Feminism(s)

Black queer feminism(s) (BQF) centers the experiences of those marginalized because of their gender and sexuality. Doing so allows us to understand the ways gender oppression compounds class and racial oppression. When we talk about BQF, we are drawing heavily on the organizing work of groups like INCITE!, the Audre Lorde Project, and BYP100 as well as the writings of public intellectuals and scholars such as Charlene Carruthers, Andrea Ritchie, Angela Davis, Beth Richie, Kimberlé Crenshaw, and others. While the term "Black queer feminism(s)" is relatively new, the ideas that it embodies are not.

Queer folks, trans folks, and women have always been the backbone of radical movements; they have imagined expansive versions of liberation and have innovated strategies and tactics to get us there. They have done this while having to fight for their lives and the freedom to be their full selves.

We talk about Black queer feminism(s) in the plural. We do this to acknowledge the many theories, viewpoints, and practices that make up the Black queer feminist tradition. We use Charlene Carruthers's definition, which she puts forth in her book *Unapologetic: A Black Queer and Feminist Mandate for Radical Movements* and repeated, during a Law for Black Lives presentation. She said: "Black queer feminism(s) is a movement to dismantle all forms of exploitation and oppression, while centering racialized and gendered oppression. It is a lineage of theory and ideology developed outside, inside and in between the academy; a lineage of practices developed across the world, across class, across gender, abilities and languages."[12] This definition tells us a few important things about BQF:

1. It is concerned with dismantling all forms of exploitation and oppression. It articulates the belief that if you put those historically marginalized in the center of your analysis, the solutions you come up with will be more comprehensive and holistic. History teaches us when we do not center Blackness and queerness, we tend to erase whichever one is not at the forefront.

2. It redefines sources of authority and expertise. By drawing expertise from a variety of forms of knowledge, BQF works against elitism, which is often racialized and gendered. We know that ideas, brilliance, and insights do not just come from academia or legal scholarship. Black queer feminism(s) has been expressed and sharpened through music. Black blues singers were at the forefront of Black feminist expression when

they "created a poetic of sexual freedom and power, a politics of protest veiled beneath songs of love and loss."[13] Similarly, author Octavia Butler's Afro-futurism, her centering of Black women as protagonists, and her reimagining of worlds where Black people are free is a form of Black queer feminist thought. Traditions that only honor expertise developed inside the academy are removed from lived realities, reinforce existing gender and racial hierarchies, and are often incomplete.

3. It emphasizes practice and organizing. This is key, as we discussed in chapter 1, because we believe it is through organizing that we build power and make change. We also believe it is through organizing that our theories are best sharpened and tested.

4. The definition alludes to a key tenet of Black queer feminism(s)—the idea that Black queer people experience multiple oppressions and that these different oppressions are compounded.

Black queer feminists have long theorized about how our multiple identities influence our lives, shape our activism, and are key to our collective liberation. Fran Beal and the Third World Women's Alliance coined the phrase "multiple jeopardy" to discuss how oppressions are interrelated and compounding.[14] Kimberlé Crenshaw later applied this theory in the legal context coining the phrase "intersectionality."[15] As Audre Lorde said, "There is no such thing as a single-issue struggle because we do not live single-issue lives."[16]

Yet Black women and queer people have constantly been asked to leave parts of their identity at the door to join fights for liberation. Black liberation fights have historically asked women to ignore patriarchy. Meanwhile, feminist and queer liberation fights have asked Black people to ignore racism. Black queer feminism(s) insists that we not deprioritize any of our identities in favor of expediency or false unity. Black queer feminism(s) allow "people and groups to bring their full selves into the process of dismantling all systems of oppression."[17] Moreover, BQF insists that collective liberation is only possible when the most oppressed among us get free. As the groundbreaking Combahee River Collective Statement, written by a group of Black socialist lesbians, put it: "We might use our position at the bottom, however, to make a clear leap into revolutionary action. If Black women were free, it would mean that everyone else would have to be free since our freedom would necessitate the destruction of all the systems of oppression."[18]

Some of the key takeaways of Black queer feminism(s) include:

- Black queer feminism(s) are focused on ending all forms of oppression. By centering those traditionally at the margins, it expands the horizon of what is possible for all of us.
- Black queer feminism(s) help us understand how all of one's identities—as Black people, women, queer people, and working-class people—impact their lived experience.
- Black queer feminism(s) help us understand how interconnected our struggles are but also the ways that different types of oppression spawn and feed other forms of oppression.
- Throughout history Black queer feminists have, out of necessity, created new ways of surviving and thriving. As movement lawyer Bryanna Jenkins details in her piece in chapter 5, about centering Black trans voices in amicus strategies, key to Black queer feminism(s) are collective action and community building. As Angela Davis writes, Black queer ecosystems are characterized by "networks, organizations and collectives. It is never a solo project."[19]
- Black queer feminism(s) help us develop a deeper understanding of violence and how state and interpersonal violence are connected and mutually reinforcing.

Anticapitalism

At Law for Black Lives we have spent years studying and sharpening our analysis around capitalism. It is clear to us that an understanding of capitalism, including its inherent racialized and gendered nature, is key to our communities' ability to thrive. Several of today's movements—including the Land Back Movement and the Black liberation movement—have identified the end of capitalism as a prerequisite to liberation.[20] Nobody has suggested this will happen quickly or will be easy. But there is growing feeling that there can be no equity within a system that values profits over people and naturalizes inequality.

We draw heavily from the teachings of organizations like Left Roots and the Center for Political Education for our understandings and critiques of capitalism. We also have collectively studied the writings of folks like Stuart Hall, Robin D. G. Kelley, Jessica Gordon-Nembhard, Cedric Robinson, W. E. B. Du Bois, Renee Hatcher, and others.

You may have noticed that unlike the rest of our politics, anticapitalism is framed in the negative. Generally we think it is important to name and focus on what we are fighting *for*, not just what we are fighting *against*. So why the exception of "anticapitalism"? We believe socialism, communism, and solidarity economies of various flavors would all more effectively and humanely serve our people. But we have not seen a clear consensus in the current iteration of the Black liberation movement around what system should replace capitalism. And we are also on our own journey of study, ideation, and experimentation. We do not have a collectively agreed upon answer to "what system should replace this one?" However, we agree with Gordon-Nembhard that whatever replaces this system must be "a non-exploitative economic system geared toward the grassroots that's indigenous, participatory and that's democratized."[21]

To answer the question of what is anticapitalism, we first must answer the question: What is capitalism?

- Capitalism is characterized by wage labor, private ownership over the means of production (things like farms, factories, machines, etc.), production for profit and accumulation.
- Capitalism requires inequality. It requires that some people own things and other people sell their labor to the people that own things. It requires laborers who do not own their labor and capitalists who make profits off the excess of the labor of others.
- Capitalism must grow to survive. This insatiable appetite is disastrous for the environment. It fuels neoliberal policies that decimate the social safety net in order to create new frontiers of profit, such as the privatization of health care, housing, education, and many other basic human services.[22]
- Capitalism is only possible because of colonialism, slavery, and imperialism. Accumulation by some comes at the expense of others and our planet. Accumulation requires the theft of land, resources, and labor. The creation and reproduction of capitalism is always violent, and often this violence is targeted at populations of people who are racialized. Racialization makes the mistreatment of some politically possible because the dominant population does not see those racialized people as equal. Examples include colonization, imperialism, slavery, and environmental destruction.
- Capitalism relies on the unwaged and undervalued labor often performed by women, Black and Brown people, and disabled people. The largest category of labor is reproductive and care labor (such as having and/or raising children, caring for the elderly, maintaining a family). These types of labor are essential for the maintenance of capitalism, not to mention the survival of humans. However, capitalism disparages this life-sustaining labor by offering no wages for it, often forcing caregivers to take on wage labor or become dependent.

- Capitalism is not natural. It was created and sustained by violence and destruction. Of the nearly half a million years of human existence, capitalism has only been the dominant economic system for about two hundred years. There were systems before capitalism, and there will be systems after capitalism.
- Capitalism is inherently undemocratic. To sustain capitalism requires that those with more capital have more power. The idea of power being derived from money and privilege is in direct opposition to democratic decision-making ideals.
- Capitalism emerged in the soil of racial hierarchy, and these hierarchies are fundamental to its maintenance. Not only does racism justify different levels of exploitation within capitalism, it also divides the working class. In the case of the United States, many poor and working-class white people ravaged by capitalism believe they are benefiting from these systems because of the symbolic and material benefits of white supremacy. However, ending capitalism does not mean racism will automatically end.
- One of the primary functions of laws in the United States is to maintain the capitalist system. The major function of the police is to protect those with capital and to protect property. Law structures these unequal relationships and enforces and naturalizes conditions of inequality.

Anticapitalism is the movement to end capitalism and transform the systems, culture, and practices that uphold it.

Capitalism is inherently harmful and that harm is gendered and racialized. We believe we must fight for a system that puts people over profits, that stewards the Earth as opposed to exploits it, and that allows people to live in their full dignity. This looks like cooperative and solidarity economies, mutual aid networks, and working to demystify capitalism while slowly creating cracks in its foundation. Some key takeaways from anticapitalism include:

- We must be in right relationship with each other and the Earth. This means that nobody has coercive power over the labor of another. It means that we cannot constantly take from the Earth for our own consumption.
- Black people cannot be free under capitalism. But the end of capitalism does not automatically mean the end of racism. We must take seriously the relationship between racism and capitalism and not erase the superexploitation of racial groups inside of capitalism.
- Patriarchy is also inevitable under, but distinct from, capitalism. Women, femmes, and gender-nonconforming people will never be free under capitalism. But again, the end of capitalism will not automatically end gender oppression.
- We are more than what we produce. Capitalism perpetuates an ableist understanding of our value being tied up in our capacity to produce for others. Anticapitalism embraces the inherent worth and intrinsic value of all people.
- We must create small-scale viable alternatives to capitalism and continue to experiment and grow them. We are already doing this! We each should figure out ways to support and scale these efforts.

Now that we have explored the theoretical groundings of our politics, let's discuss their current manifestations in social movements. The next section explores how these political ideas play out in our movements.

Our Movements

The current iteration of Black struggle builds on past movements' attempts to dismantle capitalism, anti-Blackness, and patriarchy. Current movements push many of the boundaries that limited the

Interviews with Lawyers

JULIAN HILL

What does "anticapitalism" mean to you?

Home and possibility come up when I think of anticapitalism. There is no monopolistic consolidation, or notion, of private ownership of land, housing, labor, certain ideas, or resources needed for production. Capitalists aimed to crush my working-class parents from their homes and pressure people to leave the Kankakees for the Chicagos of the world for work while displacing locals. It means possibly waking up in *una casa* on ecologically sustainable, family- and community-stewarded land, eating fruit grown by Pembroke farmer cooperatives, strolling down fully accessible blocks past community gardens, cooperative medical and conflict transformation clinics, credit unions, and barter stations on my way to teach at an education cooperative. It's an abolitionist's dream settling into reality, where direct democracy is in our politics and the workplace. It's socialist, likely some form of New Afrikan anarchism communities I belong to are still fleshing out.

What are the roots of anticapitalism?

As I understand it in my readings of folks like Claudia Jones, Amílcar Cabral, Cedric Robinson, Mariame Kaba, Robin D. G. Kelley, Ruth Gilmore, Barbara Ransby, Noam Chomsky, and others, anticapitalism is rooted in a centuries-old belief that we survive and thrive when we see ourselves in an interdependent relationship with each other and the Earth instead of a hierarchical relationship rooted in commodification, exploitation, and profit. Anticapitalism understands that capitalism is a racist economic system that justifies modern-day versions of the transatlantic enslavement practices I explored recently at the Elmina and Cape Coast dungeons. My ancestors, but not the wack ones who were complicit in oppressive regimes (i.e., "wackcestors"), fought against capitalism since we first encountered it; therefore, I believe anticapitalism is also rooted in Afrikan, New Afrikan, and so many other struggles for self-determination and alternative, solidarity, economies worldwide.

Why are anticapitalist lawyers important?
The anticapitalist lawyer provides an invaluable understanding of the legal infrastructure fundamental to upholding our existing system. They can see how contract law embodies capitalist values, corporate law prioritizes hierarchy and profit maximization, securities law fails to undermine monopolistic behemoths manipulating consumers and misusing their data, and how so many other areas of law stifle community exposure to cooperative economics, criminalize practices that challenge or undermine capitalism and protect capitalists from accountability for the economic violence wrought against vulnerable communities. Moreover, we understand the role of corporate lawyers, from law firm partners to summer associates to government lawyers, who have blood on their hands. When not captured by these elite forces, the true anticapitalist lawyer is also a collaborative dreamer who is willing to push the envelope and bend, or go beyond, the law to help do the build work necessary for bringing about the world we deserve.

What does anticapitalist lawyering look like?
Anticapitalist lawyering is memory work. It's remembering the relevant laws and their limitations. It's remembering that my family, friends, neighbors, and I all would have suffered if we did not creatively address legal challenges to mutual aid work in New York City targeting Black migrants, sex workers, transgender folks, and folks coming home from the carceral system—all of whom were excluded from government programs during the first year of the pandemic. It's looking at what is and supporting clients who ask, *What if?* and *How can we?* when building stronger relationships rooted in solidarity, care, mutualism, and ecology. It looks like forming a solar energy worker cooperative, presenting community-ownership models for land for a local community group, joining protests as legal observers or chant leaders, co-creating propaganda regarding rent relief, and directly challenging government leadership when they (often) fail to show up for us to build dual power.

horizons of past movements. Moreover, while abolition, Black queer feminism(s), and anticapitalism have always been important radical threads in Black movements of the past, they have come to the forefront in the past decade. Much of that is due to the work by organizers who have demanded a more intersectional and holistic approach to liberation. Many of us, thanks to their tireless work, have concluded that if any of us are unfree, all of us are vulnerable. Therefore, freedom for the most marginalized must be the goal.

One manifestation of the reach and scope of these radical politics can be found in the Movement for Black Lives, of which Law for Black Lives is a founding member.[23] The Movement for Black Lives is a formation of dozens of Black radical organizations. It took off in the aftermath of the police killings of 2015 and earlier. Following the killings of Rekia Boyd in Chicago, Michael Brown in Ferguson, Missouri, and Eric Garner, in New York, organizations across the country began to embrace a more abolitionist politic. Even as many called for the prosecution of the officers involved in police killings, a nonabolitionist demand, organizers began to make systemic indictments against the system of policing.

In the summer of 2016 thousands of Black people gathered in Cleveland, Ohio, for the Movement for Black Lives Convening.[24] During this gathering, a more explicitly abolitionist politic began to develop. By that time many had lost hope in reformist solutions like body cameras or implicit bias training, which poured more resources into systems that were killing Black people with impunity. The lack of indictments for the killers of Eric Garner and Michael Brown, coupled with the increasing awareness of the often-ignored Black women killed by the state, dashed any hope that the same state that inflicted this violence would somehow hold itself accountable.[25] Meanwhile, more and more of us were slowly piecing together our collective and lived knowledge. We were starting to recognize the organized abandonment of Black communities—from the underfunding of our schools and health-care systems, to the unchecked poisoning of our water and air, to the criminalization of our survival—including in moments of man-made disasters (like the failure of the levee system in New Orleans after Hurricane Katrina). The state-style executions of our people by police only added insult to injury. And many of us were ready for something more than piecemeal solutions.

At the Movement for Black Lives Cleveland Convening, organizers and some movement lawyers participated in a People's Movement Assembly, a democratic decision-making process borrowed from movements of the Global South.[26] Together we agreed we wanted to use all tactics available to us, including law and policy. Through consensus we decided to develop a political platform that addressed the systemic conditions that result in the devaluing of Black life. Over a year later we published "The Vision for Black Lives."[27] "The Vision" was a result of the work of more than fifty organizations and was a clear articulation of an abolitionist, Black queer feminist, and anticapitalist politic. While created in response to police violence, only one of the thirty-five demands was about police. "The Vision" explicitly rejected prisons, police, and surveillance as ways to keep Black people safe, but it also demanded an end to militarism and called for reparations, economic redistribution, holistic health care, and more.[28] The publication of "The Vision" and the fact that some of the leading Black organizations across the country had struggled and come to a position of abolition was significant. But the summer of 2020 was when decades of organizing around prison industrial complex abolition came to fruition. By 2020 we had continued to see Black death unabated. Not only had over twelve hundred Black people been killed by police since the protests in 2015, but we were also six months into the COVID-19 pandemic.[29] The pandemic was uncovering the systemic nature of racism in our health-care system. Black people were dying at alarming rates not only in the street but as frontline workers, who were underpaid, undervalued, and underinsured.[30]

Moreover, the previous five years had shown us the limits of criminal legal system reform.[31] While the killers of George Floyd and Ahmaud Arbery were prosecuted and ultimately convicted, these symbolic prosecutions did nothing to slow the rate of killings at the hands of police.[32] The prosecutions also did nothing to support the families who lost their loved ones to police violence or other survivors of police violence. Prosecutions of individual officers do not address the social, legal, and political conditions that lead to the criminalization and killing of Black people by the state. In fact, you could argue that the focus on individual officers distracts from a systemic analysis. Instead of addressing root causes of racism or racialized violence, the institution of policing was adapting and using our demands to justify extending its reach. In the meantime, police departments were expanding their budgets.[33] Many were requiring taxpayers to pay for the cost of ineffective reforms like body cameras.[34] The reforms put in place made it clear to many organizers that the only way to stop the killing of Black people by police was to end policing. Similarly, the only way to end the criminalization of Black people would be to abolish the prison industrial complex. Thus the call etched on streets and protest signs throughout 2020 was "defund the police." Unlike past demands, this one got to the heart of the matter. And while much has been made of the political and media backlash to the demand, it planted seeds that question the legitimacy and efficacy of police.

This movement for abolition also has clear strains of Black queer feminism. As Charlene Carruthers notes, "We Black queer and trans women have been on the front lines of anti-police and Black liberation organizing . . . we have been there after Black men and boys have been slain. . . . We have shown up, even when the masses have not, after a Black woman, girl, or trans, or queer, or gender nonconforming person has been killed."[35] For perhaps the first time the movement to center the deaths and experiences of Black women who have experienced state violence took center stage. The #SayHerName movement started with Black queer feminists Andrea Ritchie, Kimberlé Crenshaw, and others attempting to make an intervention in the continued phenomena of mass movements ignoring the deaths of Black women, queer people, and trans people. In 2015 the African American Policy Forum (AAPF), along with movement lawyer Andrea Ritchie, copublished a report that told the stories of women killed by state violence. AAPF embarked on a public education campaign that was buttressed by the dozens of local organizing efforts to uplift the lives of Black women and trans and gender nonconforming people killed and sexually harassed by state actors and vigilantes.[36] Organizing campaigns from across the country, led by groups like SNAPcO, a trans-led coalition in Atlanta, and BYP100, coalesced to amplify the names of people like Alesia Thomas, Mya Hall, Sandra Bland, Breonna Taylor, and others.[37]

This type of organizing is not new, but the popularity and resonance of it is. More and more Black queer feminist organizers are pushing those historically marginalized to the center of conversations about racial and gender violence, and their intersections. Relatedly, organizers like Mariame Kaba and organizations like Survived and Punished are calling attention to the criminalization of gender violence survivors. Women being criminalized for defending themselves or for taking steps to end gender-based violence is also not new. Kaba and others organizing at the intersection of abolition and Black queer feminism(s) are demanding that survivors of gender-based violence receive the support, care, and justice they deserve—not cages. They are continuing the decades-long work of removing antiviolence work from the purview of the criminal legal system.[38]

This generation of Black queer feminists is rebuking attempts to flatten the complexities of interpersonal violence into a problem that can be solved by the punishment and imprisonment of individual perpetrators. They are showcasing the ways that criminalization has not only failed to end violence, it has also further injured and traumatized survivors. Their work has collapsed the false dichotomy of public and private violence. In the words of Charlene Carruthers, this work has "help[ed] us understand how state and interpersonal violence operate across our lives. The BQF lens enables us to see how violence within our homes, communities and broader society are connected to the violence inflicted on us by the government and corporations."[39] Making these connections allows us to develop holistic and systemwide solutions that address the full range of violence experienced by many Black, queer, and marginalized people. It enables us to develop solutions that get to the root of these harms.

Another example of powerful intersectional organizing is the work of the National Bail Out Collective, of which Law for Black Lives is a founding member and which Gina Clayton-Johnson discusses in depth in chapter 7. The National Bail Out Collective's "Mama's Day Bail Outs" were inspired by the long history of BQF organizing, including the creation of bail funds and mutual aid projects. It was initiated in 2017 by Mary Hooks at a gathering focused on how to end money bail and pretrial detention. As the group discussed various interventions Black organizers and lawyers could make around the problematic direction of bail reform, Hooks suggested that we engage in mutual aid and bail out as many of our Black mamas and caregivers as possible for Mother's Day. The effort would highlight the impact of pretrial detention on Black communities and the parallels of bail to chattel slavery, as systems that monetize Black people's freedom.

When Hooks suggested it, we were instantly inspired. We knew a mass bail out would get people out of cages and engage them in the project of our shared liberation. We thought bailing out our mamas would highlight the reality that it is our caregivers and families that keep us safe, not cages. We decided to call it "Mama's Day Bail Out" to be inclusive not just of birth mothers and other types of mothers but also of the assortment of caregivers, including trans women, who

Southerners on New Ground's "Mama's Day Bail Out," 2017. Courtesy of National Bail Out Collective.

held chosen and blood families together. What followed was four months of chaotic planning. Lawyers across the country got in formation and were on call to provide legal support. Organizers raised a million dollars from thousands of small donors. We created safety plans for folks who would be released so they had homes, food, and support when they got out. Since the inception of national bail outs (NBOs), they have bailed out hundreds of people. They provide short-term employment for many of the people they bail out and provide housing and supportive services to a majority of those they bail out. Their efforts are not just focused on individuals. They have fought to end pretrial detention in more than a dozen locations. The work of the NBO builds up our systems of care outside of the criminal legal system, and it focuses on the humanity and importance of mamas and caregivers—a population often left out of prevailing narratives about who incarceration impacts.

All of these examples incorporated a critique of capitalism in their analysis and organizing. The popularity of anticapitalism has grown both in and outside of organizing circles, especially among young people. According to a 2020 Pew poll, 50 percent of nineteen- to twenty-nine-year-olds had a very or somewhat positive view of socialism.[40] Anticapitalism organizing has had a profound impact on popular conceptions of capitalism as well as on various movements. More and more young people and organizers understand capitalism as inherently exploitative and racialized. As a result, various movements from Indigenous movements to immigration movements to Black Liberation movements have embraced anticapitalism.[41] These movements have successfully connected the ravages of capitalism to Indigenous genocide, forced migration, chattel slavery and its afterlives, as well as various other social issues. They have exposed the reality that as long as capitalism is intact, liberation for women, Black people, and Indigenous people is impossible.

. . .

The vision of contemporary organizers is so expansive that it can easily inspire both hope and skepticism. When one begins to use these political lenses to understand the problems we face, the gravity and depth of the challenges before us become undeniable. It becomes obvious that the law is an insufficient tool, as discussed in chapter 1. If you don't believe in the power of organizing, this reality can be depressing. If you do believe in the power of people, however, the possibilities are endless, at least on a good day. But hope is a discipline. And it is best sustained by deep relationships and rigorous study. We hope that this grounding in our political lenses helps you better understand our work and our assessments. These political lenses have real implications for how we practice the law as well as for who we are in relationship with. They implicate a set of questions about how you lawyer, why, and for whom. Part II of this book explores how those implications play out in the work of movement lawyers, whatever tactics we wield.

Learn Something from This

- If you are trying to lawyer in relationship with social movements, you must be rooted in a set of political beliefs and values, otherwise you are probably lawyering in a way that maintains and legitimizes the status quo.
- The systems we work inside are not broken. They were created to do what they are doing. But despite abolition's focus on destroying harmful systems, it is as much about what we destroy as what we build. Abolitionists are constantly experimenting with new ways of being in relationship that better address harm when it occurs.
- Black queer feminism(s) is focused on ending all forms of oppression. It does so by centering the experience of Black women and queer people.[42] By centering those traditionally at the margins, it expands the horizon of what is possible for all of us.
- Black people cannot be free under capitalism. But the end of capitalism does not necessarily necessitate the end of racism. We must take seriously the relationship between racism and capitalism and not erase the superexploitation of racial groups inside of capitalism.
- Honing your politics is an ongoing journey. We encourage you to engage with organizing groups, political organizations, colleagues and comrades to explore and sharpen your politics.

Resources

Abolition

- All things Critical Resistance. Spend some time exploring the Critical Resistance website, https://criticalresistance.org. It has zines, graphics, write-ups, charts, you name it.
- Several powerful books about abolition have been released recently. A quick read is Mariame Kaba's *We Do This 'til We Free Us*. We also love Derecka Purnell's *Becoming Abolitionists* and Andrea Ritchie and Mariame Kaba's *No More Police*. Rachel Herzing and Justin Piché's *How to Abolish Prisons* provides powerful real-world examples of abolition in action.

Black Queer Feminism(s)

- As you can tell by how much we quote her in this chapter, we love Charlene Carruthers's primer on movement and Black queer feminism. Check out *Unapologetic: A Black, Queer, and Feminist Mandate for Radical Movements.*
- One of the most powerful and precise statements on intersectionality (before it was a word) and Black queer feminism comes from the iconic Combahee River Collective Statement. Google it.

Anticapitalism

- The Center for Political Education offers study guides, videos, resources, and insights about all the politics we discussed, but we have especially appreciated their trainings around anticapitalism. Check them out at www.politicaleducation.org.

Reflection

Name two or three political ideologies that shape how you see the world. How do these political ideologies impact how you want to show up in your work? What relationships, practices, or infrastructure can you create or strengthen to ensure you show up how you want to?

Notes

1. "The Left Remakes the World: Amna Akbar on Canceling Rent, Defunding the Police and Where We Go from Here," *Democracy Now*, July 15, 2020, www .democracynow.org/2020/7/15/amna_akbar_on_canceling_rent_defunding.

2. Robin D. G. Kelley, "Scholar Robin D. G. Kelley on How Today's Abolitionist Movement Can Fundamentally Change the Country," *The Intercept*, June 27, 2020, https://theintercept.com/2020/06/27/robin-dg-kelley-intercepted.

3. "BYP100: We Ready, We Coming," BYP100, 2023, www.byp100.org, accessed July 29, 2023.

4. Charlene Carruthers, "Law for Black Lives Summer School," online presentation, July 17, 2021.

5. Mariame Kaba, *We Do This 'til We Free Us* (Haymarket, 2021), 4.

6. Barbara Ransby, *Ella Baker and the Black Freedom Movement: A Radical Democratic Vision* (University of North Carolina Press, 2003).

7. Charlene Carruthers, *Unapologetic: A Black, Queer, and Feminist Mandate for Radical Movements* (Beacon Press, 2018), 11.

8. Kaba, *supra* note 5.

9. Victoria Law, *"Prisons Make Us Safer": And 20 Other Myths About Mass Incarceration* (Beacon Press, 2021).

10. Angela Y. Davis, Gina Dent, Erica R. Meiners, and Beth E. Richie, *Abolition. Feminism. Now* (Haymarket, 2022), xii.

11. See, generally, Kaba, *supra* note 5. Kaba points out that "there is not a single era in United States history in which police were not a force of violence against Black people."

12. Carruthers, *supra* note 4.

13. Robin D. G. Kelley, *Freedom Dreams: The Black Radical Imagination* (Beacon Press, 2003), 154.

14. Davis et al., *supra* note 10, at 4.

15. Kimberlé Crenshaw, "Demarginalizing the Intersection of Race and Sex: A Black Feminist Critique of Antidiscrimination Doctrine, Feminist Theory and Antiracist Policies," 1 *U. Chi. Legal F.* 139 (1989).

16. Audre Lorde, "Learning from the 60s," address at Harvard University Malcolm X Weekend, February 1982, transcript available at BLACKPAST, www.blackpast.org/african-american-history/1982-audre-lorde-learning-60s.

17. Carruthers, *supra* note 7, at 10.

18. Combahee River Collective, "Combahee River Collective Statement," in *Words of Fire: An Anthology of African-American Feminist Thought*, ed. Beverly Guy-Sheftall (New Press, 1995), 235–39.

19. Davis et al., *supra* note 10, at 13.

20. Cecilia Nowell, "The Red Nation Wants Its Land Back: The Indigenous-Led Leftist Collective Is Committed to Freeing the World from Capitalism and Colonialism," *The Nation*, August 10, 2021, www.thenation.com/article/activism/red-nation-new-mexico; "About Us," Movement for Black Lives, https://m4bl.org/about-us, accessed July 29, 2023.

21. Gordon-Nembhard interview in Keane Bhatt, "Dangerous History: What the Story of Black Economic Cooperation Means for Us Today," *Yes!*, October 7, 2015, www.yesmagazine.org/economy/2015/10/07/dangerous-history-what-the-story-of-black-economic-development-means-for-us-today.

22. Angela Y. Davis, "Recognizing Racism in the Era of Neoliberalism," *Truthout*, May 6, 2013, https://truthout.org/articles/recognizing-racism-in-the-era-of-neoliberalism.

23. Movement for Black Lives website, *supra* note 20.

24. Akiba Solomon, "Photos: Go Inside the Movement for Black Lives National Convening," *Colorlines*, July 27, 2015, https://colorlines.com/article/photos-go-inside-movement-black-lives-national-convening.

25. When we say "women," we are referring to all people who identify as women, including our trans sisters.

26. Rubén Solis Garcia, Seth Markle, Foluke Nunn, Emery Wright, and Stephanie Guilloud, *People's Movement Assembly: Organizing Handbook*, 2016, www.southtosouth.org/resources/peoples-movement-assembly-handbook, accessed April 19, 2025.

27. "Vision for Black Lives," Movement for Black Lives, https://m4bl.org/policy-platforms, accessed July 29, 2023.

28. *Id.*

29. Lauren Ingeno, "Fatal Police Shootings Among Black Americans Remains High, Unchanged Since 2015," *Penn Medicine News*, October 28, 2020, www

.pennmedicine.org/news/news-releases/2020/october/fatal-police-shootings
-among-black-americans-remain-high-unchanged-since-2015.

30. Daniel Tadeo, "There's a Reason Why COVID-19 Is Killing Black and Brown Americans: It's Called Racism," UCLA History, Public History Initiative, https://phi.history.ucla.edu/theres-a-reason-why-covid-19-is-killing-black-and
-brown-americans-its-called-racism, accessed November 1, 2024.

31. Kaba, *supra* note 5, at 64.

32. Sam Levin, "'It Never Stops': Killings by US Police Reach Record High in 2022," *The Guardian*, January 6, 2023, www.theguardian.com/us-news/2023
/jan/06/us-police-killings-record-number-2022.

33. Grace Manthey, Frank Esposito, and Amanda Hernandez, "Despite 'Defunding' Claims, Police Funding Has Increased in Many US Cities," *ABC News*, October 16, 2022, https://abcnews.go.com/US/defunding-claims-police-funding
-increased-us-cities/story?id=91511971.

34. "Research on Body-Worn Cameras and Law Enforcement," National Institute of Justice, January 7, 2022, https://nij.ojp.gov/topics/articles/research
-body-worn-cameras-and-law-enforcement#citation--0 (last visited November 1, 2024).

35. Carruthers, *supra* note 7, at 6.

36. Andrea Ritchie, *Invisible No More: Police Violence Against Black Women and Women of Color* (Beacon Press, 2018), 220.

37. Kimberlé Crenshaw et al., "Say Her Name: Resisting Police Brutality Against Black Women," Center for Intersectionality and Social Policy Studies, 2015, https://scholarship.law.columbia.edu/faculty_scholarship/3226, accessed April 19, 2025.

38. Davis, et al. *supra* note 10.

39. Carruthers, *supra* note 7, at 35.

40. Frank Newport, "Public Opinion Review: Americans' Reactions to the Word 'Socialism,'" Gallup, March 6, 2020, https://news.gallup.com/opinion
/polling-matters/287459/public-opinion-review-americans-word-socialism
.aspx.

41. "About the Red Nation," The Red Nation, https://therednation.org
/about/ (last visited July 29, 2023). Mijente, *Free Our Future: An Immigration Policy Platform for Beyond the Trump Era*, June 2018, https://mijente.net/wp-content
/uploads/2018/06/Mijente-Immigration-Policy-Platform_0628.pdf. Movement for Black Lives website, *supra* note 20.

42. Again, in these violently anti-trans times we wanted to be very clear that when we say "women," we mean all women including trans women.

3 *This Is a Call-In (Not a Call-Out)*

So far we have talked about the theories that ground movement lawyering and the political ideologies that guide us. This is important stuff. As we keep saying, without a clear idea of how change happens and the change you want to see, lawyering can be counterproductive to social movements. Using legal tools without direction can legitimize and strengthen oppressive systems and undermine communities' efforts to shift and build power. But theory and ideology mean nothing outside of practice. Figuring out the practice of movement lawyering is the hard part. The translation of theories and ideologies to practice is an ongoing (perhaps never-ending) journey. It requires self-reflection, community accountability practices, and deep curiosity.

This chapter is all about praxis—the ways our theories inform our daily practice and in turn how our daily practices inform our theories. We start with laying out some dos and don'ts of movement lawyering. Then we explore examples of movement lawyering gone wrong. The reality is that throughout our careers all of us will be guilty of some movement lawyering transgressions. We will overstep. We will underestimate how our privilege may be playing out. We will make a decision that we think is right but may have been made without the support of those we are in community with. Part II of this book features movement lawyers, both new and seasoned, reflecting on their

Interviews with Lawyers

BILL QUIGLEY

What is the most important lesson you have learned about movement lawyering?
Begin by shutting up and listening. Movement building is about power. Law school and the regular practice of law taught you and me about law. Law school and the practice of law taught us nothing about how communities organize and take back power over their own lives. Asking traditional law practice to help communities build power is like asking your car to babysit your kids. Instead, listen to community members. Listen to organizers. Listen to young people and older people who have been fighting for decades. Be willing to sit and be uncomfortable and learn. Only then can the journey of movement lawyering begin.

What is your favorite quote that guides your practice?
When I was coming up, I thought justice called me to be a voice for the voiceless. Then one day an organizer told me: "No one asked you to be a voice for the voiceless. There are no voiceless people—there are plenty of people whose voices are not heard because they are not allowed to speak or are drowned out by the people with power." Movement advocates can help quiet the room down so the directly impacted people whose voices are never listened to can tell their own stories and make their own demands.

Whose picture is in the dictionary under "best movement lawyer"?
Purvi Shah.

Whose picture is in the dictionary under the "worst lawyer ever"?
Too many to count. Including, occasionally, despite the best intentions, me.

lessons and mistakes. This chapter distills many of those takeaways and locates them in some historical examples of lawyering. We hope by highlighting some specific ways lawyers have failed movements, we can start to think through how to avoid or remedy these missteps.

The Dos and Don'ts of Movement Lawyering

We love a good list. In our shared experience of over two decades of practice, we have come up with a running list of practices that movement lawyers should adopt and some practices to avoid.

DO TAKE SERIOUSLY THE GOAL OF SUPPORTING THE BUILDING OF COMMUNITY POWER. As we discussed in chapter 1, the heart of movement lawyering is the belief that sustainable change happens when impacted people build power to change their conditions. If you are going to work with movements, you must believe in their potential or else you likely aren't in the right place. Movement lawyering focuses on how we can use legal tools toward the ends of building community power. Most of the tools that lawyers are taught to use—from direct representation to impact litigation to policy making—center the lawyer and place us in positions of power. It is easy in this context to become a gatekeeper.

The praxis of movement lawyering requires a constant questioning of whether what you are doing—from filing a motion to speaking at a press conference to accepting an award—is in fact in service of building power in the communities you are fighting for and with. Sometimes a legal loss, that might impact your prestige, will increase the power of an organization.[1] You should consistently talk with your clients or partners about whether and how what you are supporting them in is building power. This praxis is complicated by the demands of the nonprofit industrial complex, which funds organizations who claim legal or policy wins, but does not invest in the long-term organizing work needed to sustain these wins. We call these "postcard victories" or wins that you can easily claim at your end-of-year fundraiser but may or may not build power for communities. It is important as lawyers and legal workers who may find ourselves working inside of one of these organizations to remain committed to building power as a primary focus and outcome of our work.

DO BE "IN RIGHT RELATIONSHIP" WITH THE PEOPLE AND ORGANIZATIONS YOU ARE WORKING WITH AND FOR. Relationships are key. When we say "right relationship," we are referring to nontransactional relationships that are grounded in mutual respect, familiarity, and understanding. If you are in "right relationship" with someone, you know more about the person than what role they play in a particular campaign. You probably know their mama's name or their children's names and they know yours. Importantly, you have some sense of what motivates them and what they are fighting for.

When the strategy is legal, part of the role of the lawyer is to advocate for organizers to be in rooms and part of conversations that impact their fight, even when tradition or practice would have them left out. Be mindful that solely relying on legal solutions means that you are the de facto expert, which puts you in a position of power that can create dependence. You should never overpromise or inflate what the law can do, and being real about the limitations of the law goes a long way toward establishing trust and deepening relationships. People want to know that you are invested in the work you are doing together. Go to meetings and events that aren't about the case, show up as a person and comrade not just as a legal expert.

The strength of your relationships will determine, in the movement lawyering context, just how far you will go. Like all healthy relationships, this takes hard work and emotional labor. It also can fly in the face of what many of us are taught in law school—namely that we must maintain a level of objective professionalism and distance from our clients and partners. This idea of professionalism can discourage us from cultivating meaningful relationships. As a result, our professional communities can be insular and filled with other lawyers as opposed to the people we say we are fighting for and with. Strong relationships can help foster shared, or at least collectively understood, objectives. This can assist us in making sure that the legal tactics we are deploying are in service of the larger strategy. Relationships are also the backbone of accountability.

DO CREATE CLEAR ACCOUNTABILITY MECHANISMS. Lawyers have a lot of power and very few accountability mechanisms. If you are engaged in outlandish conduct, you may be disbarred or face discipline. But there are a lot of behaviors that are harmful that do not come under the purview of the Professional Rules of Conduct. For the most part, lawyers can do what they want, especially as it regards marginalized communities that have little power to hold us accountable. It is especially important for those of us who view our work as righteous to have clear accountability mechanisms. As Derrick Bell, acclaimed civil rights lawyer and one of the founders of critical race theory, has pointed out, "idealism, though perhaps rarer than greed, is harder to control."[2]

Those of us who believe we are doing the right thing may find it easy to justify our actions based on our political beliefs. Some may even glorify being out of step with others as evidence of the radicalness or necessity of our cause. However, as Bell writes, "civil rights lawyers themselves [must] come to realize that the special status accorded them by the courts and the bar demands in return an extraordinary display of ethical sensitivity and self-restraint."[3] Society also affords us extraordinary deference. There are countless stories of lawyers betraying movement aims or undermining movements and there is rarely redress. Accountability in this context may be self-manufactured, but it cannot be self-executed. Accountability cannot happen without community. We must craft accountability measures in collaboration with the communities we serve and build with. Accountability may include mechanisms such as regular and honest assessments by your partners and clients; consistent check-ins at pivotal moments to ensure continued consent and support; seeking input from partners and clients around when and how to pivot when needed; and finding principled ways to work through conflict and repair harm when it occurs.

DO DEVELOP AND NURTURE YOUR POLITICAL ANALYSIS. We have said it before, and we will say it again. You must engage in ongoing political education to ensure that you develop and evolve your political analysis. In a piece by movement lawyer Bill Quigley, he interviews several organizers to ask their reflections about how lawyers can better support communities in building power. One of the consistent reflections from the organizers Quigley interviews is that lawyers lack a systemic analysis of how the systems they are engaged with are harmful to communities. In the words of one of the organizers Quigley interviews, Barbara Major, "lawyers often believe in the system—that the system is going to work because it's the right thing to do. I don't think that they understand, when you are dealing with challenging power, the system works on the side of power."[4] This lack of awareness means many lawyers are unable or unwilling to grasp the big picture of what communities are fighting for. They may overestimate the value of their legal intervention or engage in short-term tactical interventions that undermine long-term organizing goals. If nothing else, being aware of your own political lenses and ensuring you understand your clients can result in identifying where there is alignment and misalignment and using this clarity to try to avoid long-term harm.

DO UNDERSTAND ORGANIZING. If we know that legal tools are but one tool in the toolbox for liberation, we need to understand what else is out there. At the heart of power building for impacted communities is organizing. Organizing is a field with a rich and long history. It also has a set of tactical tools that must be honed and a set of theories that must be studied. Lawyers often fail to understand the nuanced and complicated theories and practices of organizing. A lack of understanding of organizing increases the likelihood that we undermine or devalue it. We recommend joining a base building group that focuses on organizing as a tool for building power. Joining an organization helps ensure you are in right relationship with people, accountable, and politically aligned.

We should make clear that knowing about organizing does not make you an organizer. This is important. Just because you engage in study, you should not anoint yourself as an expert, especially not at the expense of those who have chosen it as their purpose or profession.

DO HONE YOUR CRAFT. If you want to be a movement lawyer, you need to be a good lawyer. Our movements and communities deserve that! The tools needed to support movements are the same tools used by traditional lawyers. However, using them to advance the goals of radical social movements, which are almost always expansive and liberatory, rather than to establish legal precedent (which is woefully inadequate and restrictive) is the key difference. That is the beauty and power of this kind of work. But it does require knowing how to use the law. That means taking the time to study, sharpen, and practice your legal skills. There are times when communities need to enlist legal skills or expertise. In those moments, having on-point legal support increases the likelihood that you help organizers, partners, and those most impacted to meet their goals or prevent further harm. Another aspect of honing your legal skills is to understand how to use them creatively and in a way that advances movement goals. This only happens with preparation and practice.

DON'T CREATE DEPENDENCE. One thing that lawyers do inadvertently is create dependency. Lawyers tend to approach situations by relying on solutions and processes that require the law. This is often done with little input from those impacted. Clients and partners are sometimes not brought into the process until the end. This gives them little insight into the options that are available, the limitations of those options and the consequences. Which means the community necessarily comes to rely heavily on lawyers' advice and expertise. Communities come to depend on courts, lawsuits, and policy change as the only means of achieving an end. This is in part due to societal narratives that tell us we will find justice in the courts. But the reality is that courts are not equipped to give many communities what they need.

In addition, some lawyers only present and advocate for legal solutions. We have heard this time and again from organizers we work with. It is essential that community members start to create capacity to deal with the issues they face as opposed to thinking everything has a legal solution. In Quigley's piece, featuring three organizers, all three touch on the issue of lawyering creating dependence. One of the organizers, Ron Chisom, said, "lawyers have killed off more groups by helping them than ever would have died if lawyers had never showed up . . . people tend to transfer their interest in the issue and the problem to the lawyer to have the lawyer solve it and this creates dependence."[5] There are ways to combat dependency. One is to be honest about the limitations of the systems you lawyer inside of. Engage in collective problem solving to identify more effective solutions, including nonlegal solutions. Even when a legal intervention is the most strategic option, it should involve other nonlegal tactics focused on growing the agency and capacities of your clients or partners. In Chisom's words one of your goals should be "giving a people a sense of their own power."[6]

DON'T MISTAKE THE MEANS FOR THE ENDS. Lawyers can become so fixated on a single legal victory or passing a single law that they lose track of the overall goals that their partner or client may have. If you believe that sustainable change happens through the building of community power, you know that no single legal victory or policy change is the end goal. Legal tools are tactics. Legal wins can be small steps toward a larger vision. But they are never the vision. If your case or legislative campaign is your idea of a north star, you are thinking too small. If you find yourself pushing organizations you work with to change their tactics, approach, or timeline because of your legal tool, it is time to pause. If you are not fully understanding how your legal tool fits into the larger goals of the campaign or movement, it is time to pause. If you are prioritizing a legal win over the power-building tactics of an organization and attempting to silence them—for example, insisting they not speak to the media—it is time to pause. If your legal tool is jeopardizing the ability of your partner or client to build or protect their membership, it is time to pause. In each of these cases you need to engage in an honest dialogue about the import and impact of the legal tool.

DON'T BE SCARED TO DISRUPT THE STATUS QUO. Lawyers and legal workers are trained to do the work in a way that positions us as defenders and protectors of the status quo. We are taught that the law is the primary tool to accomplish that goal. As noted in chapter 1, this starts with legal education that teaches young lawyers to be politically and morally "neutral" and to apply the law in that way. It extends into practice when you are bound by rules of legal ethics that are designed to prevent you from taking risks or disrespecting legal institutions. It is reinforced through the inaccessibility of the language, processes, and venues where the practice of law takes place, which grants lawyers privilege.

On the contrary, radical movements and organizers are constantly pushing the boundaries of what we think is possible to bring about long-lasting change. To be a movement lawyer, some part of you has to be bought into the goals of your partners and clients. You must be ready to use your skills and training to help shift power away from you and the power structures you were trained to protect. Doing this requires self-reflection, and taking steps to fully understand your privilege and how it impacts your decision-making.

DON'T SPEAK ON BEHALF OF OR BECOME THE LEADER OF THE GROUP. This one is straightforward. If you find yourself speaking on behalf of groups or find yourself leading a group while you are also movement lawyering on behalf of this group, it is time to reassess your role. Lawyers are often asked to speak on behalf of groups and organizations, and sometimes groups themselves will ask for this. Before you agree, you should return to the question of if your action is helping build power or capacity for this group. If you find yourself leading a group, you should ask yourself why are you best positioned to do that? Does being the leader mean that someone else is not developing leadership skills? And how does accountability about your approach or legal interventions look if you are in a position of power inside the group?

DO UNDERSTAND THE POWER AND PRIVILEGE AFFORDED TO YOU ESPECIALLY WHEN IT COMES TO YOUR LEGAL SKILLS AND TRAINING. Be aware of the other intersecting identities that you have and how those show up in your work as a lawyer. One way to help effectively build democratic people power is to understand how you may be getting in the way of that. A practice many movement lawyers cultivate is one of reflection and honest self-assessment. What kind of energy are you bringing to the space? Are you offering expertise or advice about things you don't have experience with? Are you understanding the power dynamics in the space and how much power you have? Understanding what role you play in any movement space is critical and important.

For example, if you are asked to organize a press conference, it doesn't mean that you automatically need to be a speaker at the press conference because you are the one with legal training or you are seen as an authoritative voice in dominant culture. In fact, you likely shouldn't be the primary speaker. The strength of this type of lawyering is that you don't have to have the answers, nor do you have to work alone. Working with people who are impacted means that there is plenty of expertise to go around. Organizers and members of social movements bring first-hand experience to the work of dismantling systems of oppression through various tactics and strategies. Lawyers are often invited in to assist with navigating just one of those tactics and strategies.

DO GROUND YOURSELF LOCALLY. Law for Black Lives (L4BL) is a national organization. We were founded in a moment where lawyers (and organizers) from all over the country left their homes to travel to places where uprisings were brewing and where there was revolutionary potential. For many of us that meant doing work in places that were not our home. This collaborative work is essential, but it has its drawbacks. As Iman Freeman, a movement lawyer who works in Baltimore, discusses in part II of this book, national legal organizations or even just lawyers from out of town can deplete resources, undermine local organizing efforts, and wreak havoc on local relationships. Sometimes they create dependence that when they leave becomes power vacuums or fuels resentment. When doing this work, we must be mindful of our impact and ensure that we leave organizations stronger, more trained, and better resourced than when we came.

Movement Lawyering Gone Wrong

This section explores some prototypical lawyers drawn from our study and experiences. We explore how they violate some of the dos and don'ts we just laid out.

The Cynic

Often lawyers are invited into rooms because of the perception that legal knowledge makes a person well positioned to assist when there is a problem that needs to be solved. There are circumstances where that is true. Specifically, in spaces where a legal issue, real or perceived, has emerged. While lawyers can be useful, not all lawyers should be trusted for all things. Lawyers who lack a political analysis and whose vision for what's possible is limited to what the literal letter of the law allows may be unhelpful in movement spaces, where organizers are dreaming of new horizons and new worlds. These lawyers may not be open to transformative changes but instead may be committed to the kinds of reforms that legitimize current practices and strengthen systems that cause harm. We call these types of reforms "reformist reforms" and explore them in more depth in chapter 7.

Lawyers and legal workers are trained to be risk-averse and to give deference to the current system. Many lawyers advocate for the preservation of these systems, even when clients or partners want a more abolitionist or transformational approach. Lawyers frequently have an obeisance for systems that uphold and protect white supremacy and oppression (i.e., the prison industry complex) in part because our own power and privilege is tied to these systems.[7] At the core of that commitment to what already exists is a strong doubt in the power of people organized to bring about real change. Lawyers who believe strongly in enacting the types of reforms that strengthen

Visualization of key questions from Law for Black Lives that movement lawyers should engage with as they start a new campaign or partnership. Based on a visual collectively created as part of Movement Lawyering Bootcamp. Courtesy of Law for Black Lives.

existing systems and demobilize movements may inadvertently play a critical role in maintaining inequality.[8]

Reform is not necessarily a bad thing. As Rachel Herzing writes in chapter 7, reform just means a change and there are times when movements will fight for reforms. Some types of reforms can alleviate suffering or prevent further harm. Other times the reform represents progress toward the goal of abolition or call for more transformative outcomes.[9] Nonreformist reforms, or abolitionist steps as Herzing describes them, are the types of reforms that while small serve to shrink the size, power, and legitimacy of exploitative systems like the prison industrial complex and shift power toward people impacted by those systems.[10]

When you are engaged in the type of lawyering that is accountable to movement, that is dedicated to sharing power and delegitimizing the status quo, you cannot be exclusively committed to what you think is possible. You must have some faith in movement and be bought into the project of liberation. To be successful at this type of lawyering, you have to engage with the goals and efforts of your partners and clients and see yourself as tied to one another. That means understanding the root causes of the issues, the forces and the system you and your partners are up against, and agreeing to play a role in shifting power away from that system. Otherwise you are probably in the way.

The Poser

There comes a time in some movements or campaigns when organizing efforts are successful in building power and awareness. This can result in the movement's language and demands becoming popularized and ultimately co-opted. New people feel the urge to connect themselves with the movement to advance their own goals while not fully understanding or adopting the values and politics.

Interviews with Lawyers

JARIBU HILL

What is the most important lesson you have learned about movement lawyering?
Movement lawyering is not for the faint of heart.

It must be client-centered.

It must objectively be against the status quo in all of its forms/systems/by-products (e.g., white supremacy, the patriarchy, classism, homophobia, ageism and ableism, capitalism and imperialism).

It must call attention to the historical lockout.

It must not accept the limitations imposed by the legal system but must always defy and push through barriers set up to deny basic human rights and dignity.

It must always be lawyering that lifts up the humanity of the sufferers and seeks to level the playing field. It must be the full embodiment of courage and resistance.

What is your favorite quote that guides your practice?
"If one really wishes to know how justice is administered in a country, one does not question the policemen, the lawyers, the judges, or the protected members of the middle class. One goes to the unprotected—those who need the law's protection the most—and listens to their testimony."—James Baldwin

Whose picture is in the dictionary under "best movement lawyer"?
Without a doubt, I would say the names of two lawyers who stood for freedom and never backed down. One choice is Chokwe Lumumba, New Afrikan Freedom lawyer, who staunchly represented those who were marked for death and disposal. Those who were presumed guilty. Those whose death warrants were signed at birth. I was privileged to work with this warrior and learned many lessons and adopted his resistance strategies. He would introduce his client to the jury by saying this is [name] and I am pleased to be working with him on this case. That showed me the ultimate example of the client-centered approach. My choice would also be Evelyn Williams, the aunt of Assata Shakur, who

represented Assata in her battles against this genocidal system. I remember reading her book, *Inadmissible Evidence*, in which she recounted the story of how Assata gave birth in prison, while handcuffed to the bed. Attorney Williams was a fierce advocate for our sister and the Black liberation movement as a whole. These two warriors are shining examples of true courage, brilliant legal skills, and an unflinching love for our people and oppressed people the world over. Ancestors who are still guiding us as we strike blow after blow against capitalism and white supremacy!

Whose picture is in the dictionary under the "worst lawyer ever"?
By definition, this has less to do with skill-set and more to do with the perpetual condition of spineless and cowardice behavior. Many a Black life has been destroyed by their failure to stand up for those who are targeted, profiled, and denied basic human rights. These are the professional stooges with fancy titles who are bought and paid for. Who accept titles and salaries from their masters and look the other way. They shield and protect the lynchers and hate mongers from accountability. They go above and beyond the stated assignment to even do greater damage. To see that the guilty always go free for crimes committed against the oppressed. You see them cutting deals. Ignoring public outcry. Bending over backward to provide comfort and shade for our captors. They are the modern-day overseers who keep watch and deliver us to fulfill their mission—protect and serve the free. Eliminate the sufferers. You know who you are. Black cowards. Race traitors who show nothing but contempt for those who are simply living and breathing Black. You know them! Usual suspects like Clarence Thomas and Tim Scott. Further down the chain, District Attorney DeWayne Richardson, who let Carolyn Bryant Donham die without being held accountable for her role in the kidnapping that led to the lynching of Emmett Louis Till.

Some lawyers are in that number. If you are not paying attention, you might mistake them for someone who is aligned with you. Especially because they may say the right things. But when you peel back the layers, they are just using the language to advance their own agenda.

In recent years efforts to elect "progressive" prosecutors has been described as making significant changes to the way that prosecutors' offices work. Often former public defenders, defense attorneys, or social justice lawyers run for district attorney (DA) promising to operate the office in a way that is significantly different from the DAs of the past. Vowing not to rely on harsh punishments, to use alternatives, and to hold police accountable for wrongdoing. Sometimes they even align themselves with movements for decriminalization or abolition, co-opting language and demands. They believe that their own experiences, good will, or even being a person of color makes it likely that they can produce outcomes that are more fair, less racially biased, and less damaging to the everyday lives of people who find themselves ensnared in the system. However, this is not movement lawyering, and prosecutors—no matter how progressive—are agents of incarceration, not agents of change.

As discussed in chapter 2, modern-day, Black-led, radical movements are calling for the abolition of the prison industrial complex. Abolitionists are fighting for a world where the response to social problems is not more policing, surveillance, and punishment. It seeks to build new infrastructure of care to meet human needs, to end entrenched policies, practices, and institutions of violence and to resource community-led efforts to redress harm without criminalization. A district attorney does not exist in that world. Many DAs who claim to be "progressive" won in the wake of the Black Lives Matter Movement and in no small part as a result of the organizing and public awareness inspired by that movement. Many used the momentum, language, and logic of that movement to win office but once in power continued to fuel mass incarceration and state violence. This is an example of the type of lawyer who espouses a set of beliefs or political values that they do not live by or operationalize in their work. If you are going to do work in service to a movement, you can not just use their language or take advantage of the conditions they have created, you have to be in relationship and in struggle with them.

The Power Broker

There are a lot of lawyers who are interested in being proximate to power. Some may believe that the best way to change things for the better is to use their privilege and access to influence those who have power. Others may just like having and being close to power. Either way many lawyers and legal advocacy organizations prioritize their relationships with people in positions of power over their support of movements. Relationships with those in power can be an effective and important strategy for movements. But being too reliant on this strategy and not having strong accountable community relationships can result in lawyers or legal organizations being complicit in the co-option of movement demands and the undermining of social movements.

These legal organizations may think they know what is best. They may believe that movement demands are unrealistic, and they see themselves as better equipped to determine what is possible or what should be prioritized. These lawyers may claim to speak on behalf of impacted communities or even to share some of their objectives. But these lawyers and the legal organizations they work at or run are rarely in right relationship with movement groups. In many cases they do not share the political analysis of the organizations they speak on behalf of. Moreover, they are rarely accountable to them. Nonetheless, these lawyers and legal organizations derive some of their power from the power of movements. The threat of radical movements, of protest, and of effective organizing are often why those in power seek to negotiate with these legal intermediaries. Those in power hope that by negotiating with these lawyers, they can divide the movement and co-opt the radical demands being made.

A cautionary tale about this kind of lawyering is the ACLU of Illinois's agreement with the City of Chicago around collecting data on stop-and-frisk practices in 2015. The agreement, which was negotiated in secrecy, undermined the work of Black youth organizing across the city, which was calling for an end to stop-and-frisk. While claiming the empty victory on behalf Black organizing efforts, ACLU of Illinois's willingness to negotiate a backroom deal with the City, without the knowledge or input of organizing groups, amid an ongoing campaign undermined the grassroots campaign and did not improve the material conditions of communities impacted by stop-and-frisk.[11]

The lesson of the power broker lawyer is that you should be clear about your theory of change, and you should be transparent and honest with your partners, so that they can navigate accordingly. If you believe change happens through shifts in power and organizing, you must be clear about your priorities and your allegiances. Even if you are someone who wants to be close to power or if you work for an organization that does, transparency, relationship, and accountability are essential to be an honest broker.

The Win-at-All Costs Lawyer

A lot of litigators in practice find themselves struggling to uphold movement lawyering best practices. This is in part due to the nature of litigation, which is often focused narrowly on individual remedies, as opposed to systemic analysis. As a result of demanding timelines and confidentiality mandates, attorneys sometimes feel forced to make decisions without the meaningful consent of those they represent. While they may abide by all the Model Rules of Professional Conduct, they are not necessarily in right relationship with communities most impacted by their work. In addition to the structural hurdles of litigation, the reality is that many litigators become so fixated on the outcome of their case that they lose sight of the larger movement goals that may have animated the filing of the lawsuit to start with. They get tunnel vision focused on winning the case and may stop asking themselves, *Is this building power for communities most impacted or the organizations I am partnering with?*

The most widely discussed example of when the drive to win cases overshadowed the desires of communities is the litigation around school desegregation led by the NAACP Legal Defense Fund (LDF). We discussed this litigation in depth in chapter 1. While initially the goal of desegregation was strongly aligned with parents', students', and teachers' goals of improving the educational experience of Black students after decades of trying to enforce *Brown*, with the increasing use of bussing and the ongoing traumatic experiences around integration, more and more communities began to separate integration from educational quality and wanted to prioritize educational quality for Black students. Ultimately there was a fundamental difference in theory of change. At some point LDF made the common mistake of assuming that litigation was self-actualizing and that winning court cases would somehow automatically desegregate schools.

However, as Bell pointed out, "even successful school litigation will bring little meaningful change unless there is continuing pressure for implementation from Black communities." The key lesson from this example and from many litigators is that rule change, without a political base to support it, doesn't produce any substantial results because rules are not self-executing, they require an enforcement mechanism.[12] And well-organized communities and strong social movements are one of the most powerful, and least corruptible, enforcement mechanisms. As detailed in part II of this book, a successful litigation strategy is more concerned with building the power of movement than with winning in court.

. . .

This chapter focused on tips about how to be an impactful movement lawyer and an exploration of some of the ways that lawyers can fail movements. What is clear from distilling the dos and don'ts of movement lawyering, and exploring how they manifest in practice, is that movement lawyering is a discipline. It requires a deep commitment to the people and communities you purport to serve as well as a commitment to a political and ideological lens. It requires cultivating and sustaining relationships that can help guide you and also hold you accountable when you make mistakes. It requires honesty about your political alignment and dedication to the goals of the movements you seek to serve. And it requires honing your legal skills.

In the next section we move to the complicated and rich work of serving movements. Part II of the book includes reflections from movement lawyers who are doing the work. It details how they are using different legal tactics to build the power of movement but also reflects on mistakes they have made and challenges they face.

Learn Something from This

- Movement lawyering requires us to be engaged in a relationship of trust and accountability with the communities we are working with and that takes time and effort. There is no shortcut to being in right relationship with the community—you have to put in the work.
- Understanding the theories, practices, and history of organizing are essential. It should inform your work and your thinking. But

that does not mean your primary role in movement spaces is to be an organizer. Get clear about what skills you bring and step back and let organizers do their thing.

• Hone your legal skills; our communities deserve the best and the brightest working on their behalf.

• Reforms, legal victories, or legal outcomes that aren't reflective of movements' demands or do not build power to help them actualize their demands, should not be your goal.

• You are closer to sharing power with partners and clients when you are using movement lawyering tactics to fight oppressive power and build power for communities.

Resources

• There are lots of resources for learning more about organizing. Momentum Community is an in-person and online training institute that has a helpful curriculum for new organizers. You can find out more about them at www.momentumcommunity .org. The Midwest Academy is a long-standing progressive organizing training school that has been doing its thing for fifty years. You can find out more about them at www .midwestacademy.com.

• Bill Quigley's piece "Reflections of Community Organizers: Lawyering for Empowerment of Community Organizations" is short and to the point. We quote it extensively because it is full of gems. Quigley speaks to community organizers to get their thoughts on lawyers. The advice that follows is sound and instructive. The piece appeared in the Loyola University Legal Studies Research Paper Series in 1994.

• *No Good Prosecutors*, the zine by Survived and Punished, is a powerful movement take on the problem with prosecutors, even the "progressive" ones. It illustrates the impossibility of them

being authentic movement representatives or actors. See
https://survivedandpunished.org/2021/07/12/sp-ny-zine-no
-good-prosecutors.

- To learn more about the example of the ACLU of Illinois's
backroom agreement with the City of Chicago and how it
undermined the movement to end stop-and-frisk in Chicago,
check out the open letter that We Charge Genocide, a local Black
youth group, wrote. The letter is a powerful teaching document
about how *not* to navigate organizing relationships and an
example of what attempts at community accountability may
look like. You can find the letter, dated August 12, 2015, on the
We Charge Genocide website, at http://wechargegenocide.org
/an-open-letter-to-the-aclu-of-illinois-regarding-stop-frisk/ .

Reflection

How does the list of dos and don'ts help you clarify how to show up as
an advocate? Which one or two most resonate? What plan can you
make for accountability around how you want to show up?

Notes

1. Jennifer Gordon, "Law, Lawyers, and Labor: The United Farm Workers'
Legal Strategy in the 1960s and 1970s and the Role of Law in Union Organizing
Today," 8 *U. Pa. J. Lab. & Emp. L.* 1 (2005).

2. Derrick A. Bell Jr., "Serving Two Masters: Integration Ideals and Client Interests in School Desegregation Litigation," 85 *Yale L.J.* 470, 505 (1976).

3. *Id.*

4. Major as quoted in William [Bill] Quigley, "Reflections of Community Organizers: Lawyering for Empowerment of Community Organizations," 21 *Ohio
N.U.L. Rev.* 455, 462 (1994).

5. Chisom as quoted in Quigley, *supra* note 4, at 457.

6. *Id.*

7. Tifanei Ressl-Moyer et al., "Movement Lawyering During a Crisis: How the Legal System Exploits the Labor of Activists and Undermines Movements," 24 *CUNY L. Rev.* 91 (2021).

8. See Amna Akbar, "Non-Reformist Reforms and Struggles over Life, Death and Democracy," 132 *Yale L.J.* 2497 (2023) ("reformist reforms" are reforms or ideas for reform that entrench the power of oppressive systems).

9. Angela Y. Davis, Gina Dent, Erica R. Meiners, and Beth E. Richie, *Abolition. Feminism. Now* (Haymarket, 2022), 185.

10. Akbar, *supra* note 8.

11. Kelly Hayes, "ACLU of Illinois Sells Out Chicago's Black Youth," Truthout, August 14, 2015, https://truthout.org/articles/aclu-of-illinois-sells-out-chicago-s-black-youth, accessed April 22, 2025.

12. Bell, *supra* note 2.

II *Get in Formation*

THE HOW OF MOVEMENT LAWYERING

4　*We in These Streets*

Protest and rebellion are powerful tools of organizing. They can mobilize masses and expose hypocrisies and injustices. However, as we discussed in chapter 1, we believe long-term change only happens when we leverage the energy and possibility created by protest and turn it into power building. Law for Black Lives (L4BL) was born from protest. Many of our cofounders formed relationships with each other during the Ferguson uprisings in 2014. A year after Ferguson, a group of us (including two contributors to this chapter, Purvi Shaw and Iman Freeman) came together to answer the questions *What next? How do we move from protest to power? How can we turn the networks and capacities developed during this crisis into long-term movement infrastructure?*

One of our answers was the creation of the national organization Law for Black Lives. We also supported or created local formations like the Baltimore Action Legal Team, which is described by Iman Freeman in her piece in this chapter. This combination of local, national, and ultimately international organizations, as described in the piece in this chapter by lawyers from the Global Network of Movement Lawyers, helped anchor the development of long-term infrastructure that is ready to respond to moments of crisis and opportunity.

When protests erupted in 2020, L4BL was more prepared to provide effective legal support. However, in the sustained backlash to 2020, our networks have been put to the test. In the past few years we have seen an onslaught of laws criminalizing protest and repressing dissent. The question of how to turn protest into power and how to defend against vicious backlash is more important than ever. This chapter struggles with these questions by drawing on lessons from protest movements across the globe.

Movement lawyers have an important role to play in supporting organizers during times of protest and crisis. Because of the aggressive state response to protest and the use of the law to suppress movements, there is a lot of defensive work that must be done to protect organizers and movements. And since moments of crisis create new possibilities and fresh horizons, movement lawyers must always be ready to take advantage of these opportunities.

This chapter highlights how different movement lawyers have responded to moments of crisis in ways that both protect organizers and help build power. Each author discusses the need for what the Global Network for Movement Lawyers terms an "integrated defense." The integrated-defense approach leverages community education, media, documentation, direct services, and more to support and strengthen social movements. Authors in this chapter also touch on collaborative approaches to assessing, strategizing, and solving the issues that communities in crisis face. Lastly, these authors emphasize the importance of international solidarity. The commonalities between how police in Ferguson, Colombia, and Baltimore abuse their power to violently suppress protest, or how international forces collude to silence dissent when it comes to Palestinian liberation, demonstrate that the forces we are up against know no borders. Therefore our strategies and tactics cannot be bound by national borders.

Biographical Reflection: Building Infrastructure
from the Rubble
By Iman Freeman

In April 2015, I received an email from legal workers supporting Baltimore United for Change, a coalition of grassroots organizations in
Baltimore. The email was a call to action to law students, attorneys,
and legal workers in the area requesting legal support because a man
was murdered while in police custody. When I was asked to write this
essay outlining my journey since receiving that email, I immediately
searched my inbox. I thought that reading it again would help me reflect on the emotions I felt all those years ago. I couldn't find the
email and have forgotten the exact details, but nothing in the email
could have prepared me, or the city of Baltimore, for what happened
in the days after Freddie Gray was murdered by the Baltimore Police
Department.

A decade later, Freddie Gray is a household name known for the
pain and trauma he endured at the hands of the police. Pain and
trauma eventually led to his death. The facts of the case are well-
known and all too familiar to many in the Black community. Mr. Gray
was arrested on April 12, 2015. He was put in the back of a police van
while handcuffed. He was not properly secured. The Baltimore Police
Department took him on what they referred to as a "rough ride." This
is a common practice of police departments, when they handcuff people in their custody, put them in the back of vans, do not put a seatbelt
on them, and proceed to drive erratically. At the end of this ride, Mr.
Gray had a severe spinal injury. Days later that injury led to his death.

I responded to the call for legal help even though I knew nothing
about supporting social movements. Before working in Baltimore, I
worked a few jail-support hotline shifts for organizers in Ferguson
in the months after Michael Brown's killing. But I was responding to

a request for legal support and had no clue how an attorney should show up. I just knew that I had a set of skills that could be helpful, and I wanted to figure out how to support my community in the moment.

I had just graduated from law school in May 2014, after studying law for four years as an evening student. Movement lawyering was not mentioned once during these four years. No class ever covered how to provide support to the community during times of unrest. In law school a lesson on justice often starts and ends with litigation or landmark legislation, none of which focus on what's needed to effectuate change—shifting power. The law is designed to remedy the aggrieved party, an individual. Solutions that disrupt systems and shift power don't exist. And this moment needed a shift in power from those that abuse it to the most marginalized people in our community.

To be fair, I'm not sure anything prepares you for this work. What could have prepared me to be a Black lawyer who responds to Black pain? I tell people all the time that this work requires self-reflection. You must take inventory of who you are and what motivates you and be very intentional about how you interact with the communities you work with. Being an attorney comes with a great amount of privilege. People assume you are the authority on any legal topic regardless of whether you've studied it or how long you've been an attorney. Despite going to law school and passing the bar, I felt inadequate when I worked in Ferguson, Baltimore, and later in Baton Rouge. Most of the legal workers and lawyers I encountered had been doing this work for years. Not only did they have experience in the streets, but they had knowledge of movement lawyering principles, of how lawyers have helped (and most important, harmed) communities while pursuing "justice." They knew how lawyers should show up during times of civil unrest, and they were able to articulate what was needed.

Although I didn't have the academic experience, I did have something to offer. I had my experience as a Black woman raised in

Harlem, New York. Experience dealing with loved ones being locked up. Experience dealing with inadequate housing and generational poverty. Experience living under the weight of institutions that were designed to harm me. These experiences can literally make or break you. In fact, they are designed to break you. But I wasn't broken. Despite my upbringing, I was thriving and committed to helping people who shared my story. When I was deciding how to interact with community members, I would often think about how I would want my mom to be treated by a stranger.

I came to see more and more how valuable my perspective and experiences were. This movement needs lawyers like me. Lawyers and legal workers who share life experiences with those that seek legal support. My ability to understand the needs of the Baltimore community led to me being one of the cofounders of the Baltimore Action Legal Team (BALT). When I responded to the call for lawyers in April 2015, there was no Baltimore-based organization that was meeting the needs of movement organizations in Baltimore. Many of the legal volunteers that came to support organizers during the protests were not from the area. Some did a good job of identifying volunteers who were local to the region and sharing knowledge so they could continue to do the work.

When most of the legal volunteers left, the few who remained began to discuss ways to provide a longer-term response to the lack of legal information offered to the community. The Freddie Gray protests helped us identify gaps in legal infrastructure. We began by holding monthly community education events that focused on the officers' trial. Later the workshops focused on fundamental concepts of the criminal legal and policing systems. Soon we realized that this was the first time many community residents had a chance to learn more about the criminal legal system. This was problematic since this very system shaped many lives, especially during traumatic moments. The lack of legal education isn't unique to Baltimore and often compounds the trauma and feeling of helplessness, over-whelm, and inadequacy.

In the beginning, BALT responded to a need for information. As a reminder, this happened a little more than two years after Trayvon Martin's death and less than a year after Michael Brown's death. The Black community was in pain. Pain that was compounded by recurring stories of Black people dying for being Black. The community was trying its best to make sense of what was going on and why justice seemed improbable. At the time there wasn't a legal organization providing space to answer why the justice system wasn't designed to resolve these issues. This is why BALT was started. I remember when the state's attorney of Baltimore City decided to charge the six officers for Mr. Gray's death. I can still feel the tension in the air. Early on, BALT connected with community members and helped them make sense of the moment.

One of BALT's values is agility. BALT remains flexible and ready to respond to practical and legal harms quickly and deliberately to the community. Since its inception, the organization has shifted from a collection of lawyers responding to immediate needs, to a space where community members could learn about the system and share their experiences. Today we are a service-based advocacy organization committed to abolishing systems that criminalize Black people. We do this through litigation, providing direct services, operating a bail fund, and doing policy work. We have evolved and will continue to evolve based on the needs of the people of Baltimore.

While doing this work, the staff and I struggle to balance our goal of ending a system that harms Baltimore's Black community with the fact that we work within the same system. Operating within a system you want to abolish is difficult. Every time we post bail or pay someone's electronic monitoring fees, we are propping up a system that exploits and harms our people. However, the team and I will never

10 TIPS FOR LEGAL & BAIL SUPPORT

ESTABLISH A HOTLINE NUMBER AND HAVE IT PERSONED AT ALL TIMES

A Google number can work for this and can forward to many mobile phones ensuring access, but be warned, Google voice is not secure for calls.

TRACK ARRESTEES' NAMES, EMERGENCY CONTACTS, AND MEDICAL CONDITIONS THAT MIGHT NEED ATTENTION

Track areas where most people are being arrested and the most frequent charges for those arrested.

FIGURE OUT LOCAL BAIL OR BOND PROCEDURES

What percent do you have to pay? How do you pay it? What do you get back? When?

COLLECT MONEY TO BAIL PEOPLE OUT ONCE ARRESTED

Setting up a bail fund can be a great way to get people back out into the streets. A lot of bail money is returned after court processes so the same money can bail out multiple people in the long run.

GET A MAP OF POLICE JURISDICTIONS TO DETERMINE WHERE PEOPLE WILL BE SENT ONCE ARRESTED

You can sometimes get this information by calling police stations or the Sheriff's office

DOCUMENT THE COURTS PEOPLE ARE BEING SENT TO FOR ARRAIGNMENT ONCE THEY ARE BAILED OUT

Give this information to legal representatives on hand

IF YOU'RE ARRANGING BAIL FOR A GROUP, HAVE THOSE BAILED OUT FIRST WAIT FOR THOSE BAILED OUT LAST

It is usually the most vulnerable among us who are released last and solidarity is our best weapon. Focus on freeing those who face the most risk: people with criminal records, undocumented folks, people with urgent medical conditions, trans or gender non-conforming folks, and people under 18 years old.

TAKE PHOTOGRAPHS (WITH PERMISSION) OF INJURIES

ARRANGE RIDES FOR PEOPLE BACK HOME FROM JAIL AND/OR TO COURT THE NEXT DAY, IF NECESSARY

KEEP IN CONTACT AND SHARE INFORMATION WITH OTHER ORGANIZERS AND LEGAL

Make sure everyone knows who will represent them (if representation is being provided) and where to go for court/court support.

"Ten Tips for Legal and Bail Support" poster developed by Law for Black Lives during the 2015 Black Lives Matter protests. Courtesy of Law for Black Lives.

underestimate the importance of being released from jail or having a warrant rescinded. It is important for BALT to address the community's immediate needs while not losing sight of our ultimate goal: abolishing the system. I realize that these words cannot communicate just how difficult it is to strike this balance. We are still learning every day. We do not claim to have all the answers. What we know is that our organization was born from our community's needs, and we strive to address them in accordance with our values.

Tactical Case Study: Lessons from Ferguson for Movement Lawyers
By Purvi Shah

On Saturday, August 9, 2014, an unarmed eighteen-year-old Black teenager, Michael Brown, was fatally shot by a white police officer in Ferguson, Missouri. His body lay in the street for four hours. Enraged and grief-stricken family members and friends organized an impromptu vigil. The vigil transformed into a daily protest. As the daily protest grew, protesters were met by local police wielding guns, rubber bullets, tanks, and tear gas. When the protests continued undeterred, police escalated their tactics. They set up checkpoints, imposed curfews, and arrested hundreds of protesters. The Black youth of Ferguson organically and courageously continued to protest, day after day, night after night. A rebellion was born.

When I arrived in Ferguson just a week after Michael Brown was killed, I needed to quickly gain a sense of the local context and landscape. I knew a few local activists and learned where people were gathering. I showed up at street protests, community meetings, and direct-action trainings. I visited the sites of highest conflict and talked to protesters to understand the scale and scope of police repression. I spent a lot of these early days just listening to people, making protest signs, distributing water, and running errands.

One of the most challenging aspects of working in a crisis is getting oriented and building enough trust to understand the crisis. It is important to make the right connections to have the right data points to make assessments of how legal strategies can advance community goals. I gained firsthand experience of the excessive violence of the police when I was tear-gassed multiple times hours before the state-imposed curfew. I watched, in horror, as babies, mothers, disabled elders, and entire neighborhoods were tear-gassed for simply exercising their right to protest, for simply lamenting the loss of one of their own. As a lawyer of conscience, I had to stand with the people of Ferguson.

Overwhelmed and slightly traumatized, I returned to New York and organized daily conference calls with some of the nation's most experienced movement lawyers to pool strategies about how we could protect the civil and human rights of protesters. These calls

What Movement Lawyers Can Do in the Early Stages

- Show up without an agenda and do any task that will contribute to collective efforts.
- Listen to the concerns of organic protesters and local grassroots organizations.
- Begin to map the ecosystem—that is, who are the key legal actors; what national organizations are present; what kinds of roles are people already playing; where are the gaps.
- Begin tracking the legal issues; organize conference calls to leverage the collective wisdom and expertise of many lawyers.
- Organize legal delegations to collectively document and investigate civil/human rights violations.
- Participate in local and national organizing strategy meetings— being mindful to not have discussion of legal strategies take over the conversation.

spurred two legal delegations, focused on gaining more information and insight about how legal tools could help build the power of the local movement.

After the initial investigation a team of us began providing rapid-response legal support. Our work ranged from recruiting transactional and criminal defense lawyers to providing strategic and tactical support to organizers. We convened a series of national legal calls to strategize with grassroots groups in Ferguson. We recruited experts on mass arrests, human rights, and mass defense to join the calls and provide their expertise. These calls led to the creation of the Ferguson Legal Defense Committee (FLDC), a network of people's lawyers and legal advocates in Saint Louis and across the country who were committed to supporting the protesters in Ferguson. The FLDC, in coordination with a broader organizing call to action, put out an Emergency Call to Action for lawyers in anticipation of the grand jury announcement. This call to action garnered more than five hundred responses in two weeks. Over the course of a few weeks, we created the infrastructure to best utilize and match these legal advocates with needs on the ground. We created a website, volunteer questionnaire, matching process, and assignments.

In addition, a few of us worked to set up and staff a command hub to serve as the nerve center for communications, law, and organizing for the forty-eight hours surrounding the grand jury announcement. This rapid-response work was extremely complicated and required significant systems and infrastructure to be built, including a physical space where legal volunteers could congregate. We also needed to communicate protocols between the different arms of legal volunteers (legal observers, jail support, human rights documentation, criminal defense, and civil rights) and prepare defensive and offensive legal tactics to support to protesters. Over the next year the FLDC incubated and generated a series of legal work. Here are some of the things we did:

Civil Rights Litigation

- Wrote a Demand Letter to the Unified Command alerting them to the civil rights violations.
- Drafted civil rights litigation that was filed and litigated by Arch City Defenders, the Advancement Project, and the Saint Louis University School of Law on behalf of Ferguson protestors. This litigation won a temporary injunction.
- Filed a petition to oust Bob McCulloch, the Saint Louis County prosecutor responsible for overseeing the case related to Michael Brown's death, and appoint a special prosecutor.

Criminal Representation

- Helped find counsel for six hundred municipal cases and seventy felony cases.
- Facilitated conversations between Bronx City Defenders and Arch City Defenders to discuss a holistic approach to criminal defense representation.
- Facilitated introductions for high-profile protesters to Arch City Defenders and SLU Law so they could provide direct representation.

International Human Rights

- Submitted a written report to the UN Committee Against Torture and presented findings on a historic trip with Michael Brown's parents in Geneva.
- Continued our advocacy with UN Special Rapporteurs.
- Launched a new national human rights documentation project focused on capturing information about harassment and surveillance of protesters.

. . .

Here are a few key lessons I learned from my work in Ferguson:

1. BUILDING TRUST IS YOUR PRIMARY OBJECTIVE WHEN YOU ARRIVE. Get on the ground as fast as possible and work humbly without a predetermined institutional agenda and with a movement lawyering approach.

2. DEVELOP RELATIONSHIPS WITH AND LISTEN TO THE CONCERNS AND EXPERIENCES OF A DIVERSE GROUP OF ACTIVISTS, COMMUNITY LEADERS, AND ORGANIZATIONS. A healthy social movement has many different layers of leadership, some visible and others hidden. To be effective, movement lawyers look beyond the most formalized parts of movements and nonprofit groups or high-profile activists and take time to listen to more raw, organic, and unorganized parts of the movement.

3. COLLABORATIVE CRISIS ASSESSMENT RESULTS IN BETTER ISSUE-SPOTTING. While it took parts of the legal community some time to understand the importance of the Ferguson resistance, those of us who traveled to Ferguson quickly understood the potential for a much larger transformative moment. Our initial strategy calls and delegations were instrumental assessment tools that helped us gain a clear understanding of the conditions on the ground and the ways lawyers could help. The collaborative nature of the delegations expanded buy-in beyond our organization and laid the groundwork for the Ferguson Legal Defense Committee and other long-standing relationships. With these relationships as the foundation, similar formations of lawyers came together time and time again—in Baltimore, Baton Rouge, and Charlotte.

4. ASSESS THE SITUATION FROM A BROADER LENS THAN LAW. A handful of organizers and advocates from across the country

were also traveling to Ferguson. We met there and quickly began working collaboratively to provide support to local Ferguson organizations including the Organization for Black Struggle (OBS), Hands Up United, and Missourians Organized for Reform & Empowerment (MORE).

5. RAPID-RESPONSE AND SYSTEMIC CHANGE WORK ARE TWO SIDES OF THE SAME COIN. BOTH ARE NEEDED IN REBELLION MOMENTS. Rapid-response work builds the credibility, relationships, and trust necessary for subsequent systemic change work.

6. BUILDING INFRASTRUCTURE TO CHANNEL THE CAPACITY OF HUNDREDS OF LAWYERS REQUIRES CREATIVE SOLUTIONS TO CAPACITY CONSTRAINTS. Most social justice organizations and social justice lawyers are stretched incredibly thin. Legal organizations are structured with a narrow view of their primary tactics and expertise. Many lawyers approach problems myopically, missing other more strategic, sustainable, and effective approaches to creating social change. We focused on creating infrastructure that would leverage the capacity of hundreds of legal advocates outside of any single organization—hence the idea for the Ferguson Legal Defense Committee and ultimately Law for Black Lives. The crowdsourcing approach utilized by the FLDC allowed us to facilitate a variety of imaginative and creative legal tactics that require different types of expertise, different legal tactics, and different approaches to how we work with the movement; and as a result, we were more able to ensure that needs in our communities were met.

7. INFRASTRUCTURE DEVELOPMENT IS OFTEN INVISIBLE WORK, BUT WHEN DONE RIGHT, IT CAN HAVE AN ENORMOUS IMPACT. Collaboration requires a container. In a few short

months the FLDC went from being an idea to the central hub for hundreds of lawyers to strategize about Ferguson. It yielded lawsuits, reports, documentation projects, and a community of movement lawyers working together across jurisdictions. Building a collaborative space or network that can rapidly execute strategy together requires a considerable amount of infrastructure and organizing, much of which is invisible work. This connectivity is too often deprioritized by organizations as it doesn't provide much notoriety or visibility.

8. MAKE SURE YOUR WORK IS ADDITIVE TO ANY LOCALLY CREATED LEGAL INFRASTRUCTURE, SINCE IT WILL RE-MAIN LONG AFTER YOU LEAVE. While we were getting the FLDC up and running, a local nonlawyer legal collective in Saint Louis built the apparatus to support the more than six hundred people arrested during protests. These visionary organizers had rapidly built complex jail support infrastructure to deal with bond negotiations and arraignments and had created a protester hotline. This work was precious and important. We made sure the FLDC was complementary to this work by working in direct consultation with the legal collective.

9. PRIORITIZE ORIENTING AND TRAINING LEGAL VOLUN-TEERS. IF YOU WANT PEOPLE TO COME CORRECT, YOU HAVE TO SET THE CONTEXT AND EXPECTATIONS FOR THEIR INVOLVEMENT IN THE WORK. Through the FLDC more than 150 lawyers and law students contributed to work in Ferguson. But perhaps most important, these volunteers did so in a way that supported the work of local lawyers and was not counterproductive to the movement goals of the Ferguson leaders. We did this through reviewing and vetting five hundred volunteers and assigning them to teams; creating written orientation packets; designing an online webinar and video trainings for FLDC volunteers; fielding remote

What Movement Lawyers Can Do in the Later Stages

- Produce memos with colleagues assessing the civil and human rights violations.
- Recruit, vet, and secure legal representation for mass arrests. Take some of those cases yourself.
- Recruit transactional lawyers to help set up 501(c)(3)s and to advise on the tax implications of donations.
- Call meetings of all legal actors on the ground to build a shared approach for deploying emergency-related legal services during the grand jury announcement.
- Set up national calls between local lawyers and national lawyers to imagine how lawyers across the country can best support the local movement.
- Build rapid-response legal infrastructure when needed by drafting Emergency Calls to Action. Recruit, vet, and train lawyers from across the country to provide rapid-response assistance.
- Prepare the legal infrastructure to handle mass arrests and repression, including designing human rights documentation teams and civil rights litigation teams.
- Train volunteers in a manner that creates long-term capacity for movement work. Create written orientation packets, host online volunteer webinars, and prioritize community and mentorship so that people grow through their volunteer work.
- Field remote research assignments and design a process to match assignments with best out-of-state capacity and monitor the quality and progress of work.

research assignments from Ferguson by designing a process to match assignments with best out-of-state capacity and monitoring the progress of the work; adding a racial justice training component to the legal observer trainings of our volunteers; facilitating weekly calls for the FLDC national legal team; conducting one-on-ones with FLDC members to get feedback and ensure group unity; and providing problem-solving support and mentorship to individual lawyers working on these tasks.

10. BUILD SHORT-TERM LEGAL CAPACITY IN A WAY THAT BUILDS LONG-TERM INFRASTRUCTURE. Over time, the FLDC grew to provide movement support to the burgeoning multi-city and national movements around police reform and accountability by keeping movement lawyers around the country in tune with the efforts being made in Ferguson.

. . .

The Ferguson rebellion was a historic moment. As with past Black liberation movements, this one challenged the contradictions woven into the fabric of the United States, its laws, and its institutions. The movement raised fundamental questions about the way our system of laws and law enforcement devalues Black life, and it did so in visionary ways: centering the leadership of Black folks and the experiences of the most marginalized—queer, trans, working-class, poor, undocumented, and incarcerated Black folks. Hidden beneath these tangible outcomes are a few more subtle victories that show the potential of legal work when done from a movement-centered perspective.

First, the FLDC forged and cemented connections between like-minded lawyers from across the country, who are now able to call on each other in times of crisis. The exchange between veteran movement lawyers and newer ones deepens collective strategic knowledge and ensures that we don't just work harder, we work smarter. Second, responding to a crisis moment with a movement lawyering approach ensured the FLDC was different from most rapid-response legal efforts. The FLDC kept movement goals front and center and explicitly engaged in discussions about how the law can help build power. This ensured that legal strategies were always part of a multipronged vision. Third, the FLDC strengthened local infrastructure and built long-term movement lawyering know-how in Saint Louis. The infusion of radical and progressive lawyers into Saint Louis (a fairly conservative bar) was incredibly powerful for reigniting imagination and conversation about law and social change. This, combined with the fact that local legal organizations were inspired to match the ferocity and dynamism of the Ferguson movement, has led to the adaptation of more movement-centered practices.

The Hard Stuff: Movement Lawyering in a Time of Genocide—Bolstering the Palestine Movement Through a Crisis of Repression
By Dima Khalidi

In light of the crisis that Palestinians have been facing with the genocide in Palestine and the simultaneous global efforts to attack any opposition to Israel's genocidal actions, I want to briefly reflect on the challenges of movement lawyering in times of crisis. I offer a few reflections, from my experience leading a legal organization supporting the Palestine movement, on how we respond to massive crackdowns and meet defensive legal needs, all while continuing to build power amid the destruction. As we contend with the advent of the second Trump administration in early 2025, it is clear the Palestine movement is the tip of the spear of a much broader right-wing agenda to undermine the very infrastructure of social justice movements that will likely alter the landscape dramatically for the foreseeable future.

As the genocide unfolded in Gaza in the fall of 2023, through 2024 and 2025, and promises decades of work to rebuild infrastructure as well as shattered bodies and souls, Palestinians everywhere—with millions of allies—rose up to demand a stop to the slaughter and justice for our people. The vast mobilizations calling for ceasefire, ending aid to Israel, and for Palestinian liberation were quickly painted as a threat. The draconian reactions to the unprecedented show of solidarity with Palestinians illustrate how Palestinians are rarely portrayed as wanting to live free and dignified lives in our homeland. Instead, because of decades of concerted and racist repression efforts, we are presumed to be motivated by visceral, irrational hatred and violent tendencies toward those who oppress us.

I want to address, as a preface, how navigating such racist gaslighting on a mass scale is a primary challenge of lawyers working in support of movements. All social justice movements that confront the status quo experience this in different ways. Black, Indigenous, and environmental justice movements have been painted— historically and currently—as violent, subversive, and terrorist to justify repressive measures against them.[1] For the Palestine movement in the United States, widespread doxing and harassment campaigns, repressive legislation, civil and criminal legal persecution of activists, and politically motivated deportations are all tactics aimed at undermining and thwarting the movement through the racist narratives about Palestinians as "anti-Semitic" and violent "terrorists."[2]

Such gaslighting is possible because the history of our struggles is obfuscated, denied, and outright falsified in the public mind.[3] In our work challenging the repression, it is therefore imperative that movement lawyers have a nuanced understanding of the history of oppression that a movement is challenging in order to defend and bolster its aims. For the Palestine movement this is especially critical because so much of the repression is based on the denial and falsification of Palestinian history and the role of Zionism in that history. For example, claims that protest chants for freedom "from the river to the sea" are "genocidal" against Jewish people rely on the negation of the fact that Palestinians have long identified as a people in the land between the Mediterranean Sea and the Jordan River, and that they have been dispossessed and denied their freedom in that land for the more than seventy-five years of Israel's existence.[4]

Common claims that anti-Zionism is equivalent to anti-Semitism—which form the basis of many legal attacks and smear campaigns against Palestinians and their allies—also rely on a revisionist history.[5] Zionism is an ethnonationalist movement that emerged in Europe in the nineteenth century. This movement eventually decided to actualize Jewish self-determination through the colonization of Palestine by establishing an exclusive Jewish state in that land, in part because of strong Jewish religious and historical connections to the region and the severe violence that European Jews faced culminating in the Holocaust. Zionist leaders acknowledged they would need to get rid of the vibrant Palestinian population that already existed in Palestine and replace it with Jews from around the world to establish Jewish supremacy in a land where the Jewish population historically hovered around 5 percent. Understanding this fact—and the subsequent history of Zionist colonization, occupation, and apartheid of Palestinians that continues today—is enough to destroy the logic behind the widespread effort to conflate a political ideology with a religion so as to claim that opposition to that ideology is equivalent to hatred of the religion and its followers.

Another example is the prevailing narrative of the events of October 7, 2023, when Hamas militants broke through the walls surrounding Gaza and overtook surrounding military bases and nearby Israeli settlements, resulting in the death of hundreds of Israeli soldiers and civilians. The mainstream narrative would have one believe that the attacks happened in a vacuum—unprovoked and motivated by pure evil. Any understanding of the current phase of the genocide against Palestinians requires a basic understanding of previous phases of the genocide over the past seventy-five years. After Zionist militias committed massacres, spread terror, destroyed more than 400 Palestinian villages, and caused the flight of over 750,000

Palestinians from their land in 1947–48, a state of Israel was declared in 1948 over 78 percent of historic Palestine. A Palestinian refugee population was created that continues to be barred from returning to their homes and land.

Israel has established a complex regime of apartheid since then to rule over Palestinians.[6] There is one set of laws for Jews and several other sets of laws that govern Palestinians.[7] One set of laws is for those who reside in occupied East Jerusalem; another for those living in the occupied West Bank; and yet another for those living in the Gaza Strip, which Israel has besieged since 2006. Palestinians are divided not only by walls, fences, and checkpoints that Israel erects, but also legally, with different ID cards and rules that govern what they are able to do and where they are able to go. Israel has repeatedly bombarded Gaza—where more than 70 percent of the population were already refugees—since the siege on the tiny territory began in 2006, progressively destroying homes and infrastructure in one of the most densely populated areas on Earth, to the point that the UN called the territory practically unlivable long before 2023.[8] This is what creating a "Jewish state" has meant. Palestinians have not lived one day of peace or freedom. And Palestinians have always resisted Israel's denial of their freedom and self-determination. Resistance has taken different forms: from general strikes and boycotts, to armed struggle, to nonviolent and self-sufficiency protest movements and beyond. The October 7 attacks and the subsequent fighting against Israeli forces in an obliterated Gaza are the latest episode in that long arc of resistance.

Countering the repression without a basic understanding of this history of injustice risks further entrenching harmful narratives about the Palestinian struggle, even if it might bolster First Amendment rights, for example. This is therefore an entreaty to all movement lawyers to embrace this learning as a key part of our lawyering, because we need all the great legal and political minds we can get to confront the enormous threats our movements face today. While the movement in the United States advocating for Palestinian liberation has long faced attacks from Israel and allied Zionist groups, as well as increasingly from state actors, the post-October 2023 landscape has magnified this repression exponentially. It is impacting people and groups in every arena—from K–12 schools and colleges to varied industries and at every level of local, state, and federal government. This extreme repression will have long-term impacts for our right to dissent generally, including rights of free expression, assembly, association, and academic freedom.

While I can't purport to have the answers, I share general learnings and examples to illuminate both the challenges and potential paths toward building power in times of extreme repression—even when all odds feel stacked against us.

Challenges and Lessons in Navigating Crises of Repression

In all of 2022, Palestine Legal received a total of 290 requests for legal support. In 2023 we received 1,352, more than a thousand of these between October and December.[9] In 2024 we received 2,099 requests for legal support.[10] By August 2024 that number had almost tripled. The crisis here, unlike in Palestine, is not one of life or death—although violence against Palestinians in the United States has increased, including a boy who was killed and several others who were shot or attacked.[11] It is, however, often a matter of livelihood and fundamental rights, and now of freedom as well, as Trump's agencies unlawfully abduct and detain noncitizen students solely for their speech activities. There has been a veritable purge in many places of employment, where employers are firing and otherwise investigating or disciplining employees who are often reported for social media posts or other expressions in support of Palestinians. We documented 162 terminations in 2024, among 317 total reports of people facing issues with their employers because of expressions opposing the genocide or in support of Palestinians.[12]

Universities have been the focal point of many protests as well, as students demand a voice at their universities, many of which invest enormous sums in the industries that enable and profit from the oppression of Palestinians. Rather than take their students seriously, university administrators have called in the police, which often brutally conducted more than three thousand arrests on campuses in the spring and summer of 2023, after students erected encampments to force universities to pay attention.[13] Hundreds of students across the United States have been dragged through disciplinary processes with little due process and hit with draconian sanctions that include eviction, expulsion, suspensions, and even prohibitions on being involved in student clubs.[14]

Meanwhile, congressional committees are calling university leaders to testify, stripping them of federal funds for not punishing Palestine activism enough and conducting fishing expeditions about activist groups and organizations connected with the movement, relying on frivolous accusations of support for terrorism.[15] Zionist groups have long been pushing to criminalize opposition to Israel, and have since October 2023 brought a number of civil lawsuits claiming that movement groups are "aiding and abetting terrorism" through their speech activities—attempting to expand prohibitions against "material support for terrorism" to mere words and advocacy efforts.[16] Such lawsuits have historically been precursors for governmental criminal indictments under antiterrorism laws. This crackdown on Palestine organizing is both a measure of the power of the mobilizations and also a measure of the extent to which Israel and its allies in the United States see the movement for Palestinian freedom as a primary threat to its impunity as well as to continued unconditional US support for its genocidal actions.

Palestine Legal was started at a time when this crackdown was in its infancy. And since 2012 the threat level has steadily escalated. Since October 2023, Zionist groups have put into overdrive all the tactics used against the movement at once. I offer a few reflections about lessons learned throughout our work that have been magnified in this crisis period. Needless to say, we are continually striving to learn and adjust in ever-changing circumstances.

INFRASTRUCTURE IS KEY. As a small legal organization, Palestine Legal was not built to handle the volume of legal support needed after October 2023. We had to shift our model from taking on most of the cases that came to us to doing triage and referring large numbers of cases to our network of attorneys. At the same time, we had to prioritize building up our attorney network to meet the overwhelming needs. In the span of less than a year our attorney network doubled to about two thousand individuals. Building and adjusting infrastructure in the midst of crisis is hard, because it inevitably takes time and coordination. Time feels in especially short supply. In order to manage the volume of need for legal support that started in 2023 and has persisted, we needed a new triage system to identify the most urgent issues and effectively direct issues to the right place. We had to narrow the focus of what our handful of attorneys could take on. Because we had expertise in campus issues, we narrowed our focus to student and some faculty issues.

As the volume continued at high levels, it quickly became overwhelming, and we had to dedicate significant resources to growing our network of attorneys to support advocates under attack. Hundreds of new attorneys volunteered to support, and we put in place a system and brought on capacity to vet them, identify how they could help, and provide basic tools and resources on the legal and political issues at play, along with movement lawyering principles and strategic guidance. This was critical to ensure that the attorneys we send clients to don't undermine activists' goals or operate in ways that are harmful to the movement or other social justice causes. We also had to set expectations, establish the legal and ethical relationships necessary to collaborate, and set up platforms to communicate, share resources, and strategize. These are all things that we are continuing to build out and improve nearly two years into the crisis, with long-term needs and goals in mind.

A STRATEGIC COMPASS HELPS GUIDE ALLIES. A primary challenge in dealing with this volume of needs as well as new, often unknown volunteer capacity to support is to maintain a strategic compass. When the attacks are relentless and individuals need immediate help, how do we forge both defensive and offensive strategies across many organizations and attorneys so that the movement can maintain its momentum? Strategy requires enormous coordination and relationships. Palestine Legal has a unique view of the landscape of repression, both historically and presently, and has built a wide network of relationships that it relies on to support the movement. Nevertheless, in a crisis period, with a new array of forces both attacking and stepping up to defend, strategic direction is helpful, and innovative modes of coordination are needed to share and collaborate on different strategies.

While it's helpful to have different groups contributing to the arenas where they can have most impact, it's a challenge to maintain communication and coordination across a wide variety of groups with varying agendas, capacities, and politics. Early on after October 2023, a number of overlapping groups were formed to bring together lawyers and other advocates to respond to the crisis. These helped to build relationships and also served as a way for us and others to highlight the biggest threats and areas of need. This gave us an opportunity to share what we saw as important strategic considerations. For example, there was a tendency by groups that traditionally serve

Muslim communities and that were steeped in defense against post-9/11 anti-Muslim policies to use the language of Islamophobia and anti-Muslim hate to explain what was happening. We shared with partners the imperative of naming the specifically anti-Palestinian racism that was driving Israel's genocide as well as the racist repression happening in the United States. This framing was critical to keep the focus on Palestine and Palestinians when Israel and US allies were intent on erasing Palestinians from the equation—literally and figuratively.

Forging and aligning allies on legal strategy is a particular challenge. To begin with, when we're working within a profession that relies on laws made and interpreted by and for the privileged, and focused on individual rather than systemic harms, we often don't have a lot of options. We are advocating for clients who are working for Palestinian liberation within a system that has effectively blocked it for more than seven decades. It is a small sampling of the systemic racism and discrimination ingrained in the legal system that Indigenous, Black, and Brown people have been fighting against on a daily basis for over four hundred years. We have to choose legal tools that allow us to expose the broader issues at play and challenge the fundamental injustices that our clients' organizing is focused on. For example, long before October 2023, we prioritized addressing backlash against students through antidiscrimination laws, filing civil rights complaints against universities for anti-Palestinian racism. Such a strategy would help keep a focus on the impact of repression on Palestinian and associated students as well as on the underlying issues that they were being targeted for—namely their advocacy for Palestinian rights.

The complaints allowed us to center the way that the targeting of Palestinians is inherent to Israel's Zionist ideology, which denies Palestinians' history and even their existence and paints opposition to their oppression as "anti-Semitic" and "terrorist." While antidiscrimination laws are generally focused on individual harms and have been watered down in ways that have retrenched systemic injustices, as critical race theorists have long argued, these complaints had a broader purpose.[17] They advanced a narrative that traces anti-Palestinian racism that students are experiencing back to Israel and its oppression of the Palestinian people as a whole in its execution of its settler-colonial project.

Since October 7, 2023, as the genocide clarified the deep-seated anti-Palestinian racism behind the wave of repression at universities throughout the United States, we worked to tool up allies to use civil rights complaints to hold universities accountable for their treatment of Palestinian and associated students. Dozens of complaints helped enlighten Biden's Department of Education about the way that anti-Palestinian racism manifests and that helped push back on efforts by Zionist groups to entrench in antidiscrimination laws the notion that criticism of Israel and anti-Zionism is the same as anti-Semitism.[18] While there have been a number of other challenges in forging both defensive and offensive strategies to counter the widespread repression in different arenas, this is one example of how our pre-crisis work helped to guide one aspect of a crisis response.

THE NARRATIVE IS HALF THE LEGAL BATTLE. In the context of the Palestine movement, the dominant narrative in the media as well as at institutions and in government—both before and even more so after October 2023—was hostile to Palestine advocates and protesters. This is partly because of the fact of US support for Israel and the line that is enforced in various arenas. The result is a dominant Zionist narrative that labels criticism of Israel as anti-Semitism and erases the fact of an ongoing genocide that has claimed tens of thousands of Palestinian lives, not to mention the more than seventy-five years of oppression that advocates oppose. To counter this narrative, and in line with the strategy noted earlier, we put forward framing and analysis that show the prevalence of anti-

Palestinian racism to explain the persecution of Palestine advocates. This included a report we copublished with the Center for Constitutional Rights on the anti-Palestinian origins of antiterrorism laws, which are a primary weapon being wielded against activists to criminalize a broad swath of expression and advocacy.[19]

We endeavor, in our legal work, to create avenues for activists to speak from their perspective and about their motivations for protesting independent of false accusations and narratives. We try to ensure, when clients agree to publicizing their stories, that our clients' and movement narratives are represented in legal documents as well as in public communications. A robust media strategy alongside legal work educates the general public and gives clients a voice when the primary purpose of repression is to warp their voice or deny them one at all. While getting favorable coverage in the mainstream media is difficult—especially when there is rampant censorship on Palestine in newsrooms—there are increasing opportunities in alternative media sources and via social media platforms.[20]

A parallel advocacy strategy that mobilizes community support for targeted groups and individuals while pressuring decision makers can bring new activists into the fold, turning a threat into an opportunity. Repression and censorship harm movements not only by preventing activists from sharing their message but also by distraction and isolation, forcing individuals and organizations into a defensive posture. Inviting a broader community to rally around a person or group facing backlash can serve not only to amplify the original message and demonstrate the power the movement holds but also to expand the movement and build more power.

THE POLITICAL LINE MUST DEFY ATTEMPTS TO DIVIDE. In all social justice movements there are both natural schisms that emerge and manufactured divisions that result from oppositional infiltration and governmental efforts to sabotage effective organizing.

Movement lawyers can get caught up in such ideological divisions as well as in intentional sabotage efforts. As an organization, Palestine Legal has prioritized maintaining a certain level of neutrality in intramovement divisions so that we're able to represent different elements of the movement that are under attack. We are intent on defying efforts to create movement fractures by avoiding passing judgment on different movement tactics. We aim to focus on protecting the rights of people to dissent and engage in protest against injustices and to be free from discriminatory and violent persecution for their views and protest actions, while echoing the movement's broader goals and demands. This includes uplifting the way that capitalism and imperialism shape the repression of dissent to those systems.

The post–October 2023 period witnessed numerous incidents of potential rupture and internal divisions that we had to navigate, including increasing accusations of infiltration and collaboration. We have worked to help activists and groups navigate relationships and build trust where appropriate, while stressing movement security practices to protect against surveillance and sabotage efforts. These are difficult needles to thread, and it has helped to learn from other movement experiences confronting these threats that have destroyed many a movement.

WORKING ACROSS MOVEMENTS BUILDS POWER. Palestine Legal has long sought to strengthen cross-movement collaboration in the legal arena, mirroring the cross-movement collaboration and solidarity that the Palestine movement in the United States has been nurturing for decades on the grassroots level. Such collaboration comes naturally as other movements face similar threats. The pre–October 2023 waves of legislative attacks on advocates for Palestinian rights, for example, are being weaponized against other movements. What were originally laws targeting boycotts for Palestinian rights are now templates for laws targeting boycotts of the fossil fuel industry, the prison industry, the gun industry, and companies that discriminate against LGBTQ communities.[21]

Laws attempting to codify a definition of anti-Semitism that encompasses criticism of Israel are justified in similar ways as so-called anti-CRT (critical race theory) laws that try to ban the teaching of race and the impacts of the history of systemic racism. Both efforts rely on the notion that looking critically at history—whether that of the United States or Israel—is harmful and offensive to dominant communities (i.e., white in the United States or Jewish in Israel/Palestine).[22] Similarly, legislation that is undermining collective First Amendment rights to protest is a threat to all of our movements— whether by criminalizing Indigenous and environmentalist protests of pipelines or attempting to attach criminal liability for whatever happens at mass protests on organizers. Common forces are at work pushing such legislation at the municipal, state, and federal levels, and our movements should be aligned in challenging them.[23]

The political persecution of activists through criminalization and frivolous lawsuits by private actors is reaching new heights across movements. The prosecution of StopCopCity activists in Atlanta with RICO and domestic terrorism charges is one example of the way activists are being pursued with draconian charges by right-wing prosecutors.[24] Already, since October 2023, a number of frivolous lawsuits have been filed against activist groups under antiterrorism laws that will take considerable resources to defend against, and we expect that terrorism prosecutions will soon follow.[25] This is all par for the course in the history of repression of justice movements in the United States, and making these connections allows us to see that we are not alone and that we can collectively overcome the repression as we continue to push to change the status quo of profits over people.

These are general reflections while our people in Palestine and our movement in the United States are still in the midst of a crisis period. I have no concrete answers on the best way to navigate the shifting political terrain and the extreme repression. History has taught us that many make sacrifices fighting for justice, and that certainly remains true today. As movement lawyers, we know that the law is weaponized against our movements, and that while we need to challenge the law in court with a fully political approach, we also need to extend the fight into the streets, campuses, our communities, and the media. We know that courts will not save us, because the edifice of institutional racism will remain even if one law is struck down or one client's rights are vindicated. So our task remains. We must keep bolstering the popular struggles for liberation that are organizing, changing minds, and fighting injustice from the ground up, while trying to enact the liberated futures we want to see along the way.

Praxis: Standing Up for the Right to Resist at the Global Level
By María Elvira Cabrera, Alejandro Rodríguez Pabón, Meena Jagannath, Felipe Mesel, and Jomary Ortegón Osorio

Liberation cannot be achieved within any set of borders. This is especially true given the present borders we have inherited from colonialism and imperial conquest. It is thus a moral and strategic imperative to link our struggles together globally, analytically, and practically, understanding how local issues share common root causes and how transnational collaboration produces systemic transformation.

As reactionary conservative forces gain ascendance around the world, we are seeing an authoritarian playbook take shape in places like Hungary, Brazil, India, Uganda, the Philippines, and now the United States. Right-wing US politicians like Donald Trump and Florida governor Ron DeSantis are actively pulling tactics from this playbook and experimenting in ways that transmute those tactics toward more repressive ends. This is particularly the case due to the expansion of connections among right-wing forces on a global level.

We are witnessing a worldwide upsurge in violence and repression against human rights and environmental defenders, activists, and communities of resistance. Examples include the spreading anti-LGBTQ+ hatred across Africa and beyond at the behest of US-based evangelical churches; Israel's attempt to shut down long-standing Palestinian human rights organizations in the name of "terrorism" and the genocide in Gaza; the spread of antiprotest laws to criminalize Black protestors in Florida; the criminalization of Indigenous communities' organizing in other states to resist natural resource extraction and the building of oil and gas pipelines that threaten the sanctity of our collective lands and waters; and the imprisonment of environmental defenders in Vietnam as a way to silence and suppress any civil society critique of state extra-activist efforts.

The global COVID-19 pandemic reinforced this reality in two ways: it deteriorated the material living conditions of the working class around the world, making the need to protest for a more dignified life more urgent; and many states have chosen to combat the pandemic with repressive measures that have increased the punitive power of the state as well as its legitimacy to exert this power. The pandemic created the conditions for states to propound repressive measures under the guise of a "state of emergency," passing legislation limiting the right to protest in multiple countries and deploying the police to criminalize social protest. At the same time, authoritarianism, militarism, white supremacist movements, the scapegoating of oppressed populations (Black and Indigenous people, women, LGBTQ+ people, migrants, people with disabilities), crackdowns on activism, and the absolute dominance of market forces are on the rise.

In this context the Global Network of Movement Lawyers (GNML), which grew out of a convening in 2019 and is presently stewarded by Movement Law Lab, aims to build the infrastructure necessary for movement lawyers to connect across borders, to learn from each other, and to strategize about how to address common threats, including threats to the right to resist oppression and to protest for a better and more just society. We have seen how multiple members of our network have experienced serious threats, harassment, arrest, cuts to the funding of their organizations, and invasive audits. It is crucial that we understand these events to be symptoms of a global trend toward repression of progressive movements.

With this backdrop we highlight the work of movement lawyers in Colombia—the Colectivo de Abogadxs José Alvear Restrepo (CAJAR) and Temblores—in the context of the Paro Nacional (National Strike) that took place in 2021. Colombia's Paro Nacional—which began on April 28, 2021, and lasted more than three months—has its roots in key moments of conflict and strikes triggered by the failure to implement the historic 2016 Peace Accord, which was intended to end a decades-long armed conflict between the Colombian government and the Revolutionary Armed Forces of Colombia (FARC).

A primary antecedent of the 2021 Paro Nacional was the civic strike of Buenaventura in 2017, a well-organized, Black-led mobilization formed in response to a pattern of disinvestment, extraction, and failed promises on the part of the Colombian government in that region. Despite the repressive and excessive use of force by the Escuadrón Móvil Antidisturbios (ESMAD)—a police force deployed to control protests—the mobilization continued defiantly, gaining national attention. In 2018, in the Valle del Cauca, a cycle of Indigenous protests took place in what is known as the "Indigenous Minga," later accompanied by a student movement. These flashpoints demonstrate that from the beginning, diverse racialized and historically oppressed communities in Colombian society were at the forefront of the organizing that led to the national strike and, as a result, were also those who suffered the greatest repression. In fact, one of the epicenters of the Paro Nacional was the city of Cali (capital of the Valle del Cauca), which has one of the largest populations of

Afro-Colombians in the country; half of the murders at the hands of the police documented by Temblores during the strike took place in Cali.[26]

Under the right-wing government of President Iván Duque, who took power in 2018, the government further militarized Colombian state forces and made policy decisions that exacerbated preexisting inequalities. In response to this, on November 21, 2019, the first major national strike began, characterized by several innovations in the exercise of the right to protest. First, the protest was decentralized, such that key actions not only happened in historic or emblematic sites in big cities where demonstrations usually took place, but they also spread throughout smaller neighborhoods and rural areas. The strike integrated new tactics—ranging from the provision of food through community kitchens for those who joined the strike to the renaming of certain key sites of struggle. For example, the entrances to the Transmilenio (a public transport network that connects different parts of the city of Bogota) began to be called Portales de la Resistencia (Portals of the Resistance) by the social movement, and the neighborhood of Puerto Rellena in Cali began to be called Puerto Resistencia (Resistance Port).

As the protests progressed, police repression intensified, and public discourse began to blame immigrants and those they labeled "terrorists" for what was happening. In 2020 the COVID-19 pandemic brought street mobilizations to a standstill for a few months. However, the passage of a regressive tax reform proposal that fundamentally impacted the lower- and middle-income classes subsequently served as the triggering event for the April 28, 2021, start of the massive Paro Nacional. By all accounts there was a staggering number of human rights violations and violence committed by the state police apparatus, including ESMAD. In this context lawyers accompanying the social movement, including CAJAR and Temblores, deployed a strategy of "integrated defense" (*exigibilidad integral*),

Protestors in Colombia reclaiming public space. Photo taken by July Henríquez.

which combines legal means of defense with other tactics including public advocacy with authorities, rights education, and media advocacy.

The lawyers' role included accompanying protesters directly, providing psychosocial and legal assistance (by gathering complaints of police violence and litigating those cases), building coalitions through the campaign Libertad Asunto de Todas (Freedom Is Everyone's Issue), and giving visibility to the movement's demands through both legal and nonlegal tactics. In particular, there was a tremendous effort to document, produce, and disseminate information through platforms like Plataforma Grita that reported police violence. Over the course of the more than three-month-long strikes, Temblores documented forty police killings and nine different practices of disproportionate use of force by police, including assassinations, torture, shooting at faces, eye injuries, and sexual violence. The Defender la Libertad campaign produced a comprehensive report documenting the number of human rights violations and their geographic spread over the course of the strike.[27]

Additional lawyers' support included designing toolkits for activists and for military officials who were conscientious objectors as well as bringing suits to publicly denounce police brutality and misconduct. This support incorporated political advocacy to make concrete demands of public authorities and the construction of democratic forums in public spaces so that civil society could discuss pressing issues, including a police reform plan that was presented to the government. The intention was to move from defensive demands to deep political debate and to give emotion and substance to the strike. Finally, lawyers and the movements they represented deployed international advocacy through the international press to counter the government's narrative and submitted a joint report on behalf of a coalition of organizations to the office of the United Nations High Commissioner for Human Rights and to the Inter-American Commission on Human Rights (IACHR). The successful petition led to an official visit from the IACHR to document and investigate human rights violations, which resulted in a report with forty-one recommendations to the Colombian government.[28]

Of course, the lawyers maintained a commitment to the underlying structural demands of the Paro Nacional; however, the overwhelming and shocking level of state violence and force used against demonstrators caused many of the movement lawyers to dedicate significant efforts to documenting and beginning the process of holding officials accountable for their acts of extreme repression. It remains to be seen whether state officials responsible for the human rights violations will be held accountable (i.e., face justice beyond the special forums that are biased toward the police and state forces), to break with the history of impunity that they have long enjoyed. Transformation often begins in the streets. While many of these structural issues persist in Colombia, the recent election of Gustavo

Petro and the first Black vice president of Colombia, Fráncia Marquez, marks a new political moment in Colombia, which might not have been possible without the massive mobilizations over the past few years.

As for the rest of the world, the outlook does not look as rosy. We are preparing for escalating violence and repression as economic conditions worsen across the globe, wars and climate change force migration and food insecurity, and authoritarian forces take hold of ever more countries. In this context the Colombian experience and others like it are instructive for how lawyers can deploy a range of tools—beyond legal tools—to accompany movements not only in their defense but also in creating spaces and opportunities for their demands for justice and dignity to be heard and ultimately fulfilled.

Learn Something from This

- The problems our communities face are global in nature and origins. We should be studying and building with lawyers and movements across the globe and should use all the tools, including international tools, in our arsenal.
- Effective rapid response must combine media engagement, public education, documentation of human rights abuses, defensive and offensive legal interventions, and more. We must not underestimate the power and impact of narrative and media in our legal strategies.
- Creating and sustaining spaces where people from different organizations and with different expertise can work together results in strong and sustainable infrastructures that make us better able to assess the conditions and take advantage of opportunities. But building these containers requires hard work that is

often undervalued and made invisible. We have to honor the labor it requires to build spaces like this and allocate time for it.

- We must build short-term capacity with an eye on long-term infrastructure. Especially local infrastructure. Rapid response often includes coming in from outside. We must ensure that as we do rapid-response work, we are training up local lawyers and legal workers and feeding local organizations. When we leave a place, it should be stronger and more resourced than when we came, not less.
- Relationships take time, care, and listening. There are no shortcuts. As they say, move at the speed of trust.
- A victory should be defined by whether or not we build power for our communities or increase the resilience of our movements, not whether we win a specific case or policy.

Resources

- There are a number of organizations that have extensive rapid-response resources. The National Lawyers Guild website has guides, tip sheets, and best practices for those engaging in, or representing those engaging in, protest and mobilizations. Their website is www.nlg.org. Law for Black Lives also has extensive resources for lawyers supporting protests at www .law4blacklives.org.
- Movement Law Lab and the Global Network of Movement Lawyers have a lot of resources focused on how to build across borders and issue silos. Their Webinar Series on "Tools for Safety and Protection" is especially relevant to this chapter's focus on how to move from defensive work to offensive work. Check them out at www.movementlawlab.org/webinars-with -prodesc.

- *Whose Streets?* is a powerful documentary about the killing of Michael Brown and the Ferguson uprising. It is co-directed by Saint Louis–based Damon Davis and gives powerful context to the work that Purvi Shah describes in her piece in this chapter. The movie is available on several streaming platforms.

Notes

1. Jules Boykoff, *The Suppression of Dissent: How the State and Mass Media Squelch US American Social Movements* (Routledge, 2006).

2. "The Palestine Exception to Free Speech: A Movement Under Attack in the US," Palestine Legal and Center for Constitutional Rights, 2015, https://palestinelegal.org/the-palestine-exception, accessed April 21, 2025.

3. This explains the enormous focus by right-wing forces on undermining these histories in educational institutions. The teaching of both Black studies and the history and structural nature of racism, as well as the emergent teaching about Palestine, in both elementary and higher education are under severe attack. "Legislative Threats to Academic Freedom: Redefinitions of Antisemitism and Racism," American Association of University Professors' Committee A on Academic Freedom and Tenure, March 2022, www.aaup.org/report/legislative-threats-academic-freedom-redefinitions-antisemitism-and-racism.

4. Edward W. Said, *The Question of Palestine*, 2nd ed. (1979; Vintage Books, 1992); Rashid Khalidi, *The Hundred Years' War on Palestine: A History of Settler Colonialism and Resistance, 1917–2017* (Macmillan, 2020); Ilan Pappe, *The Ethnic Cleansing of Palestine*, 2nd ed. (Oneworld Publications, 2007).

5. "Distorted Definition: Redefining Antisemitism to Silence Advocacy for Palestinian Rights," Palestine Legal, https://palestinelegal.org/distorted-definition, accessed October 30, 2024.

6. Major human rights organizations now agree, as Palestinians have long argued, that Israel practices apartheid. "Israel's Apartheid Against Palestinians: Cruel System of Domination and Crime Against Humanity," Amnesty International, February 1, 2022, www.amnesty.org/en/documents/mde15/5141/2022/en; "A Threshold Crossed: Israeli Authorities and the Crimes of Apartheid and Persecution," Human Rights Watch, April 27, 2021, www.hrw.org/report/2021/04/27/threshold-crossed/israeli-authorities-and-crimes-apartheid-and-persecution;

"A Regime of Jewish Supremacy from the Jordan River to the Mediterranean Sea: This Is Apartheid," B'Tselem, 2021, www.btselem.org/sites/default/files /publications/202101_this_is_apartheid_eng.pdf, accessed April 21, 2025.

7. "The Discriminatory Laws Database," *Adalah*, www.adalah.org/en /content/view/7771, accessed April 21, 2025.

8. "Suffocation and Isolation: 15 Years of Israeli Blockade of Gaza," Euro-Mediterranean Human Rights Monitor, January 24, 2021, https://euromedmonitor .org/en/article/4116/New-report:-Gaza-is-almost-unlivable-after-15-years-of -blockade.

9. "Reverberations of October 7: Mobilization Against Genocide Undeterred by Peak Anti-Palestinian Repression," Palestine Legal, May 2024, https://static1 .squarespace.com/static/548748b1e4b083fc03ebf70e/t/664fbc07860df7037ba 81300/1716501546613/Pal+Legal+Report+Reverberations+of+Oct+7th.

10. "A New Generation for Liberation Historic Student Protests Defy University Crackdowns: 2024 Year in Review," Palestine Legal, April 2025, https://static1.squarespace.com/static/548748b1e4b083fc03ebf70e/t /67fe79259066a5210ae06fad/1744730460662/Palestine+Legal+2024+Year+in +Review+Report.

11. *Id.*

12. *Id.*

13. Elizabeth Weill-Greenberg et al., "We Tracked 3,200 Pro-Palestinian Campus Arrests. Here's How Prosecutors Are Responding," *The Appeal*, July 1, 2024, https://theappeal.org/prosecutors-charges-protesters-arrested-gaza -colleges-april.

14. Akela Lacy, "Student Protesters Were Suspended with No Chance to Defend Themselves. Will Courts Return Them to Campus?," *The Intercept*, August 16, 2024, https://theintercept.com/2024/08/16/uc-irvine-gaza-campus-protests-lawsuit.

15. Matthew Petti, "Congressional Republicans Launch 'Fishing Expedition' Against Progressive, Jewish, and Palestinian Nonprofits," *Reason*, May 16, 2024, www.aol.com/news/congressional-republicans-launch-fishing-expedition -182003961.html.

16. Akela Lacy, "October 7 Survivors Sue Campus Protestors, Say Students Are 'Hamas's Propaganda Division,'" *The Intercept*, May 10, 2024, https://theintercept .com/2024/05/10/october-7-survivors-lawsuit-palestine-hamas-sjp-protests.

17. Kimberlé Crenshaw, "Race, Reform, and Retrenchment: Transformation and Legitimation in Antidiscrimination Law," 101 *Harvard L. Rev.* 1331 (1988).

18. Trump's decimation of the DOE and his agencies' focus on targeting the boogeymen of anti-white racism in the form of DEI and anti-Semitism in the form of Palestine activism have required a shift in strategies as well as consideration of other venues to advance claims of anti-Palestinian racism.

19. "Anti-Palestinian at the Core: The Origins and Growing Dangers of U.S. Antiterrorism Law," Palestine Legal and Center for Constitutional Rights, February 2024, https://static1.squarespace.com/static/548748b1e4b083fc03ebf70e/t /65d637d9f2843f3855780ae3/1708537837536/Anti-Palestinian+at+the+Core .pdf.

20. Jacob Gardenswartz, "U.S. Journalists Face Retaliation, Censorship for Supporting Palestinian Human Rights," *The Objective*, November 3, 2023, https://objectivejournalism.org/2023/11/us-journalists-censorship-supporting -palestine.

21. Lara Friedman, "Free Speech-Quashing Laws Based on Israel-Focused Anti-Boycott Laws," Foundation for Middle East Peace, 2023, https://scheerpost .com/wp-content/uploads/2022/07/BDS-Laws-as-Template-for-Laws-on -Other-Issues.pdf, accessed April 21, 2025; Meg Cunningham, "Model Legislation Targets Banks That Divest from Fossil Fuel Companies," *ABC News*, December 22, 2021, https://abcnews.go.com/Politics/model-legislation-targets-banks -divest-fossil-fuel-companies/story?id=81865813; Erika Bolstad, "Boycotting the Boycotters: In Oil-Friendly States, New Bills Aim to Block Divestment from Fossil Fuels," *In These Times*, March 19, 2021, https://inthesetimes.com/article/fossil -fuel-divestment-ban-texas-north-dakota-oil; Debra Kahn, "Cracks in the Anti-ESG Foundation," *Politico*, January 24, 2023, www.politico.com/newsletters/the -long-game/2023/01/24/cracks-in-the-anti-esg-foundation-00079204.

22. "Legislative Threats to Academic Freedom," *supra* note 3.

23. "ALEC Attacks," Center for Constitutional Rights, Dream Defenders, Palestine Legal, The Red Nation, and the US Campaign for Palestinian Rights, 2018, www.alecattacks.org, accessed April 21, 2025; Alex Kotch and Don Wiener, "ALEC Inspires Lawmakers to File Anti-Critical Race Theory Bills," *Common Dreams*, July 28, 2021, www.commondreams.org/views/2021/07/28 /alec-inspires-lawmakers-file-anti-critical-race-theory-bills.

24. Tadhg Larabee and Eva Rosenfeld, "The Criminalization of Solidarity: The Stop Cop City Prosecutions," *Dissent Magazine*, Spring 2024, www .dissentmagazine.org/article/the-criminalization-of-solidarity-the-stop-cop -city-prosecutions.

25. Lacy, *supra* note 16.

26. Plataforma Grita, Temblores ONG, https://www.temblores.org, accessed 2021.

27. "El sometimiento de la democracia: Un balance del derecho a la protesta social en Colombia en el año," Campaign Defender la Libertad Asunto de Todas, 2021, https://acrobat.adobe.com/link/track?uri=urn%3Aaaid%3Ascds%3AUS% 3A6710a368-d494-4597-92f9-f5a51177aa54&viewer%21megaVerb=group -discover, accessed April 21, 2025.

28. "Observaciones y recomendaciones: Visita de trabajo a Colombia," Comisión Interamericana de Derechos Humanos y Organización de los Estados Americanos, 2021, www.oas.org/es/cidh/informes/pdfs/ObservacionesVisita _CIDH_Colombia_SPA.pdf, accessed April 21, 2025.

5 Bringing Movements into the Courthouse

Lawyering is synonymous with litigation. It is seen in our society as the most powerful way for aggrieved people to "get justice." When you say you're a lawyer, often people think you wear a suit, carry a briefcase, and go to court. This notion is further reinforced by false narratives about lawyers as "rainmakers" using the courts to literally make miracles happen. Unfortunately this positioning has left many people with a false sense of what is possible inside of a system that is designed in many ways to protect the ruling class thus ensuring that inequality continues to exist. Relying on litigation alone will not bring about systemic change, but as this chapter shows it can be an effective tool for advancing movement goals and mitigating harm.

In this chapter we explore the benefits and risks of using litigation as a movement lawyer and some of the important questions that come up during the process. Authors in this chapter reflect on how they have decided when courts can be used strategically to advance movement goals as well as the pitfalls, especially because the nature of litigation is that it is insular, slow-moving, and precarious. In her piece Judith Browne Dianis discusses her adoption of a movement lawyering approach after realizing that traditional lawyering and litigation often ignores the priorities of communities and leaves them no better off, even after a win in court. Vince Warren walks through the ways that litigation can be used strategically both as a defensive and offensive tactic. Bryanna Jenkins's piece considers how choosing specific legal tools, like amicus briefs, can impact the outcome of litigation and help build power through a commitment to collective action and collaboration. We end this chapter with a piece by Joo-Hyun Kang, who reflects on her experience as an organizer working closely with lawyers in a decades-long campaign to end stop-and-frisk in New York City. Overall, the chapter is full of offerings about how to use litigation in ways that help build power and avoid some of the possible harms that can result from this expensive and time-consuming tactic.

Biographical Reflection: My Journey to Movement Lawyering
By Judith Browne Dianis

Losing will make you reflect. I know I'm a smart lawyer but if in-court win-loss records are the only indication of intellect or competence, I'm not so sure.

When I went to law school as a survivor of employment discrimination, I was committed to ensuring Black people would no longer have to endure the harms of white supremacy and racism. I grew up in a household with a community activist mother who took me to my first protest when I was three. I was a student organizer in college and law school against racism. This work is my purpose, and it is righteous work. I will never forget my first loss in a civil rights case—I cried an ugly cry. I wondered, *How could we lose this case when we were on the right side of justice?* I went on to lose a jury trial where a white realtor admitted that she would only show my Black client's homes in Black areas. Ignoring the law, jury members later admitted that's just the way it is in Alabama. It quickly became clear to me that going to court did not result in more protection for Black people.

My years at the NAACP Legal Defense Fund were filled with incredible opportunities to protect Black people, challenge racists, and utilize the laws that so many people before me had worked hard to get passed. I filed cases that tested new laws including Motor Voter and took the first mortgage lending discrimination case to trial.[1] We secured victories that set the stage for important civil rights advances. There were times, though, when lawyers led the charge and the work was misaligned with community priorities. In a school desegregation case, for example, when a new issue arose under a decades-old consent decree, I remember some community members expressing their ambivalence. They wanted to fight for running water. But that wasn't our priority. This disconnect stayed with me.

The work we did was critical, yet the times were calling for a different approach. The "social engineering" in the courts, of days gone by was just that—gone. The courts were captured by the conservative Right, and their policies and narratives were turning civil rights victories on their head. For example, the Right's commitment to ending affirmative action was not only a legal fight; they also organized and used narrative interventions. After the Supreme Court's decision in *Bakke*, the Right took their cause to voters and the court of public opinion with Prop 209 in California.[2] Misleadingly titled the California Civil Rights Initiative, and spearheaded by a Black man, Ward Connerly, Prop 209 sought to eliminate affirmative action in employment, contracting, and higher education. Legal challenges to the language were not enough.

The Prop 209 loss was instructive. Retrenchment on civil rights required more than litigation. The revolution would not be litigated. Our future could not rest in the hands of biased courts that upheld laws intended to maintain the status quo of white supremacy. We—Black people—need power. White supremacy and racism could not be defeated without it, and power did not come from lawyers and courts. We needed to center (and support) organizing to build power to secure sustainable change. Our communities needed access to all of the advocacy tools available: litigation, legislation, and strategic communications.

We established the Advancement Project to go back to what worked. Our movement lawyering model centers and follows organizing campaigns that build power to eliminate structural racism and white supremacy. For us, litigation must be in service of the goals of the people; it's a tactic. Winning doesn't always mean getting a court order that gives you the proposed remedy; it may be a strategic intervention in the organizing campaign. These partnerships require attention to the ultimate goals of community groups and devising various tactics to get them closer to amassing the power they need to win. At times this approach has meant that communities don't want to litigate because they don't want to give their power to a court. In other instances litigation has been critical to showing the community's resolve, publicly challenging the power structure, or slowing things down to make room for organizing to happen. Ultimately the lawyers are co-conspirators in shifting power and changing the rules of the status quo. As movement lawyers, we cannot move faster than, or without, the movement.

When Hurricane Katrina devastated New Orleans in 2005, it was clear that the city wanted wholesale removal of low-income Black families. Their strategy was to remove the safety net (public schools, the public hospital, and public housing), making it near-impossible for these families to return. We teamed up with Bill Quigley and Tracie Washington, two extraordinary local attorneys, to support these survivors. Because of the lack of local organizing capacity in the midst of the tragedy, we hired organizers to find residents and organize them to determine what they wanted. As a result, we filed four major lawsuits to protect the interests of Black survivors. The goal of these lawsuits was to secure the right to return and ensure Black survivors had a voice in the rebuilding. Litigation helped us slow the city down so people had time to organize and develop their demands.

Our lawsuit to stop the demolition of public housing, for example, helped bring survivors into the conversation about the future of their communities, giving them seats at the table with the city, developers, the Department of Housing and Urban Development, and Congress. To partner with the community under these unusual circumstances, we surveyed those who were displaced, organized those we could find in other cities, and met regularly with those who had returned. Their vision became our goal for the litigation. But the courtroom wasn't the only venue for this fight. Community members testified before Congress, protested outside the courthouse and at City Council meetings, utilized the media, and engaged in civil disobedience. Litigation and legal advocacy were among our tactics, but victory was measured in the power we built and the voices we uplifted.

I learned movement lawyering from movement. If we believe that power in the hands of Black and Brown communities can uproot white supremacy, we must listen to, and be accountable to, community. We must provide access to the tools necessary for power building and at times help communities analyze, diagnose, and imagine new, radical solutions to entrenched problems. Resist the urge to parachute in and file lawsuits that are unconnected to movement. It is not a power-building exercise but rather a tactic that has undermined and weakened community power time and time again. Litigation wins can be fleeting. You can win in the lower court and lose on appeal. Or a legislature might upend the victory. But when litigation is in service of building the power of the people, it can be a helpful tool. In many instances it's the movement and the narratives it creates, not the litigation itself, that has the ability to push the courts in the right direction. Our job as lawyers is to provide the vehicle for this to happen.

Tactical Case Study: The Radically Inclusive Amicus Litigation
Strategies of Centering Black Trans Voices
By Bryanna Jenkins

In September 2020, I was a first-year legal fellow at Lawyers Committee for Civil Rights Under Law (hereafter Lawyers Committee) in Washington, DC. As a first-year attorney, I was nervous because I did not know what my legal career would look like during COVID. Luckily I had a supervisor who prioritized my professional development, and he wanted me to make the most of my year with the organization. My most transformative experiences came from assisting with amicus briefs that merged my passions for transgender civil rights issues with other civil rights issues regarding race, gender equality, and public accommodations. As a Black transgender woman attorney, and often the only out Black transgender person working on these briefs, I was able to share space with other cisgender lawyers and lead conversations about the real-life implications of these cases for my community.

At Lawyers Committee I was a legal fellow in the Educational Opportunities Project (EOP). EOP strives to guarantee that all students receive equal educational opportunities in public schools and institutions of higher learning regardless of their race.[3] The first amicus brief I assisted with was *Hecox v. Little*.[4] In our amicus brief we argued that the State of Idaho's House Bill 500, which bans transgender women and girls from participating in sports, is unconstitutional and violates the due process and equal protection clauses. We argued that this law is not only harmful to transgender students, but it also harms Black women and girls in sports who routinely experience discrimination because of pervasive misogyny and transphobia that exist in sports.

Next I had the opportunity to assist with an amicus brief in *Mahanoy Area School District v. B.L.*[5] We argued the Supreme Court should hold that it is unconstitutional for schools to regulate off-campus student speech given the facts of that case, which involved a middle school student uploading an explicit social media post over the weekend. The Supreme Court ruled in favor of the student, holding that she had a constitutional right to free expression off the school campus. Although this case did not directly deal with a racial issue, had the Supreme Court ruled in the school's favor, that decision would have harmed Black and Brown students by preventing them from engaging in free speech and expression, especially when Black and Brown students critique mistreatment by their school and other issues that impact them in the outside world.

Finally, I had the opportunity to internally pitch that Lawyers Committee participate in an amicus brief for *Corbitt v. Taylor*.[6] We planned to argue that the Eleventh Circuit should affirm a lower court's decision to strike down Alabama's unconstitutional driver's license policy, which requires transgender people to undergo gender confirmation surgeries to change the gender listed on their driver licenses. Lawyers Committee declined to participate in this brief because they were not persuaded that this was a racial issue. Personally this decision was hard for me to digest because I knew that this case would have implications for Black transgender people in the Deep South. Despite my disappointment, other amicus briefs in support of the transgender appellees in this case were successfully submitted.

Amicus briefs have been and continue to be necessary for the transgender community. This is a tactic that resembles how we as transgender people organize to build our movements. When working on amicus briefs, we worked in partnership with other social justice organizations and large law firms that had access to capital and person power to draft and submit the briefs.[7] Since the transgender community is small and underfunded, it is and always will be important for entities with more access to leverage their resources, time, and labor to work in service of transgender issues. My vision, when drafting and editing briefs, was always to unapologetically bring my perspective as a Black transgender person. There is nuanced storytelling that must be integrated into the drafting of any brief, especially amicus briefs.

However, pitching *Corbitt v. Taylor* was a sober reminder to me that although amicus briefs are an important step, they are not the final step in transformative movement building. A harsh truth is that legacy social justice organizations can be shortsighted because they are designed to only prioritize one identity at a time and not to see the larger vision for more radical coalition-building. LGBTQ+ and transgender civil rights organizations also struggle with institutionalizing a radically inclusive framework that goes beyond just amicus briefs. Amicus briefs are a great tool for creating change, but they cannot be the only tactic that we use to foster change in our movement.

My experience with amicus briefs inspired me to pivot my career and center building national power for Black transgender people. As the national organizing director at Lavender Rights Project, I frequently rely on my experience working on amicus briefs. I convene groups of talented Black transgender people and Black trans–led organizations while also developing messaging that conveys our issues and policy goals. Amicus brief litigation can be used as a strategic tool to build coalitions and center the stories of transgender people. However, our collaboration and our vested interest in each other do not end with the conclusion of a case.[8]

The Hard Stuff: Resolving the Tensions in Movement Lawyering
By Vince Warren

The late Harry Belafonte compared the corrupting force of state power to a disease. He suggested that the law, which historically has functioned to metastasize the disease, could be thought of as an antibody if we "use the instruments that create power, and turn them into instruments that create power only for those who do the good works in relationship to the human condition."[9] Most lawyers, even those who support radical or progressive causes, are left to wonder how they are supposed to craft a cause of action out of all that brilliance. They're not wrong for asking.

If we're honest, combining movement lawyering and movement power building presents a conundrum. They are in many ways at opposite ends of the spectrum when it comes to tools for social change. Where movement organizing is lithe, flexible, always creating the opportunity for action, building momentum around it, catching a win, and building the next opportunity, the law is technical, methodical, and highly regulated by rules and court schedules, with cases often sitting on a judge's desk for months, if not years. Next to the powerful panther of power building, litigation—along with its attendant sparring with opposing counsel, mandated briefing timelines, arguments, and appeals—is a lumbering rhino; formidable when it makes an impact, but it often moves at its own pace.

So, if the disciplines are so different, why should they be joined? Why do we even think about movement lawyering as a viable option for social change? The answer lies in Mr. Belafonte's call for a recommitment to exploring the law's potential as a tool to support liberation rather than oppression. Movement organizing and lawyering should, in certain circumstances, be combined intentionally because the systemic nature of power that we confront when we seek meaningful social change often requires multiple and complementary tactics that can benefit from legal advocacy. However, those legal tools need to be deployed in ways that nourish the organizing strategy when done offensively and preserve the organizing strategy when done defensively. Below are two examples of the ways legal work has done its part in serving the goals of movement, one in the context of offense and the other in the context of defense.

Movement Lawyering on Offense

In 2020, rather than merely focus on the deadliness of the COVID-19 virus, organizers looked to "the deadliness of race and class oppression [which became] all the more apparent in the midst of th[e] pandemic" and "the systemic ways in which generational poverty, medical bias, and racism leave Black and Brown communities particularly vulnerable to living shorter lives than white people."[10] Robyn Maynard and Andrea Ritchie have pointed out that Black and Brown people disproportionately died from COVID-19 infections, disproportionally worked in jobs in which they were forced to be exposed in public spaces when local governments were requiring people to stay home, and paradoxically were disproportionately incarcerated in COVID-infested cages that health officials effectively abandoned.[11] Ritchie, along with Timothy Colman, Pascal Emmer, and Tiffany Wang, further frame the pandemic response in the context of abolition by saying that "instead of leaving people to die in Covid-plagued prisons, jails and detention centers, officials could free them with support to return safely to families and communities."[12] This was a powerful abolitionist charge from visionary organizers, and movement lawyers around the country saw a unique opportunity to use their skills to meet it.[13]

Although the call for releasing people locked up during the pandemic was clear, the interlocking systems of oppression that combined to thwart it were as well. The state—which has the power to make the change—will always deploy almost unfathomable resources to *stop* change from happening: the deep reservoirs of financial resources, the ability to criminalize communities, and control over policing power were all deployed in service of an ironclad commitment to preserving the status quo. Nonetheless, organizers realized that the fastest way to get people quickly released from jail was to file legal petitions for release. In the context of the pandemic they quickly and amply demonstrated that people who were locked up were forcibly subjected to the exact opposite of social distancing, sanitation, and medical care. Lawyers were able to use this valuable analysis, coupled with virtually every tool in their toolbox, to demand freedom.[14]

Typical of large-scale mass lawyering efforts in differing jurisdictions, not all (and in fact relatively few) of the lawyers share the liberatory politics of the most radical strategists in the effort. However, the mass impact can work in the organizers' favor by providing positive legal outcomes to build upon as they overcome the negative ones. In the end there were both legal successes and losses (either a refusal to release people or a requirement that released people be returned to jail), and the legal tool remains profoundly inadequate on its own (but not without power) to free all who should be.[15] Importantly, however, lawyers around the country filed cases en masse to free people from prisons, jails, and detention centers, many with an abolitionist framework that revolved around the compelling logic that if judges felt that people were "safe enough" to release, they shouldn't have been locked up to begin with. This work was an important building block toward the vision of abolition.

Movement Lawyering on Defense

When movements go on the offense, movement lawyers often need to go on the defense. This is especially so when there are mass or targeted arrests during mass protests. These arrest tactics are used by the state to slow movement momentum, marginalize its leaders, and criminalize movement formations. Unless the protestors remain out in the streets making their demands, the state can rewrite public narratives about movement goals and actors. A powerful example of this state tactic and how lawyering and organizing can provide a countermeasure when put on the defensive is the movement support legal network that was developed during the Ferguson uprisings in 2014. Montague Simmons, one of the Ferguson organizers who called for protests, says that the "explosion [of demonstrations] that happened that night happened because policing authorities refused to engage people directly. It wasn't just the anger about Mike Brown, this was accumulated over a generation . . . more than a generation of folks who actually felt powerless to do anything and to push back."[16]

In response to the Ferguson protests, the state deployed extreme and violent measures that included curfews, riot squads, the military, and the use of chemical weapons. Organizers put out a broad call to allies to counter the state's escalation. Lawyers from across the nation responded to the call.[17] Some of them, including the Center for Constitutional Rights, joined with the local organizers and Saint Louis–based movement lawyers to develop the Ferguson Legal Defense Committee (FLDC), a national collective of lawyers and legal workers committed to supporting Ferguson's movement to end racist and abusive police practices.[18] In anticipation of the grand jury decision that would fail to indict the police officer that killed Michael Brown, the Ferguson organizers called for national and sustained protest, and the FLDC itself put out an emergency call to action for more lawyers, law students, and legal workers to stand with Ferguson.

The FLDC and the hundreds of lawyers who responded to the call supported organizers by providing criminal defense representation for arrested demonstrators, researching and filing constitutional claims, conducting jail visits, providing legal observation, and helping to co-design mass arrest defense strategies. Moreover, "the family of Mike Brown Jr. and young Black leaders that emerged through the demonstrations in Ferguson chose to air their grievances before the United Nations Committee Against Torture in the fall of 2014"; they subsequently traveled to the UN in Geneva to address them on an international stage.[19] This move was facilitated by lawyers connected with and trusted by the movement who put the issues highlighted by organizers before the appropriate international human rights bodies.

In moments like those in Ferguson, the law was no longer a lumbering rhino but appeared to move closer to the speed of the movement as it furiously assessed the political and safety conditions on the ground. To be sure, some cases filed at the time took years to resolve—and in one case, even a decade—but from the beginning, veteran organizers in Ferguson developed both short-term and long-term strategies within which some of these cases resided. In that sense movement lawyers helped local organizers strengthen the political leverage to support their demands long after the frontline protesters had gone home. By working with the guidance of organizers, the legal strategy in Ferguson became an important part of the movement strategy, which kept the protestors out of jail and provided information and additional tools for organizers to deploy in defense of the deadly threat to the community.

History has shown that while people power is enough to overcome the most brutal oppression, legal intervention can be a very useful tool, when guided by movement, to articulate to power the conditions that people are living under and to challenge the legal obstacles that act as restraining forces on the freedom dreams of our communities. When done creatively and grounded in community goals, rather than those of the lawyers, we come closer to reducing the harm done to our communities and, as Mr. Belafonte dreamed, building up antibodies to the deadly disease of oppression.

Praxis Case Study: Four Organizing Lessons for Lawyers from *Floyd* Litigation
By Joo-Hyun Kang

August 2013 was a watershed moment for New York City's anti-police violence movement, with two pivotal victories against the

NYPD, New York's five police unions, and Mayor Bloomberg's administration. On August 12, 2013, Judge Shira Scheindlin issued a 195-page ruling finding that the NYPD's stop-and-frisk program violated the constitutional rights of Black, Latino, and other New Yorkers of color. A week and a half later, the local City Council overrode the mayor's vetoes of two police accountability bills that had been passed by the council in an after-midnight vote in June.

Floyd v. City of New York was the broadest, most far-reaching legal challenge the NYPD and the City of New York had ever faced regarding police violence. The ruling specifically acknowledged that "communities most affected by the NYPD's use of stop and frisk have a distinct perspective that is highly relevant to crafting effective reforms. No amount of legal or policing expertise can replace a community's understanding of the likely practical consequences of reforms in terms of both liberty and safety." *Floyd*, like the Community Safety Act legislation that was enacted into law over a billionaire mayor's veto, originated with grassroots organizers and community members who had experienced police violence and faced the same opposition: the world's largest police department, five police unions, a powerful mayor, and other conservative forces.

A new coalitional campaign called Communities United for Police Reform (CPR) spearheaded both victories.[20] The path to delivering two major blows to the world's largest police department started well before 2013.[21] This holds lessons for understanding how the law (e.g., courts and legislation) can be used as a tool for movement-building, even though by itself the law doesn't change material conditions in a liberatory way and can't replace the need to organize. When the *Floyd* litigation went to trial in March of 2013, grassroots groups and leaders within CPR understood *Floyd* as an opportunity to put the NYPD on trial in the public eye, create public awareness beyond the courtroom, and build community power. Material conditions changed for a time: Stops across NYC dropped dramatically from a high of almost seven hundred thousand in 2011 to fewer than twenty-three thousand in 2015, the first year of the monitorship after the stay was dismissed and after a Bloomberg-era lawsuit against the Community Safety Act was defeated.

We've learned a lot, which can't be summarized in a few pages, but here are four lessons for lawyers (and organizers who work with lawyers):

1. WE CAN CHALLENGE AND WIN AGAINST POLICE DE-PARTMENTS LIKE THE NYPD (AND THEIR UNIONS), BUT THOSE WINS WILL BE TEMPORARY UNLESS WE REDUCE THE POWER, SIZE, SCOPE, AND BUDGET OF THE NYPD AND POLICING AND BUILD SUSTAINED POWER THROUGH COMMUNITIES AND ORGANIZING. The dramatic reduction in reported stops by the NYPD was a result of a coordinated campaign that used various tactics including litigation but didn't rely on litigation alone and couldn't have been achieved with litigation alone. Annual reported stops continued to drop for a number of years, not because of the *Floyd* monitorship alone but because the New York City movement had expanded their political power and changed the conditions that had enabled the NYPD to carry out so many unconstitutional stops without consequence. After the 2020 national protests in defense of Black lives and against police violence, reported stops decreased to a new low of fewer than nine thousand in 2021.

But power shifts. Stops in New York City are again on an upward trend. With the election of Eric Adams, a cop mayor, the NYPD reported more stops in 2023 than it had in almost a decade. Stops almost doubled in 2023 to almost seventeen thousand stops, compared with 2021 (the year before Eric Adams became mayor), and the court monitor has continued to find significant and repeated underreporting of stops. While our side won in the courtroom back in 2013, the NYPD, police unions, and power players like the mayor had enough financial resources and institutional power to use the legal system's biases toward power to delay implementation of remedies by a year and a half and to get the original judge kicked off the case. The police unions lost their baseless legal challenges to block *Floyd* but maintained the power to shape narratives and influence court-appointed officials like the monitor and others to side with the NYPD for fear of their backlash. And due to the steadily increasing financial resources of the NYPD and their largely unchecked power, the NYPD has been able to use litigation to ensure more favorable conditions in the monitorship, resulting in the NYPD expanding its violations of *Floyd* without consequence.

The NYPD's police and union power should be understood as outsized and antidemocratic. We need organizing that expands the power of communities to challenge and end the illegitimate power of policing.

2. LITIGATION IS A TOOL THAT CAN BE LEVERAGED FOR LIBERATORY WORK WHEN IT'S PART OF A BROADER MOVEMENT-BUILDING STRATEGY, BUT IT HAS SERIOUS LIMITATIONS WHEN NOT DEEPLY COORDINATED WITHIN, AND IN SERVICE TO, A CLEAR MOVEMENT-BUILDING STRATEGY THAT ORGANIZES AND BUILDS THE POWER OF THOSE MOST IMPACTED BY AN ISSUE. Limitations include the long time frame for litigation, the constraints (and randomness) of what courts can order, the challenges of enforcement and implementation of court orders, and maybe most important, the challenge of how to ensure that litigation helps to build the power of communities instead of the power of the law, legal groups, and individual lawyers.[22]

In New York City the *Floyd* litigation was part of a broader strategy and campaign. The *Floyd* trial followed a year-and-a-half organizing campaign that flipped public opinion about police stops, organized New Yorkers into Copwatch teams, built public support for the Community Safety Act, and made stops and police violence a top-tier issue in the 2013 citywide elections. As a result, street stops reported by the NYPD decreased radically from an annual high of close to seven hundred thousand in 2011 to fewer than fifty thousand in 2014 and fewer than nine thousand in 2021. The dramatic drop in these police encounters began before the *Floyd* ruling, in late 2012, and continued with almost 50 percent decreases in the last three quarters of 2013. This was a result of the overall campaign that *Floyd* was a part of, but it would have been unlikely if litigation was the only tactic.

Litigation can't, by itself, change the material conditions of the majority of our people, but it can be part of broader strategies that improve material conditions and build the power of communities. Litigation can also bring attention to and legitimize key issues with policymakers and the broader public, amplify related policy and organizing fights, and secure key rules changes or financial resources for community struggles, especially when practiced in a way that collaborates with and uplifts democratically run community organizing groups as meaningful partners and leaders (not just as "clients").

3. LITIGATION PROCESSES, PARTICULARLY SETTLEMENTS AND MONITORED REMEDIES, ARE INHERENTLY ANTIDEMOCRATIC, INSULAR, AND FAVOR EXISTING POWER HIERARCHIES. TO BE USEFUL FOR MOVEMENT BUILDING IN LIBERATORY STRUGGLES, LAWYERS AND ORGANIZERS NEED TO OVERCORRECT FOR THIS. In the case of the *Floyd* litigation, the NYPD and Bloomberg administration never expected to lose the trial because courts generally side with police. Because of this, until Scheindlin's ruling, most of the Bloomberg administration, the NYPD, and cop unions' political attacks were against the Community Safety Act instead of the trial (with the cops

and right-wing tabloids claiming that passage of a few bills would be apocalyptic, calling the bills the "criminal safety act").

The *Floyd* moments that helped build movement and expand the power of communities were intentionally created and primarily outside of the courtroom. They were moments that connected *Floyd* to what was happening in neighborhoods and advanced noncourtroom goals like building community-level infrastructure and power to prevent and respond to police violence. The ten-week pack-the-court effort was paired with outside courtroom rallies, strategic communications, and teach-ins across the city, led primarily by young people, community members, union members, faith leaders, and other everyday New Yorkers. However, once the *Floyd* remedies process was stayed, and even once the formal remedies portion began, power moved from communities to the court-appointed monitor and the NYPD. When the original judge was kicked off the case, the monitor was able to wield centralized and largely unchecked power. While groups organized during the joint remedies process in the first few years of the monitorship to ensure that the separate court-appointed facilitator included community priorities in his recommendations to the court, the monitor sided with the NYPD and refused to support any of the reforms that would have expanded community power.

One of the useful things CPR grassroots groups did within the court's "joint remedies process" was to negotiate a reasonable confidentiality agreement with the court, allowing members to discuss key litigation developments and proposals with their organizations. However, once the community remedies process with the court-appointed facilitator was completed, the monitor pushed to reinstate a more traditional confidentiality (aka secrecy) agreement, making the process overly insular and making it inherently impossible to build democratic power without violating those clauses. The NYPD's stop-and-frisk program is still being monitored by the court because there hasn't been consistent or significant compliance. Although stops dramatically declined, they again skyrocketed under Mayor Eric Adams.

The longer a court process lasts, the less likely it is that community groups and individuals can sustain leadership and meaningful involvement without some support of financial resources. While lawyers on both sides and the NYPD are compensated by the city for their time, grassroots groups have to choose between other organizational priorities. In the case of *Floyd*, none of the grassroots groups or CPR were ever funded specifically for their *Floyd* work. The unpredictability of the timing of filings and motions, and the challenges of reading long filings in short periods of time with strict confidentiality rules in place, made it much more likely that members of community organizing groups would not be able to participate with the consistency or the time flexibility required for meaningful leadership.

The underresourcing of community organizing makes it impossible for these groups to maintain the desired level of leadership for what has become more than a decade without financial resources to support their work, just as the NYPD and the *Floyd* legal team would be unable to continue their consistent participation without resources. Litigators who aim to help build and partner with movements have to think seriously about how to help resource the movements they partner with, especially—but not only—on litigation they work on together.

4. "COMMUNITY ENGAGEMENT" AND "INPUT" ARE NOT COMMUNITY POWER. WHAT WE NEED FOR LIBERATORY PROCESSES IS TO BUILD PEOPLE POWER, NOT FALSE PROCESS EXERCISES. There's a tendency among some to romanticize "community" and to assume that providing access to public forums or creating mechanisms for public input is positive and sufficient. The reality is, it's often neither: "community engagement" by police departments or court monitors often legitimizes antidemo-

cratic processes and prioritizes those sham processes over improving material conditions and shifting power dynamics.

Any litigation process where a police department or court monitor can make decisions without a counterbalance of plaintiff-class community groups having equal or more power is a false exercise. In the *Floyd* litigation lawyers at one point wanted to propose that the court should require that the NYPD and/or monitor hold mandatory public sessions with community members and otherwise increase their "community engagement." The well-intentioned but misguided thinking was that this would give "the community" the opportunity for input. However, "input" isn't community power and is never enough when your opponent is the one with exclusive control of information and decision-making. Furthermore, holding public forums with people in power requires organizing communities if you want a liberatory or progressive outcome. Otherwise, those most likely to attend are those who are biased toward unequivocal support of police because the police will organize them. And to organize communities for such forums requires time and resources that are too often taken for granted.

It's problematic to hold a romanticized notion of "community" and "process" without a clear understanding of power and purpose. Access isn't power, input isn't power, engagement isn't power. The ability of communities to secure what we need is community power.

Learn Something from This

- The revolution will not be litigated. The courts are one venue where multiple tools can be used to complement a broader organizing strategy.
- Community engagement and input does not equal power. Do not romanticize access and mistake it for power. Power is the ability for people to make choices and decisions for themselves to get what they need.

Organizer's Corner: Litigating During the Downfall of *Roe*

MONICA SIMPSON

Courts have a long history as tools of white supremacy, almost inevitably ruling against Black people, so Black activists do not usually use litigation to defend or recover our human rights. However, for HB 481, a six-week abortion ban that was blatantly unconstitutional at the time, we had no choice. Activists across Georgia did all we could to stop the law from being passed, but our policymakers simply ignored our large protests, our compelling speeches and articles, the high-profile people we had share abortion stories, the entertainers we had cancel shows in Georgia, and more. Governor Brian Kemp signed HB 481 into law on May 7, 2019, and litigation was the only way to keep fighting it and even temporarily stop it.

We knew the ban's proponents passed it in flagrant defiance of *Roe v. Wade* in hopes of reaching the Supreme Court—recently stacked by the Trump administration with antiabortion justices—with an opportunity to overturn *Roe*. For everyone in Georgia and across the United States, we had to fight back with all we had. Even if the stacked courts meant we were bound to lose, we knew our efforts would reach multitudes, like nothing we had ever been able to do before, showing our people that we would never give up fighting for their rights and spreading our messaging far and wide to shift mainstream culture.

I am the executive director of SisterSong Women of Color Reproductive Justice Collective, a national nonprofit headquartered in Atlanta and devoted to building the movement for Reproductive Justice (RJ), the human right to maintain personal bodily autonomy, birth if and as we wish, and parent in safety and sufficiency. Already prominent in many social justice spaces, SisterSong became well known to the mainstream public when we led the protests against Georgia's abortion ban with Black women–led partner organizations. Thanks to Atlanta's numerous, strong Black women–led organizations and to the culture change already happening due to Black Lives Matter, white organizations that usually stand front and center actually stepped back to follow us, and media that usually center white voices actually centered ours instead. We were able to focus the national conversation on abortion bans as tools of white supremacy that most harm Black people. This narrative intervention was a huge win, so when the ban passed anyway, we knew we had to keep leading the fight and spreading our message. So, for the first time, we used litigation.

Although we knew losing *Roe* would be horrific, we also knew that was only the beginning, the first of many human and constitutional rights the opposition was plundering to reverse decades of national progress. With our rights attacked from all sides, we could not shirk any arena of the battle; we had to work effectively everywhere to have any hope of defending human rights. SisterSong therefore did something unusual—possibly unprecedented (though I lack the knowledge of national court history to be certain). Usually, abortion policy litigation falls to an abortion provider or someone needing abortion access as the lead plaintiff, but SisterSong became lead plaintiff as an advocacy organization representing Georgian women and trans and nonbinary people of color whom the ban would harm. We knew this would take the burden off overtaxed abortion providers and help center and amplify social justice, and especially Reproductive Justice. It also made litigation part of an organizing strategy gathering organizations across sectors, spreading powerful messages, galvanizing grassroots people and groups, and shifting culture. Our success opened a door for other advocacy organizations to do the same.

Many others became co-plaintiffs, and we filed a federal lawsuit, *SisterSong v. Kemp*, against the ban on June 28, 2019. Instead of legal jargon, it used our own bold, unapologetic Reproductive Justice language that grassroots people could understand and in which they could see their own lives reflected. The lawsuit did not water down or compromise anything. The ACLU of Georgia, our legal representation, was led by a Black woman, who understood and honored the importance of this, and we made it clear that we would do it in no other way. One article referred to our lawsuit as a "feminist manifesto." It was an excellent organizing tool, providing clear talking points and winning huge numbers of media hits that spread our message to multitudes. The great, widespread cultural influence of Black Lives Matter created fertile ground for it to be accepted and embraced by lawyers, judges, and the public.

On October 1, 2019, we won an injunction to prevent the ban from activating while our case was pending. On July 13, 2020, we won the case, since the ban was unconstitutional due to *Roe*. But, as expected, Kemp appealed. Our case was heard again after the Supreme Court decided to hear *Dobbs v. Jackson Women's Health Organization*, another of the many cases aiming, like HB 481, to empower the Supreme Court to overturn *Roe*. Our judge delayed his verdict until after the *Dobbs* decision, then followed it and upheld Kemp's abortion ban. On July 20, 2022, abortion was banned after six weeks in Georgia. SisterSong filed a state lawsuit two days later and won on November 13, since HB 481 was unconstitutional when enacted. However, Kemp won an injunction to keep the ban active while appealing, and on October 24, 2023, the Georgia Supreme Court reversed our 2022 win.

SisterSong defines "culture shift" as changing the values, beliefs, and behaviors readily accepted as the norm, and "cultural intervention" as intentional action challenging and disrupting the dominant power structures of the status quo to address the community's immediate needs and move them to action while offering healing. Our litigation work accomplishes this. It has raised understanding, statewide and nationally, of how antiabortion advocates are not striving to protect human life but to control oppressed people, and how Black liberation and racial justice require Reproductive Justice. This culture change has galvanized greater action for abortion access and Reproductive Justice.

- The legal outcome cannot be the central focus of the work; the other tactics matter a lot more.
- The speed and nature of litigation is diametrically opposed to organizing and power building. Whenever these two things come into conflict with one another, choose the movement not the court.
- Whenever you decide to litigate with or for communities, know that the process favors the court and the lawyers involved. Organizers and your clients have the most at stake. You have to be mindful of this on the front end and make adjustments and corrections for this throughout.

- If it is no longer working or there's a better way to get to the goal, don't be afraid to let it go.

Resources for Radical Litigation

- "Abolitionist Movement Lawyering Against Police and Pre-Trial Detention: A Practical Guide" is a guide to litigating with an abolitionist lens. Created by Kiah Duggins, a dedicated movement lawyer and a member of the Law for Black Lives 2022 Movement Lawyering Fellowship cohort, the guide explores ways to approach various steps in litigation from bail hearings to civil rights litigation. You can access the guide at the Law for Black Lives website under "resources": www.law4blacklives .org.
- "Know Your Fights: Using Public Records in Abolitionist Organizing" is a zine that was written by Shakeer Rahman, a member of the Law for Black Lives 2022 Movement Lawyering Fellowship cohort. The zine is a resource for both organizers and legal professionals and was created in collaboration with Stop LAPD Spying Coalition, Rahman's political home. It explores ways to request public records and how to strategically use them in a broader organizing strategy. You can access the zine on the Law for Black Lives website under "resources": www.law4blacklives.org.

Notes

1. The National Voter Registration Act of 1993 expanded opportunities to register to vote by requiring that state motor vehicle and public assistance offices provide an opportunity to register to vote when people apply for licenses and assistance. 52 U.S.C. §§ 205; National Voter Registration Act of 1993 (NVRA), U.S. Department of Justice (Aug. 13, 2024), www.justice.gov/crt/national-voter -registration-act-1993-nvra.

2. Regents of the University of California v. Bakke, 438 U.S. 265 (1978).

3. "Educational Opportunities," Lawyers Committee for Civil Rights Under Law, www.lawyerscommittee.org/project/educational-opportunities-project, accessed July 21, 2023.

4. Hecox v. Little, Nos. 20-35813, 20-35815 (9th Cir. Dec. 21, 2020).

5. Mahanoy Area School District v. B.L., 594 U.S.__ (2021).

6. Corbitt v. Taylor, No. 21-10486 (11th Cir. Feb. 12, 2021).

7. Briefs that I worked on at Lawyers Committee were drafted in collaboration with such organizations as the National Women's Law Center, ACLU National, Lambda Legal, Ropes & Gray, and Hogan Lovells, Allen & Overy.

8. I want to give a special thanks to my supervisor at Lawyers Committee, David Hinojosa, and to my colleagues Genzie Bonadies-Torres and Dorian Spence for encouraging me to participate in these matters as a first-year attorney and trusting my expertise related to the transgender community.

9. Center for Constitutional Rights, "Closing Remarks and Harry Belafonte Keynote," YouTube, August 13, 2014, www.youtube.com/watch?v=ynl-cYthnV8.

10. maya finoh, "We Must Take Care of Each Other: The Movement Response to COVID-19," Center for Constitutional Rights blog, April 20, 2020, https://ccrjustice.org/home/blog/2020/04/20/we-must-take-care-each-other -movement-response-covid-19.

11. Robyn Maynard and Andrea J. Ritchie, "Black Communities Need Support, Not a Coronavirus Police State," *VICE*, April 9, 2020, www.vice.com/en /article/z3bdmx/black-people-coronavirus-police-state.

12. Timothy Colman et al., "The Data Is In: People of Color Are Punished More Harshly for Covid Violations in the US," *The Guardian*, January 6, 2021, www.theguardian.com/commentisfree/2021/jan/06/covid-violations-people -of-color-punished-more-harshly.

13. Ariane de Vogue, "Covid-19 Cases Concerning Prisoners' Rights Hit the Supreme Court," *CNN*, May 21, 2020, www.cnn.com/2020/05/21/politics/covid -19-supreme-court-prisoners-rights/index.html.

14. "Coronavirus Resources," National Association of Criminal Defense Lawyers, March 19, 2020, www.nacdl.org/content/coronavirusresources.

15. Center for Constitutional Rights, Dada v. Witte (WDLA) (2020), https:// ccrjustice.org/home/what-we-do/our-cases/dada-v-witte-wdla, accessed July 21, 2023.

16. Freedom Road Socialist Organization, "3. Montague Simmons of OBS on the Ferguson Uprisings," YouTube, July 5, 2015, www.youtube.com/watch?v= e9KXfR9DOpM.

17. Tim Reid, "Lawyers Descend on Ferguson Ahead of Grand Jury Decision," Reuters, November 21, 2014, www.reuters.com/article/us-usa-missouri
-shooting-lawyer/lawyers-descend-on-ferguson-ahead-of-grand-jury-decision
-idUKKCN0J52H820141121.

18. "Ferguson Legal Defense Committee circa 2015," Ferguson Legal Defense, 2015, www.fergusonlegaldefense.com, accessed July 21, 2023.

19. Justin Hansford and Meena Jagannath, "Ferguson to Geneva: Using the Human Rights Framework to Push Forward a Vision for Racial Justice in the United States after Ferguson," 12 *UC Law Journal of Race and Economic Justice* 121 (2015), https://repository.uclawsf.edu/hastings_race_poverty_law_journal/vol12/iss2/1.

20. The Center for Constitutional Rights and the *Floyd* litigation were part of the citywide, multistrategy campaign that Communities United for Police Reform (CPR) publicly launched in 2012 to decrease police violence in New York City, with a focus on reducing the most common police encounters with New Yorkers. In addition to the *Floyd* litigation, the campaign included a citywide Cop-Watch alliance led by the Justice Committee (formerly known as the National Congress for Puerto Rican Rights) and the Malcolm X Grassroots Movement; Know Your Rights workshops, murals, and other community-based work led largely by community organizing groups like MXGM, JC, Make the Road NY, Streetwise and Safe, FIERCE, and others; policy advocacy for bills CPR members had written known as the Community Safety Act (largely led by community groups in partnership with policy and other groups); civic engagement around the 2013 citywide elections by community groups; multitiered strategic communications, research, and more.

21. The *Floyd* litigation's history goes back to 1999, when Amadou Diallo was murdered in a hail of forty-one bullets by the Street Crimes Unit. The late Richie Perez and the grassroots Coalition Against Police Brutality (CAPB) brought the idea of a lawsuit to challenge the NYPD's growing stops targeting youth of color to the Center for Constitutional Rights. CAPB members from the National Congress for Puerto Rican Rights and Malcolm X Grassroots Movement were plaintiffs in the lawsuit, first filed as *National Congress for Puerto Rican Rights et al. v. City of NY* and later known as *Daniels v. City of NY*—and were founding members of what became Communities United for Police Reform (CPR). Daniels settled in 2003 with reforms including mandatory reporting by the NYPD on stops and the disbanding of the infamous Street Crimes Unit. When the NYPD refused to comply with parts of the Daniels settlement, former members of CAPB advocated for the Center for Constitutional Rights to bring new litigation, which resulted in *Floyd* being filed in 2008. Again, plaintiffs came from grassroots organizing

groups, and the named plaintiff, schoolteacher David Floyd, was part of the Malcolm X Grassroots Movement.

22. While Judge Scheindlin ordered helpful items in her remedies, she also unfortunately ordered a pilot reform that nobody asked for: mandating that the NYPD run a pilot body-worn-camera program to monitor stops in five precincts for a year. By the time *Floyd* started to be implemented, Bill Bratton, commissioner at the time, was able to use this to his advantage by running a pre-pilot funded by the NYC Police Foundation, mandating body camera requirements that expanded NYPD surveillance and power.

6 Frontline Defenders for the Revolution

Since the establishment of legal services for the indigent, lawyers working in legal services corporations and public defenders' offices have been positioned inside of the legal system as "defenders" of the poor. On one hand they are the advocates for people experiencing what are often the worst moments of their lives, who would not otherwise be able to afford legal representation. On the other hand they are working inside of systems that often function as an extension of the prison industrial complex and further perpetuate racialized poverty and precarity. As a result, sometimes these lawyers are seen as lacking talent, uncaring, and too overwhelmed to do a decent job.[1]

However, frontline lawyers know the courts and venues that their clients have to navigate better than most, making many of them skillful tacticians. They carry unreasonably high caseloads and are underpaid. Studies have shown that most of the cases filed in state courts require a person to retain counsel. Of those cases nearly 80 percent needed a state-appointed attorney.[2] There are also tensions that individual lawyers who have radical politics wrestle with while doing the job. Particularly lawyers who have worked with movements or who believe that change happens through collective power building. These can be hard tensions to reconcile, but lawyers need to address them to be effective and prevent further harm.

Contributors in this chapter—all former or current legal service attorneys—unpack some of the big questions at the core of being a frontline lawyer and having radical political urges to make transformational changes inside of a system that was not created to tolerate it. This chapter starts with reflections from attorneys working at the intersection of civil and criminal legal services. Erin Miles Cloud and Tenisha Cummings explore the tensions that arise from the perspective of two abolitionist lawyers who spent a decade defending mothers who had children ripped away by what they call the child regulation system. Their piece includes powerful reflections on how one can work inside a system while supporting movements to abolish that same system. Tiffany Williams Roberts discusses how she used the public defender's office as a site of organizing and resistance. Similarly, Hannah Adams provides concrete ideas for how one can support systemic change in the housing context despite the limitations of working for a legal aid organization. Throughout the chapter we see tangible examples of how lawyers reconcile the role they play in the system with their belief in system transformation.

Biographical Reflection: Navigating the Family Regulation System as an Abolitionist Public Defender
By Erin Miles Cloud and Tenisha Cummings[3]

Public defenders are vital, but our institutional role is not radical. At its best it is a stopgap on a faucet of oppression. This does not mean individuals who are public defenders cannot have radical politics or be connected to broader liberatory movements, but it does mean we must be thoughtful and accountable to the ways our position can hinder abolition and the ways we have the power to mobilize our politics to support abolition. We write this essay to reflect on these tensions. We start by discussing the ways the state prosecutes families, and the role that family defense public defenders play. We then discuss tensions within the public defense community and its relationship to the state, and we end by offering reflections on our roles in an ecosystem of change. We claim neither to be experts nor that the ideas identified here are exhaustive. We hope people will challenge these ideas and engage with them as a springboard for the start of a very difficult yet necessary conversation.

We began our careers as family defense public defenders, representing parents charged by the government with abusing and/or neglecting their children. Our clients—predominantly mothers—are falsely blamed for outcomes created by the United States' willful abandonment of Black communities and its systemic attack on Black birthing people. While it is undoubtedly true that families can be a site of harm, we also know that the prosecutorial agency child protective services does not protect children. In fact, activists and advocates *reject* euphemistic terms like "foster care," "child welfare system," and "child protective services" for more accurate nomenclature,[4] calling it the "family regulation system" (FRS).[5] As attorneys, and more important as Black mothers, we know that the FRS is not designed to protect our children. The FRS stole Indigenous children from their parents,[6] separated thousands of Black children from their families under the racist theories of the "War on Drugs" explicitly deployed to destroy Black communities,[7] and refuses to reckon with the ways it creates the conditions for the sexual assault[8] and death[9] of Black girls. The FRS cannot, and will not, be the north star of safety that we envision for our families.

We also understand that our role as public defenders can and should be limited. When we meet our clients, they have often just experienced one of the most traumatic events imaginable: FRS has violently taken or threatened to take their children. Our aim is to assess the situation immediately and try to cauterize the proverbial bleeding. Guided by our client, we determine the best first course of action and triage begins. We ask: *What community resources can be gathered to support the family? Should we ask for a hearing to get the child back home now? Does the government have any evidence? What is this parent's goal?* The system's design requires that you work on all of these questions at once, often for multiple clients simultaneously and with relatively few resources.

This legal triage happens in an environment that is stacked against Black, Brown, and poor parents. FRS judges, whether they realize it or not, are emboldened to oppress Black and Brown families. They receive salaries and government investment that far outpaces investment in marginalized communities. They bend over backward to justify the court's intervention, not only with their platitudes of white saviorism but also by giving grace to the prosecutors who regularly are not ready for trial and make arguments that are legally incognizable. This "grace" is also extended to children's attorneys who, in our experience, often have barely met the children they are representing.

When public defenders are rooted in social justice, care for their clients, and have strong litigation skills, they can be a legal check in this oft-described "kangaroo court."[10] In our own work we have seen this bear out. Studies have shown that providing quality holistic public defense to parents decreases the chances that a family will experience permanent dissolution or face the removal of their child.[11] However, case outcomes are only one measurement of success. The rise of family defense in New York City did not coincide with equal funding increases for community-based organizations, radical activism, or organizing support. This is unsurprising. We need to be accountable to this hard truth. Public defenders are overworked. Their caseloads are too high. It is not possible to represent clients effectively with the current caseload structure, and this is by design. To mitigate the harm of the system, we must be able to do our job. This means more resources.

We must resist the impulse to fundraise only for our institutional existence and comforts. We should be working to find humane ways to decrease our caseloads, which includes supporting activists and radical thinkers who are working to build more liberatory frameworks. We envision a world where supporting resistance does not rely on prosecutors, judges, and so forth, and by consequence the need for us is eliminated. In this way we "reduce caseloads" not by constantly requesting more lawyers but by joining the fight alongside activists who are demanding that police and the FRS be defunded and are building alternatives. This is not a scarcity model, nor does it require us to sacrifice clients' immediate legal needs to support activism. We beg public defenders to have an abundance mind-set. When the communities we serve win, we all win.

We also need to shift the narrative around access to justice and expose its insufficiencies. The more we request funding for ourselves, without leveraging that privilege to request funding for the communities, the more we fulfill a false narrative that access to lawyers is the answer and that freedom is just about protecting or understanding "rights," not transforming the conditions we live in. Up until the 2020 uprisings, many of the most powerful public defenders in the nation were nervous about saying "abolition" publicly (and some still are). This fragility and cowardice only promoted the narrative that courts are the arbiters of justice. We know this is not true, and we cannot be afraid or silent about the urgent need for a total divestment of these carceral courts.

Public defenders must also be thoughtful so as to not co-opt the work of organizers, activists, and healers. We must be in community with people who are attacking injustices from multiple angles without overshadowing their work. We must prepare talking points in advance and in consultation with the community we serve, so we can ensure we are wrestling with difficult questions responsibly and ethically. Too often lawyers only discuss injustices with other lawyers. This will neither promote accountability nor creative solutions. Instead, we need to address tactical issues in coalition. This helps us become an ecosystem, not an echo chamber, while ensuring that we recognize our professional privilege and utilize it to serve movements, not to undermine them. We must do this humbly, without abandoning our own intelligences. Being humble does not mean we stand back from our knowledge; it means we must be firm in our offerings without succumbing to the white supremacist notion that we have all the answers.

We also need to be accountable to the narratives we prop up when we advocate. As public defenders, we are often negotiating liberty with the most difficult and racist institutional players. They want us to validate their racist narratives in our arguments. They want us to blame someone's harmful actions on their horrible Black mother. They want us to validate the "war on drugs" by pathologizing drug use. While these narratives may garner an individual trial win and at times our clients may choose this path, we must be conscious that these narratives are only successful because they build on the tropes of white supremacy. It is our duty to be more creative, to work hard to build narratives that are expansive and represent the humanity of the communities we serve. This fidelity to a liberatory vision is not just important for trial attorneys, it is also vital for public defense managers and directors.

We both experienced working in public defense offices that are also large nonprofits. We ask all leaders in public defense to consider their responsibility to resist building nonprofit public defense organizations that are based on racial tropes. Please stop ignoring the complexities of intersectionality, harm, and multiple truths within the communities we serve as you build and protect multimillion-dollar nonprofits. We have seen this happen time and time again. For example, in the 1980s and 1990s a large institutional public defense provider in New York City decided to abdicate its responsibility to the Black community by negotiating city contracts to represent children in neglect and abuse cases, even though there was no comparable defense for parents.

At the time the common narrative was that Black and indigent children are violently harmed by their parents, and it was unfathomable that Black and poor children could be aligned with their parents in the way that white middle-class families are commonly perceived to be a familial unit. This decision resulted in decades of missed advocacy opportunities both in and out of the courtroom. Inside the courtroom these "public defenders" had a new name—they were called "law guardians" and were legally allowed to prosecute parents. There was no requirement that they even listen to their clients, who were mostly Black children. Even though this is the antithesis of public defense, which is rooted in client self-determination and zealous advocacy, the institutional leaders protected them.

We believe these decades of prosecution and the abandonment of Black mothers consolidated the prevailing white supremacist narratives around Black families. Moreover, it resulted in missed opportunities to challenge the narrative. Public defense offices have the privilege of being in the position to coordinate impact litigation, provide statements to large media outlets and politicians about social justice issues, and build legal strategies that increase the probability of success for individual litigants. However, this did not happen. Today we see this flawed thinking continue in other jurisdictions: nationally legal directors still perceive the institutional roles of parent and children defense as so fundamentally different and misaligned that there cannot be united litigation, strategies, or tactics. These beliefs are inconsistent with how Black, Brown, and poor communities feel about and experience their families, and yet lawyers continue to prop up these false dichotomies.

These divides exist not just in the family context. Prosecutors rely on the public narrative that they are saving communities from the harms of rape, intimate partner violence, and gun violence. They use this to justify their existence. Public defenders must not be afraid to take back this narrative, and the leaders must acknowledge the complexity of these issues and seek community guidance and support. It is hard; it is complicated; however, abolition theory gives us the space to make these arguments and reorganize our institutions in ways that are more ethical and responsible.

Finally, we ask public defenders and everyone to rest and give grace. Public defense is designed to make you tired. It requires our brains to activate triage modes, which often hinder our ability to take in new information and dream. It is okay to be honest about that, and it is okay to rest. It is not okay to be complacent. Allowing for rest may look different, but we need spaces to learn and dream. To this end, we need to find a balance between self-preservation—especially as Black lawyers—and the needs of the communities we serve. If we do not rest, we will become less-effective advocates, which can weaken our advocacy and our patience with fellow Black people who are our clients. It also may shift us into a space where we spend more time lobbying for individual professional needs than for liberation.

This request to rest and give grace calls for an understanding of self and others—grace for those who may be new to the movement(s) and those who are seasoned alike. When survival is at stake, it is understandable that tempers may rise and flare. Make space for the feelings. There is no cookie-cutter solution for how this transformation takes place or what it looks like in its various iterations. We understand this completely, which is why we think it is important to continue to do the work and move toward solutions that allow for room to pivot, as things are ever-changing.

We make this plea with the consciousness that the culture of urgency is uniquely oppressive for our clients. We ask that people exist in this tension: that they have a duty to show up for those who are most oppressed, and also that they must be able to sustain this fervor and their own health. We believe that we can make this happen and it will be hard. We must creatively explore structures of work that have more planned breaks and include this demand in every contract negotiation. We must remember that we are not in it alone. If we are bold in our asks and strong in our community, we only risk winning it all. If we are not, we risk losing some of our most important legal minds to the grind of oppression while maintaining the status quo.

Tactical Case Study: Navigating Organizing as a Public Defender
By Tiffany Williams Roberts

Public defenders, despite working alongside people most impacted by the racist harm of the criminal legal system, are not de facto community organizers. The tension created by the limitations of litigation may be difficult to manage for young lawyers seeking ways to impact society beyond the courtroom. I went to law school not knowing what kind of lawyer I would be. Working for criminal defense attorneys as a paralegal before my first year primed my interest in criminal law, but I thought that representing clients facing such dire consequences would be too heavy. To my surprise, summer internships at two public defense agencies in Atlanta, and the deep connections I forged with the clients I interviewed, made it impossible for me to imagine being anything other than a public defender. I began my career at the Atlanta Judicial Circuit Office of the Public Defender shortly after taking the bar exam. I practiced under the student practice rule and assisted senior attorneys with suppression motions and argued bond motions. The paralyzing fear I once had of criminal defense now propelled me to fight alongside people whom many of my law school classmates believed to be dispensable.

One motion I wrote was on behalf of a client who was targeted by the Atlanta Police Department's notorious and now disbanded RED-DOG Unit (Run Every Drug Dealer Out of Georgia). The judge granted our motion without argument. When I obtained my bar license a few months later, I was troubled by seemingly endless constitutional and humanitarian offenses stemming from REDDOG raids, arrests, and harassment. I began to dream of a project that would share the narratives of Atlantans long plagued by this corrupt and violent police gang. The stories in the news like REDDOG's murder of ninety-two-year-old grandmother Kathryn Johnston on a falsified warrant barely scratched the surface of the harm they caused in the Black community.

Around this same time Atlanta became immersed in a crime wave narrative surrounding the tragic death of a young white bartender in Grant Park—a rapidly changing historic neighborhood near downtown. Mostly white intown residents created a group called Atlantans Together Against Crime (ATAC), and despite being motivated to improve public safety, the policies they championed amounted to wide-net criminalization of Black youth. My colleague, also concerned about the group's growing influence, came by my office and invited me to share my REDDOG project concept at a meeting of young people targeted by the city's latest tough-on-crime campaign. The diverse group of parents, teachers, social workers, and residents that met that night became Building Locally to Organize for Community Safety (BLOCS). Our tagline was "Safety isn't built by prisons and police. It's built by us, one block at a time." We worked earnestly to support education and policy focused on reframing what "safety" meant.

By understanding that systems designed to fortify white supremacy unequivocally undermine safety for Black people in Atlanta, we refused to omit police misconduct and state violence from the conversation. Our early wins included strengthening civilian oversight, forcing community input in the selection of the new police chief, and dismantling the REDDOG Unit—all extremely modest reforms intended to meet Atlantans where they were. We received opposition from likely and unlikely places. We were often questioned about whether we were speaking on behalf of the office when organizing—

we weren't. Our work (and the resistance to it) spoke to me about the tension between public defense and grassroots organizing in three keyways:

1. PUBLIC DEFENDERS CANNOT EFFECT SYSTEMIC CHANGE THROUGH LITIGATION AND OFTEN DESIRE WORK THAT EMPOWERS THEM OUTSIDE OF THE COURTROOM. The inability to transform systems through litigating individual cases can be very frustrating and lead to burnout for public defenders. I found that organizing with and learning from like-minded people helped to alleviate some of that dissatisfaction. By exercising autonomy and building community support infrastructure outside of the system that had been handed to us, we were able to think creatively about change and bring that thinking into the workplace. In addition, through conversations with community members, I often learned to think about my clients' stories in a more nuanced way. That improved the quality of representation I was able to provide because it acquainted me firsthand with facts that police reports and witness statements often omit.

2. PUBLIC DEFENDERS WHO CARE DEEPLY FOR THEIR CLIENTS OFTEN DO SO BECAUSE THEY ALSO CARE DEEPLY ABOUT THE ROOT CAUSES OF MASS INCARCERATION AND STATE VIOLENCE. Criminal defense attorneys are often taught to distance themselves emotionally from their clients because of the impact of vicarious trauma. For Black public defenders who may see the faces of their loved ones reflected in the people they represent, it's not so easy. For those of us who became acquainted with systemic oppression by being on the receiving end of it, the drive to defend our clients can feel personal. That passion can be extinguished when we experience defeats in the courtroom as personal defeats. Organizing can serve as a complementary effort that feels fruitful. It can allow us

to never disregard how our clients found themselves in the crosshairs of the criminal legal system because it forces us to center their human experience, not merely facts, theories, and case law.

3. PUBLIC DEFENDERS WHO TAKE TIME TO WORK OUTSIDE OF THEIR OFFICIAL DUTIES ACQUIRE SKILL SETS THAT MAKE THEM BETTER LAWYERS AND PEOPLE. Law school does not adequately prepare students to practice as part of a community—often the focus is on teaching students how to exist as part of the profession. Navigating our world of colleagues and institutions is important, but for public defenders it is also important to learn what skills are required to serve communities—whether they be defined by geography, race, class, or other demographics. Community organizing is the act of building relationships of trust with other human beings who envision thriving together in the same way. It requires listening with humility and finding courage in unlikely places. These skills translate positively into consultation and interview rooms, to our clients' benefit. They also make us people who do less harm to those we serve because we are constantly confronting the myriad of social issues our clients and their families face.

· · ·

I ultimately left public defense to organize and practice private civil rights and criminal defense law, landing in policy advocacy. The quiet tension between our advocacy and our office's political vulnerabilities felt too stressful for me to maintain a healthy relationship to the work. My transition from public defense was not a departure, however. The work of public defenders and their clients is integrated into nearly all fights we wage in this sphere because American criminal courtrooms are the theater where the terrifying power of the state is on display in jarring fashion. In many ways the lawyers and clients are part of our organizing base by virtue of their experiences. We who engage in harm-reductive organizing and policy work must persistently interrogate our tactics to ensure we are not causing harm to people fighting for their lives before judges and juries. We must cultivate hospitable spaces for others wishing to enter the work. Although we are not trying cases, we certainly must flank those brave souls committed to doing so until this cruel system no longer exists.

The Hard Stuff: The Ethics of Frontline Legal Defense in a Housing Crisis
By Hannah Adams

Like so many of us on the Left, the thing that motivated me to become a lawyer was not any idealistic belief in the potential to transform society through the legal system. It was the realization that the legal system was responsible for creating and upholding the deep racial and economic disparities that plague my community. Nowhere is this clearer than in the proverbial trenches of eviction court in South Louisiana. As a housing attorney at a federally funded legal aid organization, the laws I have to work with were designed to protect landlords, not tenants. And it is impossible to disentangle the current eviction crisis from our nation's history of legalized racial discrimination and disinvestment. Black neighborhoods in New Orleans that were legally redlined out of the housing market in the mid-twentieth century have an average eviction rate *seven times higher* today than neighborhoods that were not historically redlined.[12] One in four renters in majority Black neighborhoods have experienced a court-ordered eviction.[13]

At the same time, the lack of affordable housing is acute. In the least expensive zip codes in New Orleans, a person still needs to make over eighteen dollars per hour to afford a two-bedroom apartment.[14] But efforts in the 1970s to pass rent control, and in the early

2000s to pass a higher minimum wage, were blocked by the courts.[15] When it comes to changing the laws and institutions that harm my clients, most legal aid organizations are restricted. We are barred from participating in political action, legislative lobbying, organizing, solicitation of clients, and class action lawsuits. Instead, we are supposed to keep the focus on "saving" individual clients from their singular legal crises, rather than addressing the institutions designed to keep them in crisis. As a legal aid lawyer, I often feel like a firefighter trying to put out a forest fire with a watering can.

What does it mean to be a movement lawyer in a system designed to harm the people I represent? How do you do systems-level work rooted in relationships with impacted community members at an organization that is federally restricted from lobbying, organizing, and class representation? Here are some things I have learned that help me approach these difficult ethical questions. A great deal of systemic advocacy work can be done within the restrictions imposed on most legal aid organizations. It is true that I can't go to the state capitol to lobby for a particular change in the law. But there's nothing barring us from providing information on proposed legislation or rulemaking in response to a specific request from a government official or agency.[16] When you build strong relationships in the community, these requests will come.

Where something can't be changed through legislation, we just must get creative. Unable to change criminal background screening requirements through the conservative state legislature, we participated in a grassroots effort to convince our state Housing Finance Agency to require the thousands of properties it subsidizes to employ inclusive admissions policies. Strategic appellate practice is another way to create more favorable law. Prioritizing this type of work is possible and a necessary part of serving our clients, who will continue to experience the same problems repeatedly unless we push for systemic change.

There's no such thing as a routine case. As legal aid attorneys who often have unmanageable caseloads, we must triage crises constantly and develop emotional boundaries for the work to be sustainable. As a result, it becomes easy to quickly dismiss the merits of a case that looks hopeless at first glance. But sometimes systemic issues are buried deep inside what seems like a routine case. I learned this lesson years ago, when what seemed like a routine eviction case walked through the door. A Black family was getting evicted from a home that they had owned for nearly a century in a rapidly gentrifying area of the city. They had failed to pay property taxes, so the city sold the property to an investor. At first glance there was nothing we could do. But the client was adamant that the sale was improper. After a title search we learned that his property had been adjudicated for nonpayment of a few hundred dollars in taxes in the 1990s without constitutionally sufficient notice. We did our research, got creative, took a leap of faith, and sued the city. Years later we won on summary judgment. The city was forced to cough up tens of thousands of dollars, and the family was able to obtain financing to save their home. Had we dismissed this case as a routine eviction, we would have missed an opportunity to expose and address the city's practice of auctioning off Black land that had been improperly adjudicated decades ago.

At the end of the day it's important to remember that real, sustainable, effective change isn't possible without grassroots work. In New Orleans we now have a Right to Counsel ordinance guaranteeing tenants lawyers in evictions because our local Renters Rights Assembly (RRA) campaigned on the issue. We were able to effectively intervene in the foreclosure and bankruptcy of a notorious slumlord only because tenant organizers built relationships with dozens of aggrieved residents through door-to-door canvassing and neighborhood meetings, harnessing the power of media to shine a light on the conditions that tenants were living in. Collaborating with pro bono partners, we were able to obtain a nationally significant court decision halting the demolition of public housing because the public housing resident council we represented was organized and its members were prepared to share their experiences and vision for their community.

As lawyers it is our job to take a backseat to organizers and grassroots leadership, but that doesn't mean that we don't have something valuable to add. Part of the way that tenants build power is by knowing their rights and understanding what is possible within our current legal infrastructure, and this is an important place where lawyers can plug in. Though Legal Services Corporation–funded legal aid organizations cannot participate in organizing, we can take direction from organizers that have their fingers on the pulse of the community's needs and visions for change. We can support organized tenants by representing groups in strategic litigation.

Working for racial justice and equity means supporting the survival of Black people and people of color in the world we have today in addition to fighting for the world we want tomorrow. In law school I encountered a certain negative attitude about legal aid within my leftist cohort. The idea was that legal aid upholds a system designed to perpetuate the oppression of poor people by helping folks just barely survive, without challenging the underlying institutions that keep them poor. These critiques of legal aid certainly have merit. However, we cannot lose sight of the fact that while we dream up and fight for a more just society, people still need to survive in this one. As lawyers we have the training, knowledge, access, and privilege to help people survive their encounters with the legal system. The more evictions I can stop, the more of my clients may have the bandwidth to attend a community meeting, talk to a reporter, or speak at a city council meeting. And that's where real change happens.

Learn Something from This

- Being a frontline lawyer does not necessarily make you a radical lawyer; you are probably playing a role inside of a system designed to further marginalize and punish people. You must constantly interrogate your work to ensure you are not causing or perpetuating harm.
- It is inevitable that you will find yourself trying to manage the expectations of an individual client and the demands of movements. Try to prepare for that moment by being clear about your values and your politics.
- Counsel clients on the range of arguments, including social justice arguments.
- Do not underestimate the power of planting seeds in arguments in one case that may change the outcomes for someone else in the future.
- When working inside of institutions and raising money or resources, be mindful that you are not hoarding funds. Consider what it would look like to advocate both for your organization and also for funding that serves the communities where your clients come from.
- Organizing and lawyering can go hand in hand even when you are working inside of established legal organizations where there is no culture of working this way. Finding creative ways to partner with organizers and impacted people can make you more effective.

Resources

- Silicon Valley DeBug started participatory defense hubs as a way of supporting members of their organization who were facing prison time. The participatory defense model situates criminal courts as organizing targets and encourages community members and families to move from passive observers to participants who are able to advocate for their loved ones. The video "Meet the People Fighting for True Justice" spotlights the participatory defense approach. The film follows employees from Silicon Valley DeBug as they help keep people out of jail or reduce time served by pairing family members and organizers with lawyers. This video can be found on YouTube and is linked on Participatory Defense Network's website: www .participatorydefense.org/about.

Notes

1. During the Law for Black Lives listening tours in 2019, this idea of negative associations with public defenders came up a lot as a challenge faced by public defenders and legal services attorneys. This was of particular concern in our listening tour, convened by L4BL at Gideon's Promise on October 23, 2019, in Atlanta, Georgia.

2. John Gross, "Reframing the Indigent Defense Crisis," *Harvard L. R. Blog*, March 28, 2023, https://harvardlawreview.org/blog/2023/03/reframing-the -indigent-defense-crisis.

3. Special thanks to our children who are (mostly) patient with us as we take time to write, and to Adam Cloud, Lisa Sangoi, Zainab Akbar, Porsha Sha'fon Venable, and Rebecca Oyama, who graciously took time to look through edits of this essay.

4. "Black Families Matter: Dorothy Roberts," *Race and Regulation* podcast, May 25, 2022, https://penntoday.upenn.edu/news/dorothy-roberts-black-families -matter-race-and-regulation-podcast.

5. Emma Ruth, "'Family Regulation,' Not 'Child Welfare': Abolition Starts with Changing Our Language," *The Imprint*, July 28, 2020, https://imprintnews .org/opinion/family-regulation-not-child-welfare-abolition-starts-changing -language/45586.

6. Rajani Chakraborty, "How the US Stole Thousands of Native American Children," *Vox*, October 14, 2019, www.vox.com/2019/10/14/20913408/us-stole -thousands-of-native-american-children.

7. "Whatever They Do, I'm Her Comfort, I'm Her Protector: How the Foster System Has Become Ground Zero for the U.S. Drug War," Movement for Family Power, June 2020, www.movementforfamilypower.org/s/MFP-Drug-War -Foster-System-Report.pdf.

8. Stewart Nikkita and Benjamin Weiser, "Troubled Girls Were Sent to This Town to Heal. Many Were Lured into the Sex Trade Instead," *New York Times*, December 13, 2018, www.nytimes.com/2018/12/13/nyregion/sex-trafficking -hawthorne-cedar-knolls.html.

9. Fabiola Cineas, "Why They're Not Saying Ma'Khia Bryant's Name," *Vox*, May 1, 2021, www.vox.com/22406055/makhia-bryant-police-shooting -columbus-ohio.

10. Jane M. Spinak, *The End of Family Court: How Abolishing Family Court Brings Justice to Children and Families* (New York University Press, 2023).

11. Lucas Gerber et al., "Effects of an Interdisciplinary Approach to Parental Representation in Child Welfare," 102 *Child & Youth Serve. Rev.* 42–55 (September 2019).

12. Davida Finger, "New Orleans Eviction Geography: Results of an Increasingly Precarious Housing Market," Jane Place Neighborhood Sustainability Initiative and Loyola University New Orleans College of Law, Law Clinic, March 2019, https://ssrn.com/abstract=3456929.

13. *Id.*

14. "Out of Reach: The High Cost of Housing," National Low Income Housing Coalition, 2022, https://nlihc.org/oor, accessed September 21, 2022.

15. Javers v. Council of New Orleans, 351 So.2d 247 (La. Ct. App. 4th Cir. 1977); New Orleans Campaign for a Living Wage v. City of New Orleans, 825 So.2d 1098 (La. 2002).

16. This work can only be done with non–Legal Services Corporation funding per 45 C.F.R. §1612.6. This piece is not intended to be a comprehensive treatise on permissible activities under LSC regulations; advocates should review regulations carefully before participating in the activities described herein.

7 *Policymaking for Radicals*

Policy can be an important tool for lawyers and legal workers fighting for transformation. Policy has the potential to be systemic and can be an exciting avenue for impactful and even visionary change. However, as we discussed in chapter 3, reformist policy can undermine transformation. Despite its potential, policy is often used to entrench the status quo and co-opt the energy of social movements. Reformist policy solutions misdiagnose the problems we face, propose incomplete solutions, and take the wind out of movement by claiming false victories. In addition, the policy process itself can undermine movement. It often includes unequal access to information and backroom dealing, which alienates those most impacted and entrenches existing power dynamics, exalting some people (often lawyers) as experts while sidelining others. Policy outcomes can throw some communities under the bus at the expense of others, which divides and weakens movements.

How do you make sure that policy campaigns expand the horizon of what is possible? How do you imbue policy fights with power-shifting strategies? What specific things should movement lawyers do to avoid the pitfalls of traditional policymaking? This chapter includes reflections on these questions from movement lawyers and organizers who have chosen to wield policy as a means of change and power building.

Throughout this chapter you will read about policy work that is participatory and centers movement lawyering and the other political values we described in chapter 2. Gina Clayton-Johnson reflects on how Black queer feminism can help guide policy work with its commitment to "leadership from many" and its valuing of relationships as a source of power. Rachel Herzing, one of the cofounders of Critical Resistance, reflects on making abolitionist policy and provides some helpful reminders about the importance of political clarity and organizing in creating, implementing, and maintaining policy. Joey L. Mogul discusses what is made possible when those most directly impacted are centered in policymaking and when we explore both what we want to dismantle and what we want to build. This chapter also includes honest reflections about the limitations of policy, especially for movement lawyers trying to navigate advocacy spaces while remaining accountable to movement organizations and communities. In her piece Christian Snow explores how differences in urgency, goals, and accountability can create divisions between organizers and traditional advocacy lawyers.

Policy can be a tool of power building if it is done collaboratively, centers those most impacted, and is grounded in our politics of abolition and Black queer feminism(s). At its best, policy complements the bold visions of movement and is authored, advocated for, and implemented by those most impacted. As the contributors in this chapter explain, policymaking must be paired with organizing and narrative change to be meaningful.

Biographical Reflection: Black Feminist Lessons in Representing and Organizing Women with Incarcerated Loved Ones
By Gina Clayton-Johnson

"How much did it cost for you to get your nails done?" the judge asked with condescension. My client Holly answered humbly that she had done them herself. I was representing Holly as she and her young daughter were facing eviction from their apartment. Their landlord wanted them out. Holly's abusive ex-boyfriend had stored a small amount of drugs in her dresser, and she'd fallen behind on rent. My client had asked me earlier if her young daughter could observe the hearing; her daughter wanted to be a lawyer one day.

To my surprise, the judge was berating my client, and my stomach was sick with regret that Holly's daughter was witnessing it. The judge continued with many more shaming questions: "If he was abusing you, why didn't you report it to the police? Don't you care about your daughter?" Despite the judge's bullying, we ended up with a strong result that day—Holly was able to keep her housing, and I was proud of what we'd been able to achieve. Nonetheless, leaving the courtroom I knew I'd lost something. My client had been degraded and humiliated in front of her daughter. A lesson crystalized for me that day in court. In the words of civil rights activist Esther Cooper Jackson, I understood that "no small amount of change would do."[1]

I was angry at the behavior of that judge, but I knew that simply removing her would not solve the underlying issues that led to that moment. Our suits, the courthouse's domineering architecture, the guards, and the judge's elevated position ensured that we all played roles that brought about disempowering results for our clients, even if we won. I began to notice these results regularly in my cases. In Holly's situation the legal claims were related to unpaid rent and drugs in her apartment. From our talks I knew she needed help to find her agency and real choices to exercise that agency. Holly needed stable housing, healing services, trauma-informed interventions for domestic violence, and free childcare. What Holly and my other clients deserved was a radical approach to social and interpersonal problem-solving. However, the prevailing operations of our courts and statehouses are adversarial, punitive, and reactionary. We need a system that prioritizes radical problem-solving, healing, and accountability.

Black feminism holds the radical approach needed for effective transformation of our criminal legal structures. Fundamentally it is an analysis and practice that jointly addresses the interlocking systems of oppression—racism, sexism, classism, and heteronormativity—that Black women face.[2] Moreover, Black feminism is inherently queer and abolitionist. As the Combahee River Collective's foundational statement posits, Black women's freedom "would necessitate the destruction of all the systems of oppression." I've frequently heard advocates lament the fact that focusing on only one root cause of harm often leads to strategies that may carry a veneer of impact but ultimately do not produce meaningful change. Here, Black feminism offers us guidance.

Two Black feminist concepts have proven key in my gender justice organizing. First, Black feminism values leadership from many rather than from a single individual. Civil rights luminary Ella Baker famously stated: "I have always thought that what is needed is the development of people who are interested not in being leaders as much as in developing leadership in others." The need to develop the leadership of others is a core contribution to Black feminist thought, and creates breadth, sustainability, and individual empowerment in our movements. Second, Black feminism teaches that our connection to one another is the source of our power, as bell hooks offers: "One of the most vital ways we sustain ourselves is by building communities of resistance, places where we know we are not alone."[3] These communities of resistance are laden with potential to envision new and more comprehensive solutions. In addition, as Angela Davis said in a 2021 address: "If we don't have that collective imagination, there's no way we can generate the kind of passion to move along a trajectory that promises us radical social transformation."[4]

We must facilitate leadership and connection now more than ever. And yet this strategy is not new. My great-grandmother Essie Bailey was raised on a sharecropping farm before moving west in 1938. I was curious to know how she was able to overcome the obstacles of poverty, Jim Crow, racism, and sexism. Sitting at my grandmother's kitchen table, I asked her how Essie did it. She answered, simply: "Baby, she had sisters!" To her it was obvious. My great-grandmother was connected to a community. It was her leadership in connection with a community of sisters that made winning against odds possible. Black feminism is not abstract, it is ancestral; it is our work as organizers to access its wisdom in this moment.

Addressing the root causes of what brought us to court that morning with my client Holly means cultivating the leadership of people like her, who have lived experience of racism, sexism, and classism. It means ensuring she's connected and not isolated in that lived experience. However, my role was limited—the traditional attorney-client relationship positioned me as "expert," and Holly as "needy beneficiary." Moreover, I couldn't easily connect my clients to one another without violating ethics rules. I set out to better understand how I could generate the leadership and connection of people like Holly in hopes that it would hasten the pace of transformative change.

Women with incarcerated loved ones hold exciting potential for people power that can translate into big change. During my first year of law school, I got an unforgettable phone call—someone I love had been sentenced to twenty years in prison. "Twenty years?" I repeated into the phone. Through my experience of organizing Black communities in South Los Angeles, becoming a woman with an incarcerated loved one, and by representing women like Holly, I had identified that patterned, systemic, and state-sanctioned harm is occurring to women who have incarcerated loved ones. New statistics emerged to show that incarceration has reached such levels that one in four women and one in two Black women in the United States have a loved one behind bars. Women are also the fastest-growing segment of the incarcerated population. For many people, mass incarceration is an issue about Black men, not women. As a result of this narrow view, millions of women are left out of criminal justice reform. This exclusion leads to missed opportunities, unmet needs, and bad policy. I began to develop a theory of change that women being harmed by mass incarceration, if organized, could prove to be a formidable force in the intersecting fights of women's rights and criminal justice.

I founded Essie Justice Group in 2014 to connect women with incarcerated loved ones and build power for transformative change. I started small by hosting brunch meetups for women with incarcerated loved ones so I could listen. Their ideas helped create our nine-week Healing to Advocacy program for women with incarcerated loved ones to meet each other, heal, learn, and graduate into a membership body we call our "sisterhood." In the tradition of Ella Baker, we train graduates of our program to lead the next program cohorts. Since we first gathered together in those early circles, Essie Justice Group has run hundreds of sessions for women with incarcerated loved ones—graduating more than forty cohorts of the program. Our members lead in campaigns on issues including sentencing reform, jail closure, prison visitation, and pretrial liberation.

The base-building work we had been doing for years paved the way for the systemic results I sought. Our bailout action is an example. A few years after starting Essie Justice Group, I joined a group of Black organizers in the founding of a historic national tactic envisioned by Mary Hooks from Southerners on New Ground.[5] Since then, Essie Justice Group has freed Black women from California jails every year to be home with their kids in time for Mother's Day. April, mother of a three-year-old daughter, had been incarcerated for violating her probation when Essie members came to bail her out of Lynwood Jail in Los Angeles. When April saw the collection of Black women gathered outside of the jail to meet her, she was shocked. She

Essie Justice Group's Healing to Advocacy program. Courtesy of Essie Justice Group.

hadn't expected this outpouring of warmth and care—women greeting her with open arms, "Welcome Home" signs, and a care package. April would soon be reunited with her daughter to fight her case from the outside.

When I met April for coffee a few days after her release, we talked about Essie Justice Group. I told her what we tell every woman who is invited into our membership: we need your leadership. I explained that we are an organization of women and gender-nonconforming leaders, not a charity. If she wanted to join us, it would be as a partner, not a beneficiary. Next, April joined a Healing to Advocacy cohort and met more women who had also been incarcerated and who had loved ones behind bars. She made friends and created a new network; she received training on how to tell her story to move other people into action. When April's next court date arrived, the judge did what no one expected. Upon seeing how connected she was to a loving community, he terminated her probation on the spot. She would no longer live with the threat of incarceration hanging over her head.

Later that spring, connected to her leadership and community, April confidently took the mic at our press conference to make demands for policy change. She insisted that Los Angeles County fund pretrial services and thirty-six hundred mental health beds, which would dramatically reduce incarceration and lay the foundation for the closure of Lynwood Jail. In contrast to other reforms on the table, including racially biased risk assessment tools, expansions to judicial discretion, and pretrial surveillance, April's demands speak directly to the root causes of the harm at issue: "We don't need probation, we don't need jails," she said. "We need care and we need it now." We should reject the myriad reforms that tinker with the system and embrace a Black feminist approach.

With soaring isolation, brought on by a societal addiction to punitively separating people from one another through incarceration and exacerbated by public health, climate, and economic crises, we need Black feminism in our organizing and policy work.[6] In June of 2020, as a response to the murders of George Floyd, Breonna Taylor, and Tony McDade, I led an all-Black team of predominately queer women to create the BREATHE Act—a large federal bill that answers the question: What will it take to ensure Black people can be safe? Centering Black feminist strategies catalyzes radical policy such as campaigns for jail closure in Los Angeles and the BREATHE Act. The fate of race, gender, and criminal justice movements depends on how diligently we advocates apply ourselves to a Black feminist strategy in our campaigning for a liberatory future.

Tactical Case Study: The Grassroots Struggle for Chicago Police Torture Survivors
By Joey L. Mogul

For more than twenty-five years I have had the honor and privilege to represent and organize with people tortured, raped, and abused by police and governmental officials in civil rights and criminal cases and to work with organizers seeking radical social change. On this journey I have learned, changed, and evolved into an abolitionist of the entire prison industrial complex (PIC). My devotion to movement lawyering has grown with my deepened understanding that centering the experiences and efforts of those directly affected by violence and other organizers is essential to securing the transformative, sustainable change we desire in this world. As part of my ongoing evolution, I share my personal perspective on the more than forty-year campaign for justice and redress in the Chicago Police (Burge) torture cases.

The Chicago Police (Burge) torture cases involve the systemic torture of over 125 Black people by former Chicago Police commander Jon Burge and predominantly white detectives under his command from 1972 to 1991, during the rise of the "law and order" agenda and mass incarceration in the United States. The racially motivated torture was deployed to extract confessions that were introduced as powerful pieces of incriminating evidence at survivors' trials. Seeking to suppress their confessions, survivors courageously testified about the torture they endured, laying bare the details of their painful, terrifying, and degrading interrogations, while the white detectives cavalierly denied any coercion occurred. Judges and juries routinely credited the detectives' testimony over the word of Black survivors, facilitating the admission of confessions that were used to secure convictions, lengthy prison, and death sentences.

Testifying in criminal and civil cases, including at Burge's federal prosecution for perjury and obstruction of justice, was traumatizing for survivors, as opposed to being a validating and cathartic experience. They were forced to relive their harrowing interrogations while being disparaged in anti-Black racist ways—cast as criminals and gang members who were unworthy of belief, sympathy, or care. Decades later, even after Burge was convicted, survivors continued to grapple with the knowledge that they were disbelieved by judges, jurors, attorneys, and even some family members. For years, the struggle for justice revolved around the criminal and civil rights cases of individual survivors. The civil litigation, initially pursued by the People's Law Office (Flint Taylor, myself, and others) was important and necessary to support survivors.

The civil litigation was pivotal to uncovering that Burge and his disciples were engaged in a racist pattern of torture. Given the individual and atomized nature of the court system, this was not a collective effort but often a siloed one. Survivors were unaware that others had been tortured like them. There was very little coordination among the growing number of attorneys representing the survivors. In the absence of political organizing, the litigation did not have a larger impact beyond getting an individual person some relief in a criminal or civil case, which took decades to achieve. Moreover, the material needs of the torture survivors remained unsatisfied. Many survivors were unable to get any financial compensation for the torture they endured because the statute of limitations had expired on their civil claims. The survivors continued to suffer psychologically, experiencing flashbacks and nightmares, but there was no place for them to obtain any trauma-informed psychological counseling or assistance.

In 2010, after decades of representation and several organizing endeavors—some successful and others not—I initiated and cofounded Chicago Torture Justice Memorials (CTJM), comprised of torture survivors, artists, educators, and organizers. Our initial goal was to uplift and support the demand for reparations made by Standish Willis, a member of the National Conference of Black Lawyers and others from Black People Against Police Torture. As a white person I was reluctant to be central to organizing for reparations for Black people, but I wanted to support and show solidarity. It later became apparent to me, given my relationship with several survivors and their desire to pursue reparations, that I had essential knowledge and skills to lend to the struggle. Therefore it was incumbent on me to actively work in support of this and other reparations efforts.

CTJM's goal was to focus on the element of reparations known as satisfaction, which requires official apologies and public memorials. We created a participatory art project that invited everyone to unleash their radical imaginations by creating speculative memorials to the Burge torture survivors and the struggles for justice. In doing so, we created a new container for organizing, separate from the courts and law. It centered the voices, experiences, needs, and desires of the torture survivors, their families, and other Black community members. It created a space where we as creators and legal workers worked with torture survivors, side by side, rather than speaking for the survivors in the litigation or media.

As part of an art show in 2012 exhibiting speculative memorials, I drafted a proposed reparations ordinance. I never imagined in my wildest dreams that we would file it in Chicago's City Council or later build a grassroots campaign to get it passed. Then, in the fall of 2013, in response to organizing efforts, Mayor Rahm Emanuel made what many considered a half-hearted, insincere, and dismissive apology when he acknowledged that the Burge torture cases were a "dark" chapter and a "stain on the City's reputation." He said: "I am sorry this happened. Let us all now move on." His remarks infuriated many and motivated us to file the reparations ordinance in Chicago's City Council. Upon doing so, I did not think the proposed ordinance would pass but would be another adventure in doing the right thing.

Over time, CTJM formed a multiracial, intergenerational grassroots coalition co-led by CTJM (and me), Mariame Kaba (the all-time best organizer and movement theorist of the twenty-first century) and Project NIA, We Charge Genocide, and Amnesty International USA to secure the passage of reparations legislation in the fall and winter of 2014–15, in the midst of the municipal election. It was also during the first tidal wave of the Black Lives Matter movement in the aftermath of the police killing of Michael Brown in Ferguson, Missouri. The campaign used multiple tools from the organizing toolbox—demonstrations, teach-ins, pop-up memorials, CTA train takeovers, Twitter power hours, and a light installation outside Mayor Emanuel's home declaring "Reparations Now." The organizing forced Emanuel and his administration to the negotiating table. After a series of heated and contentious meetings, wherein several demands were met and painful compromises were made, we reached an agreement on the reparations legislation.

On May 6, 2015, Chicago's City Council unanimously passed the reparations legislation, which included the following: torture survivors receiving up to $100,000 each; the creation of the Chicago Torture Justice Center (CTJC, a psychological counseling center providing trauma-informed services to all impacted by the police violence and domestic torture); free tuition at Chicago's City Colleges for survivors and family members; a formal apology from the City of Chicago; the creation of a permanent public memorial; and a history curriculum on the Burge police torture cases titled "Reparation Won" taught to all eighth and tenth graders in Chicago Public Schools (CPS).

Chicago made history passing the legislation, becoming the first municipality in the United States to provide redress for racially motivated law enforcement violence. The organizing and passage of the legislation created communities of care, allowing the survivors to be surrounded by audiences of people who believed, respected, and cared for them, providing them intangible support and healing. Survivors took active roles in organizing for and implementing the legislation—developing the curriculum, memorial, and CTJC—which provided them agency, purpose, and empowerment. The first of its kind in the nation, CTJC employs several police torture survivors creating support for others, and it is a hub of organizing against carceral violence in Chicago. The enactment of the legislation has

"Reparations Now" light installation outside of Chicago Mayor Rahm Emanuel's house as part of protests demanding reparations, 2015. Photo taken by Kelly Hayes.

led to a dominant narrative change about the Chicago Police torture cases, which is changing the dynamics in criminal cases, leading to survivors' release from prison as well as vacated convictions and exonerations.

The legal system failed the survivors and Black communities every step of the way. The courts failed to stop Burge and others from torturing Black people and preventing the use of coerced confessions to obtain wrongful convictions. Prosecutors failed to hold Burge and other detectives fully accountable for their international human rights violations. The civil legal system was incapable of providing the holistic redress needed by all of those harmed by Burge and his men. The courts failed to yield the measure of justice and redress achieved in these cases. Lawyers could not have litigated this to success. Lawyers needed to recognize that litigation alone, in the absence of a wider political and social organizing campaign, was going to be largely unsuccessful. Rather, there needed to be dramatic change in the dominant narrative, making it clear that this was a racist pattern and practice of torture endemic to structural anti-Black racism. Recognizing that politics in the court of public opinion influenced the atmosphere in the courts of law required an entire reframe as to how lawyers were approaching the litigation. Lawyers needed to step aside and disregard the advice that instructs those directly affected by carceral violence to remain silent because their words may be used against them. It was a lesson I learned early on. We had to let the survivors speak for themselves because they were the best at communicating their own experiences and persuading the people to support their release and reparations they so richly deserved.

Lawyers, however, were critical to the success of the reparations campaign and played necessary roles by drafting the legislation, digesting and sharing information gleaned from the litigation, developing campaign materials, participating in negotiations with the City, drafting Memorandums of Understanding (MOUs, formal nonbinding agreements), and working with others to implement the legislation. The reparations legislation we secured was not a perfect solution. Pursuing reparations required that we create a class of police torture survivors that was both inclusive and exclusive of others with similar experiences. We continue to struggle to secure reparations for other survivors of police torture and violence. It has been a struggle to implement the reparations package requiring CTJM to recruit many others to support the efforts to create the CPS curriculum, the Chicago Torture Justice Center, and the memorial. CTJM had to organize for an additional eight years and was fortunate that Mayor Brandon Johnson was elected in Chicago before CTJM could secure $3 million to build the memorial on June 19, 2023. That said, the reparations package provided the money and resources we needed to plant seeds—the history curriculum, the Chicago Torture Justice

Center, and the memorial—to further educate the public and inspire generations to come to fight police violence and grow alternatives to policing, prosecution, and punishment.

Reparations legislation is not a panacea for stopping and redressing racist police violence. It is hard to imagine any legislative effort that would successfully reduce police violence, short of demands that strip law enforcement agencies of power and resources. That said, for decades we have witnessed this perpetual cycle of racist police violence, righteous responses, and failed prosecutions of killer and torturing police officers. A call for reparations that are expansive in scope and that center the needs of people targeted for police violence may be a new way for us to think about accountability and justice for police violence in the face of our fatally flawed legal system.

I am so grateful for these experiences and lessons, and I continue to learn from working with Black and non-Black survivors and organizers. I am fortunate that, in the words of renowned organizer Mary Hooks, I have been transformed in the service of this work.

The Hard Stuff: "Radical" Means Getting to the Root—Navigating Policy Advocacy in Support of Transformative Social Change
By Christian Snow

We who seek liberation know we need transformative social change to reach our goal, but how we get there and exactly what it tangibly looks like often comes into debate. The role of policy in our struggle for liberation is highly contested. When it comes to enacting transformative social change, policy is a limited tool, because policy changes are rarely "radical" in the Ella Baker sense of the word, getting down to the root of the problem.

I have spent much of my life watching my people—Black and working class—live under oppressive policies and practices enforced by the police through violence and upheld by the courts under the guise of neutrality. I witnessed and experienced how these practices and policies cause daily harms that have a lifelong impact. All I have ever wanted was liberation for my people. So I have spent my life exploring the best pathways to liberation and where my labor would make the greatest contribution. Over the past decade I have been a community and youth organizer, a director of a Black radical base-building organization, and a movement lawyer working in the areas of criminal defense, civil rights, and policy (sometimes at the same time), exploring the different theories, definitions of the issues, the approaches to the work of liberation, the available tools, and the pitfalls. One thing has been painfully apparent throughout my work: we will not achieve liberation without addressing the current material conditions our people are facing right now.

Policy change is worth an investment from movement, quite simply because policy changes alter the material conditions under which we all suffer and struggle, and if we intervene in policy advocacy, we can push for altering them in ways that open up resources, politicize others, and position us closer to liberation. And we have to survive under and navigate the current systems to build the world we want to see. The stakes make policy advocacy a valuable tool and a meaningful space where those dedicated to transformative social change should intentionally spend time intervening and shaping the outcomes.

Movement organizers have to build intentional coalitions with policy advocates in ways that allow for accountability and an opportunity to intervene in the policy space and push for change in alignment with a liberatory vision of transformative social change. Movement organizers and policy advocates have to build intentional coalitions. I extended my work from movement to policy because I wanted to develop an understanding of how to form deeper connections between movement organizers and policy advocates so that these intentional coalitions could be built and material conditions could be altered in ways that addressed current harms and pushed us closer to liberation. My experiences have taught me valuable lessons about navigating the policy advocacy space for transformative social change: namely that advocates and organizers have different root cause analyses, ways of determining what policy change is possible, measures of accountability, and approaches to building trust.

I hope you gain insight from the lessons I have learned in trying to build intentional coalitions between movement and traditional policy advocates. My experiences have more intimately exposed me to the limitations of policy advocacy as a tool for liberation. They have reaffirmed that although policy changes can address material conditions in ways that aid the journey toward liberation, we will not get free through policy changes alone. We have to strategically engage in those efforts in ways that make room for the liberatory work of organizing community. At the end of the essay I leave some advice for those thinking about engaging in intentional and strategic ways.

Lessons Learned

Context is critical to a full understanding. When I am referring to policy advocates and movement folks, I am specifically talking about those who are dedicated to their work and principled in their dealings with one another but struggling to align strategies, boundaries, and values. Any of us who do this work know that we always have to navigate opps, fickle friends, and pseudo-allies in our spaces, but they are not the focus of this essay.

My road to policy advocacy was deeply impacted by the COVID-19 pandemic, when it was clear that the oppressive regime Black folks, particularly the working class, perpetually lived under was only going to get worse under the circumstances. During the early stages of the pandemic I lived in Chicago, in the predominantly Black neighborhood of Austin, and the suffering was clear. Neighbors not only lost family, fell ill, and lost employment, but transportation became even more unreliable, resources even more sparse, and the neighborhood even more surveilled. Families were stressed about the safety and well-being of incarcerated loved ones. And there seemed to be no real solution to oppressive policies enacted at that moment: raised bridges, the deployment of tanks and garbage trucks to block my community in, and the halting of train routes. Something clearly had to shift if we were going to survive despite the state's actions, and I was determined to find the best way I could contribute to liberation's forward motion while addressing material conditions.

During that time I worked as a newly minted attorney in a radical civil rights and criminal defense law firm. I was also a few years into my role as the executive director of Assata's Daughters (AD). Seeded in 2015, AD was a political home for young Black people in Chicago, created and guided by radical Black women deeply affected by organizing in response to police brutality and murder. AD sought to provide consistent political education, organizing training, and revolutionary support to those young Black people, their families, and communities as a way of deepening, escalating, and sustaining the movement for Black liberation. We believed to successfully organize for Black liberation, we needed to build deep relationships with everyday Black folks. Like the Black Panther Party, Assata's Daughters operated under the theory that it wasn't enough to attempt to mobilize folks in the time of a mass uprising. We had to prepare folks for those moments so that we could strategically take advantage of them.

The year 2020 put AD's theory to the test. The pandemic and the impact of the government's response intensified existing inequities within our capitalist, racist systems, making the ground ripe for an uprising. In preparation the organization rapidly expanded its network of revolutionary support, political education offerings, organizing trainings, and contributions to movement's demand to "Free them All" and provide for the people. In May 2020 that match came in the form of George Floyd's death at the hands of police. Organizers who had been deepening the movement ecosystem since 2015 flocked to provide support for the uprising, which was primarily filled with young folks and those newly activated, who were often uncoordinated and unaware of the potential harm they faced. In many ways it was a beautiful confirmation of our theories of power-building, as those who had been engaged in political homes, including AD young people, took the opportunity to provide coordination and political education in the midst of a chaotic uprising. They drove home demands that had been crafted over the years, like "Defund" and "Free them All," and guided people under an abolitionist banner.

The experience was exhausting and traumatic to many people but particularly to community organizers. We navigated neighborhood blockades, violent police repression, raised bridges, and stopped trains, mass arrests, and mental exhaustion from holding theoretical lines of what was truly meant by the call for abolition. As the appetite for taking to the streets waned and movement turned toward moving newly activated people into political homes, I looked around at my burned-out, traumatized comrades and wondered what, outside of a more mobilized base, we had tangibly won for the sacrifice of our minds and bodies. Many people, particularly policy advocates, pointed to the passage of the watershed Illinois criminal legal system reform bill HB 3653 (otherwise known as the Safety, Accountability, Fairness and Equity Act, or SAFE-T Act) that, among many things, ended the use of cash bail. Some credited the uprisings and the work of the movement ecosystem with creating the pressure and conditions necessary for the bill to be signed into law. The bill was an incredible feat that many people had been working on for years and would forever change the material conditions for oppressed people engaged by the criminal legal system.

But it was a small chip in the prison industrial complex. I found myself in conversation with other exhausted organizers wondering if all our pain and sacrifice to build political will could not have led to more transformative social change like the SAFE-T Act. What we could witness from the ground were increased police budgets, continued police surveillance and repression, deepened community economic deprivation and divestment, and very little effort from policy advocates to address them. In addition, we felt hyperaware that despite movement being credited for creating the conditions for radical policy advocacy, many organizers continued to be alienated from decision-making spaces where their demands were being watered down or lost in translation in the name of negotiation and compromise. It was clear to us that there was a disconnect between the magnitude of movement demands and the scope of policy wins. We believed we needed to and could make an intervention in the policy field to bring policy advocates into as much alignment with movement as we could. Given my unique positionality as a lawyer and organizer, I thought that I could find a way to bridge the gap so I transitioned into a program director role with the Illinois Justice Project (ILJP), one of the major policy organizations responsible for influencing criminal legal system policy across the state.

At ILJP, I was originally tasked with advancing their Justice 20/20 initiative, a multiorganizational project focused on taking advantage of the openings provided by the pandemic to make tangible criminal legal system policy change. Instead, I attempted to build a container for those interested in building and executing a coordinated statewide strategy for ending the cycle of criminalization and incarceration. Organizing had taught me the importance of containers, and I thought creating one in the policy space would be the best way to organize people from different disciplines and sites of work around an abolitionist vision (explicit or not). I optimistically believed that with political education, long-term planning, relationship-building, and finding and working around common goals, we could bring the progressive policy advocacy community in line with the demands of movement. I believed we could make room for grassroots organizers at the table, as a way to intervene in the policy space, push for accountability, and push for policy changes that alter material conditions in alignment with a liberatory vision of transformative social change. I still believe this is the call to action for movement folks engaging with the space; however, my experiences organizing this container left me with critical lessons.

LESSON #1: POLICY ADVOCATES AND BASE-BUILDING OR-GANIZERS HAVE DIFFERENT APPROACHES TO ANALYZ-ING ROOT CAUSES, WHICH GUIDE THE SOLUTIONS EACH GROUP WORKS TO ENACT. A root cause analysis calls for you to identify the source of an issue and address it. This analysis should guide all discussions about action steps and policy solutions because in theory addressing the source should take care of the original issue identified. When policy advocates conduct a root cause analysis, they start by identifying the issue as whatever particular harm is occurring. They identify the current policies, mechanisms, and practices that allow for the harm to exist. They rarely look beyond to the systems that allow for the harm to exist in the first place. As opposed to organizers, who also identify the specific harm and the current policies, mechanism, and practices that allow for the harm to exist, but who then interrogate the systems that enable the harm.

For example, quite often when I held space for progressive advocates and organizers to strategize around harms of the criminal legal system, all parties could agree that crime and harm would decrease if people had their material needs met. However, progressive policy advocates would link the harm of people not having their needs met to poverty and end their analysis there. Their solutions would typically rest on the assumption that we just had to enact policy changes and practices that helped folks tangled in the criminal legal system get out of poverty—for instance, fund more job training and entrepreneurship programs or prioritize vendors from marginalized backgrounds in government contracts. But organizers go further in their root cause analysis. They would agree with the policy advocates that if someone is living in poverty, their needs are *not* being met. However, they would identify the current economic system as the source of poverty—for example, under capitalism poverty will always exist. Their proposed policy solutions would relate to chipping away at capitalism as a way to solve poverty and ensure that everyone has their needs met: invest in solidarity economies or provide a guaranteed basic income.

Recognizing that policy advocates and movement organizers were conducting two different root cause analyses was a key learning for how I approached coalition building between the two groups. The differences in root cause analyses can become friction when building coalitions between the two groups. In our coalition it led to debates about the functionality of the criminal legal system overall. Through those debates I learned that many progressive policy advocates were okay with the systems organizers named as wholly oppressive: they believed that most policy issues were ones of "equity" or "equality" that caused the system to malfunction, and their role was to tinker with it until it was balanced. They want to know if there is "political will," how long it might last, and what blocks or challenges might be levied by traditional forces of power. Organizers have to push these progressive policy advocates to take their analysis one step further if they are going to generate and advocate for policy solutions in line with a liberatory vision for transformative social change.

LESSON #2: POLICY ADVOCATES AND BASE-BUILDING OR-
GANIZERS HAVE DIFFERENT APPROACHES AND ANALY-
SES FOR IDENTIFYING POSSIBLE POLICY SOLUTIONS. IN

FACT, THEY ARE USING DIFFERENT FRAMEWORKS FOR DETERMINING WHAT IS "POSSIBLE." Policy advocates and organizers have different ways of assessing possible policy solutions to address oppressive material conditions. More specifically, they have different understandings of what "possible" means. Both groups consider the current system and political climate: they want to know if there is "political will," how long it might last, what blocks or challenges might be levied by traditional forces of power, and what resources are needed to enact the change. However, I found that progressive policy advocates are typically making these inquiries to determine if the proposed policy solution is viable—that is, one worth spending their political capital on. But organizers approach the process by identifying the material conditions needing change and strategizing ways to build the power to do so.

Organizers' assessment of the current system and political climate is part of how they build their strategy, understanding that they will always have to build the political will to enact transformative social change. Policy advocates use their assessment to reject acting. For instance, in many of our meetings, even after getting some of the progressive advocates to acknowledge capitalism as a cause of poverty or simply to agree that no one should experience poverty, these same advocates would often remark that ending poverty or capitalism was an impossible task because there was no political will for it. And if there is no political will, our proposed policy solutions should focus on helping people get better at navigating capitalism. Organizers believe in the possibility that we can get out from under these systems, and therefore their proposed solutions are bolder. Organizers have to encourage progressive policy advocates to expand their imaginations if they are going to generate and advocate for policy solutions in line with a liberatory vision for transformative social change.

LESSON #3: PROGRESSIVE POLICY ADVOCATES AND MOVEMENT ORGANIZERS FEEL DIFFERENT LEVELS OF URGENCY. One of the most frustrating parts of my experiences has been navigating the lack of urgency from policy advocates to do all they can to address the material conditions causing harm. My experiences taught me that the lack of urgency was also due in part to their distance from the problems. Many of the community organizers I engaged with felt the urgency to enact long-lasting solutions because they could see the impact of the systems of oppression up close, often personally. For example, many of the organizers I worked with were barely surviving under capitalism and were deeply impacted by the global pandemic, particularly if they were out supporting the community. For many of the policy advocates I encountered, even the discrete problem they sought to address was a theoretical one, not felt by anyone they had close ties to. The lack of impact contributed to their lack of urgency, and it was a struggle to get folks to commit to the labor necessary to move the needle on even the problems they committed to addressing. Organizers need to address this lack of urgency if they are going to generate and advocate for policy solutions in line with a liberatory vision for transformative social change.

LESSON #4: PROGRESSIVE POLICY ADVOCATES AND MOVEMENT ORGANIZERS HAVE DIVERGENT LOYALTIES AND HAVE DIFFERENT APPROACHES TO BUILDING TRUST AND NAVIGATING ACCOUNTABILITY. In my experience the most impactful organizers prioritize building relationships with individuals in the community they are working to organize with. This is where they gain their power, their ability to organize folks around a common goal or mobilize them to defeat an obstacle, and this is who they must be accountable to. Good community organizers know how to learn and study alongside their base; they aren't just seeking to impose their will. No matter how much you have studied an issue, someone's lived experience with it may come along and shift your whole theory about the solution. It is important to make room for this. When organizers make demands, they must be rooted in these experiences, otherwise you lose the backing of the base you are building.

My experience in policy spaces left me with a persistent question: Who are policy advocates accountable to? When they negotiate about laws and policies that affect the lives of everyday individuals, who do they check in with? Who will they have to explain themselves to if they negotiate away a provision that others who will experience it wanted to keep? There were many times when I attended meetings about the implementation of a bill when those representing organizations closer to community questioned why it contained certain provisions or lacked certain protections. Instead of explaining "This is what we felt we could negotiate for," advocates tried to spin it into a win, or claim it was something people should be able to live with.

And while there is rarely an occasion when everyone is pleased, the question of accountability only deepened when it became clear that organizers and groups were being purposefully shut out of negotiations because policy advocates wanted to maintain their relationships with traditional forms of power—namely legislators and executives. Policy advocates would openly discuss how the "radical" beliefs of community and what they viewed as an inability to compromise would ruin negotiations and lead to those advocates losing their own access. Policy advocates prioritized a relationship with these traditional power sources because their exclusive access to them added to their value. Whereas value in organizing spaces was often defined by the ability to build and mobilize people power, and therefore organizers prioritize their relationship with the people, value in the policy space was often being defined by the ability to gain the attention of someone "influential" in whatever process you were trying to intervene in and getting them to give you a piece of what you were asking for.

What sacrifices you had to make for that continued access, or whether the piece was worth it without the whole, rarely seemed to enter into the calculus. I witnessed the fear of losing this access change the entire approach to a particular issue, change the goals of projects, and change the value of external relationships. My attempts to bring more organizers into collaborative spaces with policy advocates were often rebuffed because the willingness of policy advocates to make concessions without consultation left organizers wondering if they or the vision they carried on behalf of community would be sacrificed on behalf of policy advocates' desire to maintain their relationships with traditional power. Organizers have to find ways to increase policy advocates' understanding of and loyalty to those most experiencing harm from oppressive policies, but that is truly easier said than done. In order to generate and advocate for policy solutions in line with a liberatory vision for transformative social change, organizers will have to navigate these tensions with care.

Conclusion

Policy changes tend to address an issue within the confines of the current system. At best, the policy change may be an intervention, but rarely is it meant to be a meaningful transformation of the system itself, even when the system is so often the problem. At worse, the policy change entrenches the very problem it hoped to address, creating new harms needing a remedy and new structures to dismantle. The potential pitfalls and extensive harm leave no wonder why some contest the utility of focusing on policy change and dedicating movement's limited time, people, and resources to policy advocacy.

But for those who, like me, believe that the potential to alter material conditions in ways that align with a liberatory vision for transformative social change is worth the intervention, I leave you with this advice for navigating the space:

KNOW YOUR VALUES AND BOUNDARIES. All coalitions and collaborations require some degree of compromise. In coalition with policy advocates you will navigate different and at times opposing politics and values. It is important to know which of your values are non-negotiable and where your boundaries are when engaging in these coalitions. If you value transparency with the community, you have to advocate and work for the coalition to adopt transparent practices. If you will not support any proposed policy solution that puts money into the criminal legal system, you have to know that so you can advocate against any proposals that would do so.

FIND YOUR PEOPLE. In a coalition you will not always agree. In a coalition with progressive policy advocates, you are likely to disagree frequently. But to struggle together toward a more liberated future, you have to build trust that you will work out your differences that are halting the agreed-upon work from moving forward. If you cannot trust the people you are in coalition with, you are in the wrong space and these are not your people. In addition, you never want to enter into a coalition with progressive policy advocates without other people who share your values, politics, boundaries, and approach. It is the easiest way to fight an uphill, losing battle, and not a good way to be in service to transformative social change.

PLANT SEEDS AND BUILD RELATIONSHIPS. You should approach policy advocacy places with care and understand that your goal in these spaces is to bring about the policy change that will shift material conditions toward liberation. However, that does not mean you should hide your values, beliefs, or politics. It is important to radicalize the space as much as possible because you want progressive policy advocates to adopt a liberatory analysis and apply it to their work even when you are not in the coalition. You want them to be transformed through their work with you. You may not convince everyone to pick up the banner for liberation, but you should plant seeds along the way through conversation, suggested readings and training, principled debate, and deeper exposure to the movement community. You have to build relationships with strong enough ties to promote accountability to the vision.

KEEP YOUR FOCUS ON THE POINTS OF ALIGNMENT, ACKNOWLEDGE THE POINTS OF TENSION, AND KNOW WHEN TO WALK AWAY. You will navigate many differences when you are in coalition with progressive policy advocates, including different root cause analyses and ways of approaching the work. You want to ask yourself, *What can we accomplish together?* and *What must I accomplish in a different space?* You may not get everyone to agree that capitalism is a great evil that must be abolished, but can you align on policy solutions that align with a liberatory vision like guaranteed basic income? If you can, see that work through. When you are out of points of alignment, move on to the next space where you can have the most impact.

. . .

It is worth the effort for folks dedicated to transformative social change to navigate and impact the complex and shifting terrain of policy advocacy because doing so successfully could shift the material conditions folks are surviving and struggling under in ways that push us closer to liberation. No, rent control will not end the system of capitalism, but it might free up enough resources, time, and energy for the folks struggling to pay rent to focus on building solidarity economies. No, ending electronic monitoring will not abolish the prison industrial complex, but it will reduce the number of folks under the control of the state, all folks capable of being radicalized and organized for transformative social change. Those possibilities make the intervention meaningful and in fact critical. To make it to the future, our people must survive the present. To survive the present, we must alter the material conditions.

Praxis: Crafting Prison Industrial Complex Abolitionist Policy
By Rachel Herzing

Policy, especially in strong coordination with grassroots organizing, can be key to advancing prison industrial complex (PIC) abolitionist goals. Here are some things to keep in mind when crafting policies toward abolitionist ends.

ABOLITION REQUIRES A MODIFIER OR ACTS AS A MODIFIER (e.g., PIC abolition; abolition democracy). If you're invoking the idea of abolition, ask yourself, *What is to be abolished? What is to be nurtured? And what is the relationship between what is to be abolished and what is to be nurtured?* Policy proposals that seek to include abolitionist language should include responses to these questions and should clearly establish why abolition of something is the best approach to take.

THE PRISON INDUSTRIAL COMPLEX IS THE TARGET. Even though it's helpful to pick a place to begin to fight against the harms of imprisonment, policing, surveillance, and sentencing, it's important to not lose track that the real target is the prison industrial complex in its entirety. Keeping that target in mind will prevent you from engaging in policy fights on specific aspects of the PIC that inadvertently undermine efforts focusing on other aspects of the PIC or make those fights more difficult. The best policy options are those that erode the prison industrial complex's overall legitimacy, size, scale, and scope.

THE PRISON INDUSTRIAL COMPLEX CREATES AND MAINTAINS THE PROBLEMS ITS PROPONENTS CLAIM IT SOLVES. Investing in aspects of the prison industrial complex will not lead to its elimination. Policy proposals aiming at PIC abolition must be made with this in mind. Being mindful of this proposition can be challenging when we are fed a steady stream of propaganda saying the prison industrial complex is a remedy for almost anything we might imagine. History has demonstrated, however, that when the prison industrial complex is used as a response, it leaves behind more damage than repair. Criminalizing people who are housing insecure, for instance, has increased their vulnerability to fines and fees, surveillance, police violence, and imprisonment but has not made more stable, affordable housing available.

If we bear in mind that the PIC routinely creates, maintains, and exacerbates the very problems its proponents claim it solves, we are less likely to develop policies that imagine pieces of the prison industrial complex (e.g., courts) can be effectively leveraged to achieve relief from the harms that are the very foundations of the PIC. This particular set of master's tools cannot be effectively used to dismantle the master's house.

PRISON INDUSTRIAL COMPLEX ABOLITION SUGGESTS A HORIZON RATHER THAN AN END POINT. We must actively seek the elimination of the use of the PIC as a response to what are more correctly understood as social, economic, environmental, and political disparities. In so doing, we can't forget how important it is to dismantle the prison industrial complex's institutions, policies, practices, and cultural signifiers. That said, our task is not complete even if every place of confinement and agent of law enforcement is eliminated. We will need to continue to practice new ways of relating to each other and the world around us. We'll need to maintain our abilities to resist backsliding into the logic of the prison industrial complex. We'll need to resist efforts by state and nonstate actors to rebuild aspects of the PIC under new guises.

This will be an ongoing and indefinite process. Rather than being discouraged by this, I suggest we think about it as a continually unfolding series of opportunities to develop new tools and ways of being, and to practice them, building our skills as we go. For committed PIC abolitionists, this duality is always present in PIC abolitionist politics. Dismantling and nurturing must always be understood in relationship to each other. Any policies we promote in support of PIC abolitionist politics must recognize and engage with that duality.

REFORM VERSUS REFORMISM. While a reform is simply a change, the goal of reformism is distinct from that of abolition and must be treated as such. Reformist steps move us toward the goal of an adjusted system left otherwise intact, while abolitionist steps move us toward the elimination of the system. While the two need not be in bitter opposition to each other, it's essential to remain clear about the distinct end games of each orientation since reformism may create obstacles to long-term abolitionist goals. Making a piece-by-piece plan is not antithetical to PIC abolition, but we must choose each piece carefully. Keeping our long-term goals clearly in focus will help prevent us from inadvertently putting pieces in place that lead us in the wrong direction or create new barriers.

PRISON INDUSTRIAL COMPLEX ABOLITION IS PRACTICAL. Any policy proposal that takes PIC abolitionist politics seriously must embrace not only the ideology undergirding the politics but also the movement that activates those politics in the world. PIC abolition politics is both a practical organizing approach and a political ideology. Decades of organizing have demonstrated that these politics offer a sound, pragmatic foundation from which to seek change. However, if policy advocates start from a belief that PIC abolition is a lovely ideal but not a pragmatic approach, they will undercut the viability of the politics. Policy advocates must rigorously apply the politics to the here and now. Furthermore, organizing for prison industrial complex abolition requires a community base to support the implementation and maintenance of any policy wins. Policy advocates cannot make durable gains without the labor and engagement of organizers and impacted communities.

LEGAL WORKERS ALSO HAVE A ROLE. Legal workers have important roles to play in advancing PIC abolition policymaking. In 2013, Joey L. Mogul, an attorney with People's Law Office in Chicago and a participant with the Chicago Torture Justice Memorials project, drafted a reparations ordinance that the city adopted in 2015 in acknowledgment of the torture and forced confessions perpetrated by Chicago cop John Burge and his subordinates that sent some of Burge's torture survivors to prison. New York's Sylvia Rivera Law Project, founded by abolitionist organizer and legal scholar Dean Spade, was initiated to address the disproportionate impacts of imprisonment on transgender people (particularly trans and gender-nonconforming people of color) and advocates for changes to prison policies to meet the needs of the organization's members and constituents.

The organization sometimes backs up its advocacy with impact litigation and other legal approaches. Founded in 2014, Amistad Law Project combines legal advocacy, policy advocacy, and grassroots organizing to eliminate the harms of the prison industrial complex. The organization organizes and advocates, for instance, for an end to death by imprisonment (the sentence of life without the possibility of parole) and alternatives to policing. These examples are a very small sample of groups using legal strategies to fortify policy advocacy and applying the law to abolitionist ends.

. . .

Legal tools are among those most sought by and withheld from people in closest proximity to the harms of the prison industrial complex. For legal workers advancing PIC abolitionist politics, unlocking legal tools and using them to support community advocacy and organizing is an important contribution. While legal approaches are not inherently abolitionist, they can take on an abolitionist character when used in service of the long-term goal of eliminating the PIC. Legal advocacy has been a component of abolitionist campaigns against prison construction through lawsuits compelling states, counties, or municipalities to mitigate environmental harms associated with construction. Legal action has helped eliminate shackling of pregnant and birthing prisoners, put limits on the use of solitary confinement, and increase access to compassionate release, visits, mail, books, and art supplies. Although these cases have not resulted in the abolition of imprisonment, they are steps that decrease the legitimacy of prison policies, increase the possibility of release, and increase the capacity of imprisoned people to sustain themselves and, by extension, advocate for abolition from inside prison walls.

Movement-aligned lawyers also play crucial roles in delegitimating policing and protecting political dissent. Lawyers defend organizers' and activists' ability to protest and dissent by acting as legal observers, offering legal representation to people arrested during demonstrations, and advising on legal strategies. Legal representation for people targeted by the violence of policing from people named in civil gang injunctions to people who are the focus of stop-

and-frisk practices and other forms of harassment challenges the legitimacy of these policing practices, helps targeted people defend themselves, and bolsters resistance to the violence of policing. Integrating legal approaches into PIC abolitionist policy is a complicated and slippery proposition, since the legal system is a central pillar of the PIC. Abolitionist legal workers should proceed cautiously and soberly, and in rigorous collaboration with organizers to develop policy recommendations aimed at abolitionist ends.

Learn Something from This

- Two important characteristics of Black queer feminist policymaking are that it prioritizes a leaderful movement, and it recognizes that power comes from community and connection. Therefore, two of its strategic priorities are cultivating relationships with those who are directly impacted and developing their leadership.
- Communities cannot be accessories in policymaking; they must be central actors who are consulted, engaged, and relied on throughout the creation, passing, and implementation phases. This requires patience, relationships, and accountability structures.
- Making policy that reflects the demands of movement and communities is hard. Implementing your wins can be even harder. Both require prioritizing organizing and relationships.
- Abolitionist policymaking requires that you tend both to what you are trying to dismantle and to what you are trying to build.

Resources

- Critical Resistance is an incredible resource for all things abolition, including abolition policymaking and lawyering.

Critical Resistance has created a series of charts that help you determine whether specific reforms are abolitionist or are reformist, meaning they actually move you further away from an abolitionist horizon. Check out these tools and others at https://criticalresistance.org/resource-type/infographic.

- Law for Black Lives (L4BL) has developed a Radical Policy Checklist that is a tool to help you figure out if the policy you are developing is helping build power and effectuate change that starts to grasp at the roots of the problems we face. You can find the checklist and lots of other helpful resources at www .law4blacklives.org.

Notes

1. Erik S. McDuffie, "'No Small Amount of Change Could Do': Esther Cooper Jackson, the Popular Front, and the Making of a Black Left Feminist," in *Want to Start a Revolution? Women in the Black Revolt*, edited by Dayo F. Fore, Jeanne Theoharis, and Komozi Woodard (New York University Press, 2009), 25–46.

2. Combahee River Collective, "Combahee River Collective Statement" (1977), published in *How We Get Free: Black Feminism and the Combahee River Collective* (Haymarket, 2017).

3. bell hooks, *Yearning: Race, Gender, and Cultural Politics*, 1st edition (Between the Lines Books, 1990).

4. "Angela Davis Hosted by the University of Arkansas Distinguished Lectures Committee," YouTube, February 17, 2021, www.youtube.com/watch?v=n6uq2kalhNU.

5. National Bail Out, www.nationalbailout.org, accessed November 1, 2024.

6. Gina Clayton et al., "Because She's Powerful: The Political Isolation and Resistance of Women with Incarcerated Loved Ones," Essie Justice Group, May 2018, www.becauseshespowerful.org/wp-content/uploads/2018/05/Essie -Justice-Group_Because-Shes-Powerful-Report.pdf.

8   *Teaching the Revolution*

For some of us law school felt like a hazing experience meant to condition us to injustice and powerlessness. As Kayla Vinson and James Forman Jr. note in their piece, law school "was meant to shape our ideological commitments and to narrow our sense of what the law could and should do about inequality." Many of us, especially Black and Brown people and poor and working-class people, were already intimately familiar with the law. It was a violent and often irrational force that caged people we loved, justified us being evicted from our homes, and protected police and others who abused us. The experience of having the law taught to us as a rational and objective set of rules, often by people who had no such firsthand knowledge of it, was confounding. The lack of context and even acknowledgment of its often-devastating impact was painful. The dismissal and devaluing of our lived knowledge felt disrespectful.

But beyond one's individual experience of law school, the institution serves an important function. As Jeena Shah discusses in her piece, "a core function of law is to naturalize power distributions . . . [and that] distribution of power is in service of racial capitalism." Law school is a site of reproduction for racial capitalism. It perpetuates hierarchies that maintain current power imbalances and the logics that legitimize them. Because law school trains the next generation of lawyers and because it is where power is reproduced and theorized, it is an important site of struggle. This chapter features insights from law professors who are working inside these institutions to train a cadre of lawyers who, as Angélica Cházaro puts it in her piece, learn to "think against the law," and in Jeena Shah's words, "ask the right questions." It explores how professors, especially but not exclusively clinical professors, can use the institution against itself and support social movements from the academy.

The chapter is full of pedagogical interventions, best practices, and reflections that help us better understand how to navigate the tensions of teaching about the limitations and possibilities of the law, particularly in institutions that are deeply invested in its traditional function of upholding and justifying inequality.

Biographical Reflection: Dispatches from the Clinical Undercommons
By Renee Camille Hatcher

After all, the subversive intellectual came under false pretenses, with bad documents, out of love. Her labor is as necessary as it is unwelcome. The university needs what she bears but cannot bear what she brings. And on top of all that she disappears. She disappears into the underground, the downlow lowdown maroon community of the university, into the undercommons of enlightenment, where the work gets done, where the work gets subverted, where the revolution is still [B]lack, still strong.

—STEFANO HARNEY AND FRED MOTEN[1]

Who are your people?

Ella Baker would often ask the question: Who are your people?[2] To answer, we must locate ourselves in family, community, culture, and networks. The question implores the respondent to consider: Whose story or whose struggle do you carry forward? Who are you committed to? And with whom do you choose to align yourself? Our identities are shaped by our relationships to people, organizations, and histories. The axiology of this relational thinking is rooted in an African-centered worldview that rejects the dominant paradigm of Western individualism and personal attainment. Moreover, it rejects the propagated thinking of lawyer as hero and client as beneficiary, or law professor as subject and law student as object. The simple refrain—Who are your people?—can provide clarity for those of us navigating the legal profession, specifically legal academe, who are committed to liberatory futures for "our people." In other words, our personal and political grounding can be the north star to the choices we make.

In the first part of this essay, I ground myself and my experiences in the relationships and communities that I come from and remain committed to. I offer this brief positionality account both as context and as a clarion call for lawyers committed to liberation, navigating the contradictions of the academy. I explore the double-double consciousness of Black legal academics and some of the challenges of navigating the contradictions of "being in the academy but not of the academy." Finally, I discuss the ways in which I've been able to contribute to movement from the perch of the academy, focusing on my clinical work in partnership with Law for Black Lives and frontline organizations advancing Black land sovereignty. I conclude with some key considerations for those in or interested in legal academia, specifically clinical faculty, who are committed to movement lawyering.

My first professional experience in legal academia was in the city of Baltimore. It was 2015 in the wake of the Baltimore Uprising. Sparked by the police murder of Freddie Gray, the mass protests shifted into new formations of coalitions and community experiments, such as Baltimore United for Change (BUC) and the Black Church Food Security Network (BCFSN).[3] Baltimore was radiating with political energy and new iterations of organizing. Upon arriving in the city, I felt ablaze. As a clinical fellow in University of Baltimore

(UB) School of Law's Community Development Clinic, I had the opportunity to work with new formations of community-owned, community-controlled projects—from worker cooperatives to community-controlled development organizations. Baltimore was both familiar and beautiful.

Growing up in Gary, Indiana, in the 1980s and 1990s to parents committed to the Black Freedom Movement, I feel most at home in Black communities of resistance.[4] Like Baltimore, Gary has a rich legacy of community organizing and Black resistance. The city, initially founded by U.S. Steel in 1906, attracted many Black residents during the Great Migration who were looking for work at the steel mill. For most of the twentieth century both the steel industry and the city itself were formally segregated. By 1960, Gary's Black residents constituted roughly 40 percent of the city's population, and yet they were relegated to the city's Midtown neighborhood. The Black community often faced acts of violence from local law enforcement and were unable to access public amenities in the city. My father, Richard Hatcher, moved to the city after receiving his law degree from Valparaiso University. He started organizing with several Black-led organizations and cofounded the organization Muigwithania, inspired by the Kenyan liberation movement. Muigwithania organized locally against anti-Black policies and racial discrimination and provided food and other forms of mutual aid.

After being elected to Gary city's council in 1963, my father introduced and successfully passed an open occupancy ordinance, desegregating housing in Gary. In the face of many challenges, he became the first elected Black mayor of a US city in 1967. Much of his administration's policies (inclusive hiring practices, construction of new affordable housing units, investment in public amenities, etc.) sought to improve the lives of Black and poor folks in Gary. In 1972, Gary hosted the historical National Black Political Convention: more than ten thousand Black folks from across the country gathered to create a national Black agenda and strategies to improve the lives of Black Americans.[5] The year before, many of the city's downtown businesses and white residents effectively seceded from the city, facilitated by Indiana special legislation that eliminated Gary's "buffer zone," allowing the creation of Merrillville at the city's southern edge.[6] In the intervening decades, Gary's shrinking tax base was compounded by additional layoffs at U.S. Steel and federal austerity measures.

Years later, I ventured to law school to develop a deeper understanding of the ongoing structural extraction and disinvestment in my hometown, hoping (perhaps naively) that my legal training would confer new tools for justice and transformation. Instead, I left feeling dispirited and disoriented, not sure how the law could make any meaningful contribution to the change I care deeply about. Nonetheless, after graduation I secured a position at the Chicago Lawyers Committee for Civil Rights, where I developed and directed a place-based community development law project, INWIN, focused on Gary and the surrounding communities. Working closely with community organizers, neighborhood initiatives and community benefit agreement campaigns taught me more about legal systems and structural oppression than any law school course. Many of my early experiences in Gary continue to guide how I navigate my work now in legal academia.

The Souls of Black Folk by W. E. B. Du Bois was the last book that I read before entering law school in 2008. I didn't know it then, but the book would come to embody much of my experience there. In the book Du Bois explores the concept of double consciousness—the internal conflict experienced by African Americans when embracing their African identity within a dominant society characterized by white supremacy and racial hierarchy. In effect, Black people (and other racialized peoples) are often compelled to view themselves through the lens of the dominant culture that devalues and discredits

Blackness. Du Bois writes: "It is a peculiar sensation, this double-consciousness. . . . One ever feels his two-ness,—an American, a Negro; two souls, two thoughts, two unreconciled strivings; two warring ideals in one dark body, whose dogged strength alone keeps it from being torn asunder."[7]

These words ring true for many Black law students navigating the law school terrain. On the one hand, the law is presented as neutral and objective. Law students are asked to analyze cases, extrapolate black-letter rules, and apply them to fact patterns using established methods of analysis. All the while, the cases, rhetoric, and very foundations of US law are predicated on a worldview steeped in racist ideology and designed to protect racial capitalism.[8] As a law student, I struggled with this reality. My courses, with few exceptions, did not incorporate any critical discussion of the centrality of race to legal canons. The spaces that did exist were always distinct from core curriculum courses. By not naming racism as foundational to US law, legal education inadvertently legitimizes our collective history of de jure racial oppression. As a result, Black law students are confronted with hegemonic teachings that sterilize the ways in which the law (and legal systems) historically and perpetually harm Black people.

As a Black law professor, my experience in legal academia is shaped by what James Davis III refers to as "double-double consciousness."[9] The term, originally theorized by Davis to describe the psychological experience of Black prisoners, conceptualizes the experience of Black people within dominant institutions that form new strata of internal conflict in Black identity through institutional pressures and expectations. To be clear, in no way am I comparing incarceration to the privilege of holding a law faculty position. Instead, I'm applying the concept, aptly articulated by Davis, to other contexts in which Black folks are forced to navigate the dichotomy of participating in dominative institutions while resisting the ways in which those institutions reinforce racial hierarchies and undermine Black life.

In the context of the conscious Black law professor, this tension exists both in and outside of the class. As a law professor, my responsibility in teaching a course is to ensure that students master the relevant doctrinal concepts and are prepared to apply them, first on the bar exam and eventually in practice. At the same time, it's vital that we give students the tools to deeply critique all aspects of the law and legal systems, particularly the ways in which race and power shape the very law they are tasked with mastering.[10] Furthermore, one primary responsibility of the conscious Black law professor is to prepare students with not only the analytical skills to critique "what is" but also to reimagine the status quo and develop strategic interventions to address unjust legal systems—what Sameer Asher refers to as the "pedagogy of prefiguration."[11]

While there are commonalities among law faculty, there is wide variation among the employment arrangements, statuses, and privileges afforded to law teachers. Since the integration of clinical education, clinical law professors have historically held a lesser status within law school faculty, reflected in everything from fewer faculty voting rights to less pay. Yet, within any given context, there are choices that we make as clinical faculty professionals: client and project selection, course curriculum, lawyering approach(es), approach to student supervision, how we engage with community, if at all, and scholarly agenda or public writing. Through the choices we make in these spheres of work, clinical faculty can find intentional and meaningful ways to connect to and contribute to social movements. Due to the brevity of this essay, I will limit my own reflections to project selection.

Since 2018, I've directed a community development law clinic at the University of Illinois Chicago, UIC Law (formerly John Marshall Law School–Chicago), called Community Enterprise & Solidarity Economy Clinic (CESEC). CESEC provides transactional legal support to community-based organizations, prioritizing client organizations (both for-profit and nonprofit) that are community-owned or community-controlled. In addition to providing direct legal services, the clinic partners with local and national organizations to provide legal research and support on projects that advance economic and racial justice. Our projects have included providing research support to a local reparations campaign and drafting cooperative law reform in Illinois. Typically the clinic takes on one or two project-based matters every semester that students work on in small groups. Many of our past projects were facilitated by Law for Black Lives Movement Lawyering Squad, which was started in 2018, formerly known as the L4BL Clinic Cohort program. The program seeks to "leverage legal and academic institutions to support the needs of organizations in the fight for Black Liberation. The Movement Lawyering Squad supports organizations by co-developing materials, answering research questions and engaging in legislative analysis to support ongoing campaigns."[12]

As a participating clinic, CESEC worked with L4BL to connect with various movement organizations to provide legal research support. Upon accepting a project, L4BL staff and community organizational partners provided background reading materials for clinical students and project memos to guide our work, outlining the needs of the organization and the relevant context. Clinical students attended webinars hosted by L4BL and partner organizations to ground students and answer questions. Much of CESEC's work as a participating clinic has been providing research support to Black-led organizations on issues related to Black land stewardship and land loss prevention. For example, a few of our project memos explored various legal avenues to collectively steward, protect, and preserve Black-owned land, covering legal subjects ranging from property to business organizations. Students working on L4BL projects conduct cutting-edge legal research, engage materials related to movement praxis, and are afforded opportunities to develop relationships with organizers, activists, and movement lawyers. Often our organizational partners push students to think beyond the current state of the law, as they are frequently tasked with developing out-of-the box solutions or providing a roadmap for potential law reform. While this method of clinical support is limited in time, depth, and scope, the work we produce substantively informs the strategy of our organizational partners.

I close with the following probing questions and considerations for movement-aligned clinical faculty:

- Who are your people? Who do you choose to align yourself with? And who are you accountable to beyond your students, faculty, or dean?
- What is your positionality in the world? What is your positionality in the work of your clinic?
- Does your clinic have a theory of change? If not, might you develop one in collaboration with the external community you are accountable to?
- If your clinic has a theory of change, how is it communicated to students and relevant stakeholders?
- In what material ways do you engage community? In what material ways do you engage movement spaces?
- What political project do you seek to contribute to?

These prompts are some of the questions I've used to guide my own reflections as a clinical law professor committed to liberation. They are not offered as a blueprint but as a guidepost to sharpen the clarity of our choices in the undercommons of the legal academy.

Tactical Case Study: Bridging Academy and Community
By Kayla Vinson and James Forman Jr.

One of us (James) spent his first six years out of law school working as a public defender and another three years starting a school for young people who had been arrested or incarcerated. Those jobs reflected his life's twin passions—making the education and criminal systems fairer for Black people at the margins. Leaving those jobs for law teaching—especially in an elite institution—was difficult. When he did, he made this pledge to himself: that he would devote himself to making law schools a better place for the students who walked their halls and for the low-income communities where they were located.

The other one of us (Kayla) was trained in secondary education before becoming a lawyer, first in a teacher preparation program during college and then in a graduate education program. K–12 teachers-turned-lawyers often joke that law school isn't "school" at all. K–12 teachers are often trained in backward design. We start by thinking about what we want students to be capable of by the end of their time with us. Then we work backward to decide how we can help them get there and what assessment and reflection opportunities they will need to direct their own learning. It is jarring, then, to enter first-year law school classrooms that seem designed to trick and confuse and to create hierarchies among students. On the whole, law school felt more like an acculturation than a learning experience. It was meant to shape our ideological commitments and to narrow our sense of what the law could and should do about inequality. The logics of domination were ever-present, even if (or perhaps especially when) not explicitly spoken.

In law school teaching at Yale University, Kayla strives to join the ranks of law teachers who offer students a different set of "possibilities of life as a lawyer."[13] She wants to create space for students to imagine a professional life less determined by the title "lawyer" and more by the desire to be useful to social movements and to be good stewards of their talents/training. She wants students to nurture a radical imagination about how they might close the gap between the world as it is and the world as they believe it should be. This commitment to challenging subordination in the law school and in New Haven, Connecticut, guides our work together in the classroom. We co-teach Access to Law School (A2LS), an experiential course that allows students to learn about and intervene against educational inequity. Many of our students came to law school to develop skills that will be useful in addressing issues of subordination, and many have direct experience with it in their own lives. While they hope law school will give them skills to take with them to wherever they begin their careers, we all live in New Haven, with savage inequalities all around us.

In A2LS our students run a pipeline program that supports New Haveners who want to go to law school (whom we call "fellows").[14] (In three years we have helped eighteen fellows gain admission to law school, and twenty-two are preparing to apply.) At the same time, through coursework students learn about the history of New Haven and Connecticut, with a particular focus on the university's role in racial and class subordination. Students deepen their understanding of how race and class inequality manifest in the higher-education experiences of racialized, first-generation, and other underrepresented students. Our classroom is its own small community, and as members of that community, we hold ourselves to the same ethic of care that we expect of our students in their relationships with Access to Law School fellows. Following the model of Charles Lawrence III, we invite students to use experience—their own and those of the people they care about—as a legitimate origin for critical analysis.[15] We take their reflections and feedback very seriously, inviting students to raise concerns and challenges that we work through as a group. We treat student concerns as a site for collective problem-solving and an opportunity to "experience the liberation of giving authority to ideas by acting on them."[16]

Through our course we hope to demonstrate to students that a prerequisite to radical lawyering is being a good neighbor in your community. This includes the community where they earn their law degree. Most Yale law students are New Haven transplants whose time in the city is bookended by orientation and graduation. Even with the relatively short time they will be in New Haven, the best place to begin is right where they live. This is even more true given their inside access to an institution that often acts as a gatekeeper. Our students yearn for more opportunities to feel more like New Haveners than Yalies. Many do not feel at home at the law school either. Over the past decade Yale Law School's student body has become more diverse in various dimensions, including race and class, with many more students who are the first in their families to attend college or professional school. Being an insider at Yale Law School presents these students with special challenges. Some can't shake the feeling that they are guests, not hosts, at their own law school. For others the path to upward mobility through law school seems to require them to move away from the commitments that brought them to law school. Still others expected law school to be a "necessary evil" but are caught off-guard by how much harder it is to chart their own path than they imagined.

It may seem odd, then, that these students would end up in our class, helping other people get into law school. But they are drawn to the opportunity to develop meaningful relationships and to use skills that are not always rewarded in law school classrooms. Equally important, they have hope about what could be. They understand how expanding access to law school fights against racial and class subordination and, most acutely, how it could improve their own law school experience.

Through A2LS, students and fellows impact the life of the law school. Fellows have been guest speakers in our class as experts in local activism and served as panelists for a symposium on long prison sentences and reentry. Their presence makes the walls between the law school and the community more porous. Fellows and students participate together in conferences such as Rebellious Lawyering. Other student organizations that would like to open their events to the community—but lack relationships—come to A2LS to spread the word. It is not just that our fellows get access to the building or that our students get to see more people whose experiences reflect their own. The conversations are informed by a wider range of lived experience and more capacious notions of what equity and justice require. Students (including fellows who have now started law school) feel less alienated from law school, more empowered to challenge the status quo. To use Daniel Farbman's articulation, A2LS is an opportunity for law students to "open a commons in the master's house."[17] The work is both disruptive and transformative.

Our classroom also gives students the opportunity to find each other—to form community with other law students who feel alone in their law school experience. For students who pursued a law degree wanting to grapple with questions of power and inequality, A2LS helps them stay close to their motivations for going to law school. In these ways the program ends up being a powerful way of making the law school experience more meaningful, and frankly sometimes just more tolerable, for our students. In relationship and fellowship they find a strength that buoys them and that we believe will buoy our fellows once they enter law school with their own plans to transform the legal profession.

The Hard Stuff: Navigating a Collision Course
By Angélica Cházaro

Since 2014, I have been involved in abolitionist campaigns in Washington State, attempting to shift the common sense in the Pacific Northwest away from punishment and toward collective care. I have fought alongside others to end immigration detention and stop the pipeline to deportation, to try to stop the construction of a new youth jail (and now to try to shut it down), and most recently to defund the Seattle Police Department and create a city budget that responds with funding commensurate with the crises we are facing.

For nearly all of those years, my paid work has been as a law professor. Transitioning from nonprofit legal services to academia created the space for me to contribute to abolitionist fights, in large part because I transitioned away from spending most of my waking hours in a high case load immigration practice. But joining legal academia necessarily highlighted unresolvable tensions. Radical politics are on a constant collision course with legal institutions reluctant to deviate from their traditional task of training new lawyers to uphold and replicate the status quo. People with identities like mine (a first-generation queer immigrant Latina) symbolize the possibility of resolving this collision through our very existence in elite workplaces like law schools, where our presence is heralded as a triumph of liberalism. My primary task as a legal educator is thus one of refusing to be cover for harmful systems and making my teaching, writing, and advocacy reflect the liberatory politics required for our collective survival.

What does this look like in the classroom? I begin every course by spending much of the first class creating group agreements with my students. This practice, familiar to most community organizers, can be a radical one in a law school classroom: setting up a dynamic where we agree that no member of our class is disposable or will be "cancelled," and that we will not ignore conflict and harm that may arise when discussions of race, gender, disability, class, and so on occur. This shifts the dynamic for the weeks of learning that follow and models abolition in practice. I also bring both my past practice experience and my organizing dilemmas into the classroom. Some examples include:

- In Professional Responsibility, I ask students to advise me on the ethical implications of my meetings with detained immigrants during the 2014 hunger strike at the Northwest Detention Center. Was I breaking ethical rules by meeting and supporting people who were acting collectively in protest against their detention, but who were also represented in their individual immigration cases by attorneys who believed the hunger strike would hurt their clients' chances to avoid deportation? What would they do in my place?

- In Critical Race Theory, I ask students to write a letter advising an LGBTQ campus group that is trying to decide whether joining a campaign to support the labor demands of laundry workers at the university hospital has anything to do with queer issues. What does it mean to organize intersectionally? What does it mean to reject the limited categories of solidarity the law offers?

- In Abolition and the Law, in place of a traditional final exam, I have students work in groups to create a plan for ending misdemeanor punishment in Seattle, with groups assigned to imagining an end to (1) misdemeanor DUI cases, (2) misde-meanor domestic violence cases, or (3) crimes of poverty (the three types of cases in our municipal court).

Through these exercises, learning to "think like a lawyer" becomes an exercise in learning to think *against* the law, against single-issue organizing, against a presumption that lawyers' only appropriate intervention is to reduce the harm of the current system or to tinker around its edges so it more closely aligns with due process and the rule of law.

In my organizing work, the task is similar. I support community groups in discerning between token reforms that preserve the status quo and those that build toward a liberatory future where, among other things, Black communities experience public safety for the first time. In practice, this means that I help mobilize the refusal of easy outs for a region that prides itself on its progressive politics. No, we won't accept a youth jail (that mostly cages Black and Indigenous youth) with "holistic" and "wrap-around" services for young people as a win; we will instead demand everything—from housing, to health care, to educational supports, to access to the arts—for our young people. No, we aren't okay with immigration detention if "only" people with criminal convictions are being deported; we demand that the State of Washington take every possible step to stop the flow of our residents to the Northwest Detention Center until the facility is shut down. No, an investment in "relational policing" for the Seattle Police Department will never replace defunding the police and reinvesting that money in Black communities; we demand a Black-led participatory budgeting process that puts "public safety" spending in community hands.

The fit between my role as a law professor and my role as a community organizer is not always an easy one. It is tempting to buy into my own positional authority and the deference I receive as a professor. But ultimately, in both my teaching and by example through my organizing, I am urging my students: Do not become apologists for a social order predicated on the death and disposability of millions of living beings. Swear allegiance not to ossified institutions but to our collective survival. Swear allegiance not to norms of respectability and civility but to the disruptive experimentation that will be needed if we are to dismantle the institutions that created the crises we face. Your legal degree is a tool; figure out how to be on tap for the fights to come instead of becoming a defender of the current state of affairs.

As Audre Lorde reminded us, "Change did not begin with you, and it will not end with you, but what you do with your life is an absolutely vital piece of that chain. The testimony of your daily living is the missing remnant in the fabric of our future."[18] Choose to be awakened by your legal education and commit to action that leaves no one behind, because none of us are safe until all of us are safe.

Praxis: Understanding Law and Power
By Jeena Shah

Every practice produces a theory, and that if it is true that a revolution can fail even though it be based on perfectly conceived theories, nobody has yet made a successful revolution without a revolutionary theory.

—AMÍLCAR CABRAL[19]

Successful people's struggles have all required the political education of those carrying out the struggle.[20] But a sharp turn away from this approach after the anticolonial and other revolutionary struggles of the 1960s and 1970s led to an era of social justice work that "eschews theory, emphasizes and privileges activism."[21] By doing so, this approach to social justice "tak[es] for granted" the assumptions necessary for the oppressive structures of the political economy to operate, addressing only their symptoms and thereby becoming complicit in their operation.[22]

Often, in a similar way, the *teaching* of movement lawyering is limited to movement lawyering "in action," usually on projects or cases in experiential settings. Less often, students may have the opportunity to learn about past and present people's movements in seminars. Either setting, however, risks separating what students learn about the role of lawyers in liberation struggles from what they learn about the law itself. Without a deep and specific understanding of the relationship between law and power, new lawyers risk engaging in activities that appear to be movement lawyering but do nothing to shift power.[23] When students learn the law, they learn doctrine, how to argue "two sides" of an issue within that doctrine, and they are offered space to critique the doctrine itself. Sometimes those moments of critique are supported by the historical context of an individual case or a critique of the rule put forth by the case. What is often missing is a broader understanding of how the doctrine serves certain power structures and how those power structures operate.

Without such analysis, lawyers risk mistaking their tactics for strategies,[24] employing doctrine in ways that leave unchecked or even reinforce current distributions of power, leading to pyrrhic victories.[25]

Margaret J. Wheatly recounts a narrative that is helpful in illustrating how this kind of problem comes about: "In the twentieth century, physicists faced, for the first time, a serious challenge to their ability to understand the universe. Every time they asked nature a question in an atomic experiment, nature answered with a paradox, and the more they tried to clarify the situation, the sharper the paradoxes became."[26] Analogously the more we try to grasp the role of lawyering in the struggle for social justice, the sharper the paradox of using an instrument of oppression for the purposes of liberation becomes. Wheatly continues:

> In their struggle to grasp this new reality, scientists became painfully aware that their basic concepts, their language, and their whole way of thinking were inadequate to describe atomic phenomena. . . . It took these physicists a long time to accept the fact that the paradoxes they encountered are an essential aspect of atomic physics. . . . Once this was perceived, the physicists began to learn to ask the right questions and to avoid contradictions . . . and finally they found the precise and consistent mathematical formulation of [quantum] theory.[27]

How do we train our students so that they may approach the law in ways that unravel this paradox of using the law for liberation?

Doctrinal courses could approach their specific doctrines in a way that exposes how they each operate in their entirety to support a certain structure: that of the United States as racial-capitalist state with settler-colonial and imperial dimensions. This is a structure that requires unequal populations maintained by racialization, cisheteropatriarchy, and ableism. When we see the US legal system in this way, we begin to understand how inequality is inherent to its logic. Such analysis exposes how rules or decisions that seem paradoxical or contradictory are in fact consistent, and thus victories within these rules can never in and of themselves end injustices against oppressed peoples.

Therefore, understanding not only that "a core function of law" is to naturalize power distributions, but also that the distribution of power is in service of racial capitalism, helps students understand why using the law for the purposes for which it was created cannot bring about social change.[28] Rather, legal tools must be manipulated to redistribute power, by "expanding the bargaining and political power of oppressed groups" to "create conditions where it's harder for the existing social order to reproduce itself."[29] In order to do so, the existing order of racial capitalism, along with settler-colonial and imperial dimensions, must be understood.

Such an education in students' doctrinal learning can help them move into experiential courses with a foundation to develop, refine, and reinforce two critical skills of a movement lawyer. First, this type of knowledge can help students observe the world more clearly, in turn allowing them to define more richly what it means to listen to and follow the leadership of oppressed people. Second, this type of knowledge can help them understand why organizing is central to liberatory struggles, facilitating their ability to consistently approach the decision-making that abounds in legal work in a way that seeks to build oppressed people's power.

Movement Lawyering Skill: Informed Listening

When movement lawyers are directed to listen to oppressed peoples, this listening is more than simply deference.[30] The level of "listening" required is captured in what Ruth Wilson Gilmore has described as follows:

Kwame Ture . . . said [redacted text] Marx and Engels, they didn't invent communism. They "noticed" it. They saw it. They saw what people were doing. . . . Ture saying "notice" just totally caught me . . . because, among other reasons, I'm a Brechtian . . . and what Brechtians do, or should do, as part of our work . . . is to notice, and to think about what people do and to think what they're doing as telling us something more important perhaps than the words that they use to describe what they're doing. And therefore to have a framework that enables that noticing to happen and that enables us to accumulate what we notice into some kind of understanding of what we can do next.[31]

This framework that Gilmore talks about is something that political education in doctrinal courses can help prepare students to develop as they move to practice settings.

As an illustration, the political education offered by the Law for Black Lives conference in 2015 allowed a group of clinic students to take an entirely different approach to issues of policing in Newark, New Jersey, than local lawyers were taking at the time. In this era of uprisings against police violence in Ferguson and Baltimore, there was an effort by lawyers in Newark to create a campaign for "police accountability." However, the clinic students were armed with an understanding that abolition is, as Gilmore describes, "a horizon of possibility where people in a variety of different kinds of configuration make the world and remake the world so that group-differentiated vulnerability to premature death is minimal."[32]

With this knowledge the students set about noticing what communities were actually doing in response to public safety issues. At one local community-organized meeting, they observed that in a several-hour discussion about public safety, community members did not mention the police once. They discussed efforts the neighborhood was already involved in to make sure people knew one another and could develop trust with one another, and to help people call in and support those who may be engaging in activities that could be harmful to the community. The clinic students similarly listened to other such community meetings happening across the city and designed a project that followed the "invest-divest" framework of the Movement for Black Lives, specifically tailored for communities in Newark. As part of this project, students considered the different ways laws operated to prevent or present obstacles to this very localized making and remaking of the world.

Movement Lawyering Skill: Informed Decision-Making

Power, as Gilmore defines it, is "a capacity composed of active and changing relationships enabling a person, group, or institution to compel others to do things they would not do on their own."[33] To redistribute power, oppressed communities build their own power through organizing. The political education described above allows students to come to legal work with an informed understanding of why organizing is central to social change and why the law can only be an effective tool for liberatory struggles if it is used to support organizing that seeks to "create conditions where it's harder for the existing social order to reproduce itself." Armed with this understanding, new lawyers are able to make better tactical decisions about the use of the law, including choosing whom to work with or represent, what legal tools to use, and when and how to use them.[34]

Lawyers assess this by asking, for example, whether a particular legal tool "builds the base of the organizing project, such that more members of the impacted communities are organized; it offers ways for the organized community to exercise the power they have built; and it builds structures that allow the organized community to exercise power on an ongoing basis." Or whether the legal tool helps individuals organize their communities or supports political education to help a community sharpen its analysis of the problems that they are facing.[35] Evaluating the role of a legal tactic in this way can better help guide the lawyer in identifying the tactics they may present to organizers, assessing with organizers the pros and cons of each tactic, and assessing the different ways the tactic can be used to meet their goal.[36]

Challenges

The biggest challenge to this approach to the doctrinal classroom is that without an experiential component, where students are interacting with organizers and organized community members, this exposure to the law in the context of the full horrors of racial capitalism, settler-colonialism, and imperialism tends to push students toward despair and legal nihilism, or to reject this analysis altogether, finding it debilitating and therefore impractical.[37] As Stuart Hall recounts in the opening of one of his books about this critique:

> "[A]nalysis is all very well—but where are the remedies, the practical reforms?" It is a widespread but fatal trap—precisely, a trap of a "liberal opinion"—to split analysis from action, and to assign the first to the instance of the "long term," which never comes, and reserve only the second to "what is practical and realistic in the short term." . . . [I]f someone says to us: "Yes, but given present conditions, what are we to do now?," we can only reply "Do something about the 'present conditions.'"[38]

In short, neither idealism nor nihilism allows us to make change. Mariame Kaba reminds us that "hope is a discipline." So I tell my students, if the tool they chose to support the emancipatory struggles is the law, then how can we see ourselves like the physicists of the twentieth century? In other words, how does the type knowledge I've described help us begin "to learn to ask the right questions"? We can only get the right answers if we start asking the right questions, and our lives depend on getting the right answer.

Learn Something from This

- Legal institutions are deeply invested in maintaining the status quo. The work of movement lawyer professors is to teach students to "think against the law" and start to imagine and work toward a new status quo.
- Practical experience working with movements is necessary for law students. There are lots of ways to encourage students to engage with movement in both clinical and doctrinal settings.
- Movement lawyer professors must be focused on how to teach their students to see, understand, and ultimately shift power.
- Law schools are an important site of struggle if we want to transform the majority of lawyers from gatekeepers to co-conspirators. Exposing the seemingly contradictory doctrine to explain its relationship in upholding racialized capitalism gives law students and future lawyers an important analytical framework.

Resources

- A number of movement lawyer professors, including contributors Amna Akbar and Bill Quigley, collectively created a resource called "Guerilla Guides to Law Teaching." The guides provide insights on how to break out of traditional approaches to legal pedagogy and instead engage movement work and knowledge in a number of law school courses. Check out the guides at https://guerrillaguides.wordpress.com.

Notes

1. F. Moten and S. Harney, "The University and the Undercommons: Seven Theses," *Social Text* 22(2) (2004): 101–15, https://doi.org/10.1215/01642472-22-2_79-101.

2. B. Ransby, "Quilting a Movement," *In These Times*, April 4, 2011, https://inthesetimes.com/article/quilting-a-movement.

3. Baltimore United for Change (BUC) is a coalition of organizations and activists with a long track record of working for social justice in Baltimore. The BUC coalition came together three days after the murder of Freddie Gray. "About BUC," Baltimore United for Change, https://bmoreunited.org, accessed November 1, 2024. Black Church Food Security Network (BCFSN) was birthed at Pleasant Hope Baptist Church in Baltimore, Maryland, in the midst of the Baltimore Uprising. "About Us," Black Church Food Security Network, https://blackchurch foodsecurity.net/about-us#our-story, accessed November 1, 2024.

4. Renee Camille Hatcher is the daughter of Richard Gordon Hatcher and Ruth Marie Hatcher. Richard was a civil rights attorney and Black political leader based in Gary, Indiana. He was active in many organizations and movement campaigns including Freedom Summer, the anti-apartheid movement in South Africa, and Black political power organizing. Ruth is a retired dedicated public school teacher based in Gary, Indiana. She spent her career going above and beyond for her students and community.

5. "The Gary Declaration: Black Politics at the Crossroads," address delivered at the National Black Political Convention, Gary, Indiana, 1972, www.blackpast .org/african-american-history/gary-declaration-national-black-political -convention-1972.

6. M. Rice, "The City That Split in Two," *The Awl*, November 25, 2014, www .theawl.com/2014/11/the-city-that-split-in-two.

7. W. E. B. Du Bois, *The Souls of Black Folk: Essays and Sketches* (Fawcett, 1968).

8. T. A. McMurtry-Chubb, "Still Writing at the Master's Table: Decolonizing Rhetoric in Legal Writing for a 'Woke' Legal Academy," *The Scholar: St. Mary's Law Review on Race and Social Justice* 21(2) (2019): 255–91, https://commons .stmarytx.edu/cgi/viewcontent.cgi?article=1018&context=thescholar.

9. J. Davis III, "Law, Prison, and Double-Double Consciousness: A Phenomenological View of the Black Prisoner's Experience," *Yale Law Journal* 128 (2019): 1126–44, www.yalelawjournal.org/forum/double-double-consciousness.

10. A. Akbar, "Toward a Radical Imagination of Law," *New York Law Review* 93(3) (2018): 405–79, https://nyulawreview.org/issues/volume-93-number-3 /toward-a-radical-imagination-of-law.

11. S. Asher, "Pedagogy of Prefiguration," *Yale Law Journal* 132 (2023): 869–903, www.yalelawjournal.org/forum/pedagogy-of-prefiguration.

12. "About the Clinical Cohort," Law for Black Lives, www.law4blacklives.org/clinical-cohort, accessed November 1, 2024.

13. D. Kennedy, "Legal Education and the Reproduction of Hierarchy: A Polemic Against the System," *Michigan Law Review* 82(4) (1984): 961–65, https://repository.law.umich.edu/cgi/viewcontent.cgi?article=3524&context=mlr.

14. "Access to Law School," Yale Law School, https://law.yale.edu/centers-workshops/law-school-access-program, accessed November 1, 2024.

15. C. R. Lawrence III, "The Word and the River: Pedagogy as Scholarship as Struggle," *Southern California Law Review* 65 (1992): 2231–98, https://scholarspace.manoa.hawaii.edu/server/api/core/bitstreams/b9dba0fb-a733-4feb-a42e-42e502bf32cf/content.

16. *Id.* at 2247.

17. "It may be impossible to revolutionize the institutions we work in as insiders, but it is possible for institutional actors to hold deliberative space within their institutions for transformational and radical imagination." D. Farbman, "A Commons in the Master's House," *Fordham Law Review* 90(5) (2022): 2061–87, https://ir.lawnet.fordham.edu/flr/vol90/iss5/8.

18. A. Lorde, "Commencement Address at Oberlin College," May 29, 1989, speech transcript, available at Queer History, https://queerhistory.com/radical-graduation.

19. A. Cabral, "The Weapon of Theory," in *Revolution in Guinea: An African People's Struggle* (Monthly Review Press, 1969), 73–90.

20. H. Hakamäki [@Huck1995], "Why Political Ed. & Historical Knowledge is KEY to Activism/Organizing," Tweet, Twitter, September 11, 2011, https://twitter.com/Huck1995/status/1569096177655627776.

21. I. G. Shivji, *Silences in NGO Discourse: The Role and Future of NGOs in Africa* (Pambazuka Press, 2007).

22. *Id.*

23. Some examples of this that I've described elsewhere: "In addition to filing a lawsuit, such a lawyer may seek to shift narratives in the media by writing opeds, appearing on news shows, and educating journalists. They may develop 'Know Your Rights' trainings so that impacted communities learn how the issues in the lawsuit or a victory in the lawsuit affect them. Finally, such lawyers may find other advocacy partners, usually other professionals working at non-profits like the lawyer's but in other disciplines, to create a coalition that advocates around the issue, such as lobbying for the passage of certain legislation." J. Shah, "Rebellious

Lawyering in Big Case Clinics," *Clinical Law Review* 23 (2017): 775–815, www.law
.nyu.edu/sites/default/files/upload_documents/Jeena%20Shah%20--%20
Big%20Case%20Clinics.pdf.

24. R. Knox, "Strategy and Tactics," *Finnish Yearbook of International
Law* 21 (2012): 193–229, https://papers.ssrn.com/sol3/papers.cfm?abstract_id=
1921759.

25. D. Bell, "Serving Two Masters: Integration Ideals and Client Interests in
School Desegregation Litigation," *Yale Law Journal* 85(4) (1976): 470–517.

26. M.J. Wheatly, *Leadership and the New Science: Discovering Order in a
Chaotic World* (Berrett-Koehler Publishers, 2006).

27. *Id.*

28. Akbar, *supra* note 10.

29. D. Denvir (host), "SCOTUS, Politics, and the Law," episode, *The Dig* podcast, October 9, 2020, https://thedig.blubrry.net/podcast/scotus-politics-and
-the-law.

30. R. Tuhus-Dubrow, "On the Uses and Abuses of Identity Politics," *Chron-
icle of Higher Education*, May 11, 2022, www.chronicle.com/article/on-the-uses
-and-abuses-of-identity-politics?sra=true.

31. R.W. Gilmore, "'Everybody changes in the process of building a movement'—Ruth Wilson Gilmore on Abolition Geography," episode, *Millennials
Are Killing Capitalism* podcast, August 5, 2022, at around 53 min., https://
millennialsarekillingcapitalism.libsyn.com/everybody-changes-in-the-process
-of-building-a-movement-ruth-wilson-gilmore-on-abolition-geography.

32. *Id.* at around 58 min.

33. R.W. Gilmore, *Golden Gulag: Prisons, Surplus, Crisis, and Opposition in Glo-
balizing California* (University of California Press, 2007), 247–48.

34. As Mariame Kaba cautions: "Just having an identity that is oppressed is
not the same as having an analysis of the forces that oppress us." Quoted in Micah
Herskind, "Some Reflections on Prison Abolition," *Medium* (December 7, 2019).

35. M. Grinthal, "Power With: Practice Models for Social Justice Lawyering,"
University of Pennsylvania Journal of Law and Social Change 15(1) (2011): 25, 54,
https://scholarship.law.upenn.edu/cgi/viewcontent.cgi?article=1136&context=
jlasc.

36. C. Elsesser, "Community Lawyering: The Role of Lawyers in the Social Justice Movement," *Loyola Journal of Public Interest Law* 14 (2013): 45–74, https://static1
.squarespace.com/static/57f66423440243a162891041/t/584829852e69cf
464f49bab4/1481124229659/Community+Lawyering-+Elsesser.pdf.

37. A. Rasulov, "'The Nameless Rapture of the Struggle': Towards a Marxist Class-Theoretic Approach to International Law," *Finnish Yearbook of International Law* 19 (2008): 243–94, 277, https://papers.ssrn.com/sol3/papers.cfm?abstract_id=2264220.

38. S. Hall, C. Critcher, T. Jefferson, J. Clarke, and B. Roberts, *Policing the Crisis: Mugging, the State, and Law and Order* (Palgrave Macmillan, 1978).

Contributors

Editors

AMECA REALI (she/her) is an attorney and advocate who is deeply inspired by the work of women like Ella Baker and bell hooks. She currently serves as the executive director at Louisiana Fair Housing Action Center, a civil rights organization committed to eliminating discrimination in housing across Louisiana. For four years prior, she served as the membership director at Law for Black Lives (L4BL), where she helped to mobilize thousands of attorneys in service of movement organizations across the country. Ameca received her JD from Loyola University New Orleans College of Law, and she graduated with honors with a BA in communications from SUNY Buffalo. Ameca lives in New Orleans with her daughter, partner, and dog.

MARBRÉ STAHLY-BUTTS (she/her), now an associate professor at the CUNY Law School, cofounded and directed Law for Black Lives (L4BL) for over seven years. In her role as executive director she worked closely with organizers and communities across the country to advance and actualize radical policy. She cofounded and served on the Leadership Team of the Movement for Black Lives Policy Table and was one of the chief architects of the Vision for Black Lives Policy Platform. She was also a cofounder of the National Bail Out Collective. Before her role at Law for Black Lives, Marbré worked as deputy director of racial justice at the Center for Popular Democracy (CPD). She joined CPD as a Soros Justice Fellow in Fall 2013. Before graduating from Yale Law School, Marbré received her master's in African studies from Oxford University and conducted research in Zimbabwe, where she focused on community responses to violence. She also taught in South Africa at Nelson Mandela's alma mater. Marbré graduated from Columbia University. In addition to her work to support social movements, she is busy trying to raise two young children to be joyful and purpose-filled people.

Authors

HANNAH ADAMS (she/her) is an attorney with Southeast Louisiana Legal Services in New Orleans, Louisiana. Hannah represents seniors, disabled renters, and other marginalized people facing eviction and living in substandard housing. She received her JD from Northeastern University School of Law.

AMNA A. AKBAR (she/her) is a professor of law at The Ohio State University Moritz College of Law. Amna teaches and writes about social movements, social change, policing, racism, and incarceration. She was a founding member of Law for Black Lives (L4BL) and currently serves on the advisory board.

AL BROOKS (he/him) is an organizer and attorney with Medina Orthwein LLP, an abolitionist civil rights firm in Oakland, California, where he pursues carceral state abolition and fights employment discrimination with a Black queer feminist lens. Al has worked at or interned for the Lawyers' Committee for Civil Rights, the Phillips Black Project, the Legal Defense Fund, the Bronx Defenders, the Capital Appeals Project/Promise of Justice Initiative, and the Legal Aid Society of New York. During law school he directed the NYU Law Prison Teaching Project. He is an adjunct professor of law practice at Tuskegee University. Outside of work, Al has organized with BYP100, the Black Freedom Project of New York, and Unlock the Bar.

MARÍA ELVIRA CABRERA (she/her) is a lawyer and sociologist. A human rights defender interested in sociolegal research, she is currently a researcher at the Policarpa Ambulante Justice Clinic of Temblores NGO.

ANGÉLICA CHÁZARO (she/her) writes, organizes, and teaches about immigration, abolition, and the carceral state. She is the Charles Stone Professor of Law at the University of Washington School of Law and is the author of "The End of Deportation" (*UCLA Law Review*). For seven years she worked as an attorney with the Northwest Immigrant Rights Project in Seattle, specializing in representing immigration survivors of violence. She has organized with La Resistencia to end immigrant detention in Washington State, with No New Youth Jail to stop the construction of a youth jail and court in King County, Washington, and most recently with Decriminalize Seattle and Solidarity Budget to defund the Seattle Police Department and increase investments in Black and Brown communities. Both her scholarship and advocacy focus on shrinking reliance on policing, punishment, and incarceration as a response to social problems.

GINA CLAYTON-JOHNSON (she/her) is a Black feminist organizer, writer, and the founder and executive director of Essie Justice Group, the nation's leading advocacy organization of women with incarcerated loved ones. Gina has spent over fifteen years advocating for Black communities and is the recipient of numerous fellowships and awards. She is a leader of the Movement for Black Lives Policy Table (where she served as the central architect of the BREATHE Act), a founding Advisory Council member of the National Bail Out Collective, and a leading advocate for bail reform in California. She holds a BA from the University of Southern California and a JD from Harvard Law School. Gina is an avid runner, composter, and lives in Los Angeles with her husband and two young children. She would like to acknowledge all the women and gender-nonconforming people impacted by incarceration who infused love and skill into the writing of her piece, in particular Emma Ayers and Bianca Williams-Alonzo.

ERIN MILES CLOUD (she/her) is the codirector and cofounder of Movement for Family Power and a former family defense public defender. She is a Baltimore native and the mother of two beautiful children.

TENISHA CUMMINGS (she/her) was born and raised in East Harlem, New York. Tenisha graduated from Fordham Law School in 2010 as a Stein Scholar. She is currently a supervising attorney at the Neighborhood Defender Service of Harlem and mother of an eighteen-year-old.

JUDITH BROWNE DIANIS (she/her) has served as a lawyer, professor, and civil rights advocate in the movement for racial justice. Hailed as a voting rights expert and godmother of the movement to dismantle the school-to-prison pipeline, Judith helped establish Advancement Project and Advancement Project Action Fund, where as executive director she leads movement lawyering work in combating structural racism in education, voting, policing, and criminal justice. She began her career as a Skadden Fellow at the NAACP Legal Defense and Educational Fund, eventually becoming managing attorney of the Washington, DC, office and director of the Fair Housing Program. Judith is a graduate of the

University of Pennsylvania and Columbia Law School. She often appears in the media and was one of *Essence Magazine*'s Thirty Women to Watch, a finalist of The Grio Heroes Award, and the recipient of Penn's Inaugural Alumni Social Impact Award. In addition, she was awarded a Prime Movers Fellowship for trailblazing social movement leaders.

JAMES FORMAN JR. (he/him) is the J. Skelly Wright Professor of Law at Yale Law School. He teaches criminal law and Access to Law School (A2LS), a pipeline program serving first-generation and underrepresented minority students from New Haven, Connecticut, who wish to pursue a legal career. He is the faculty director of Yale's Center for Law and Racial Justice. His book, *Locking Up Our Own: Crime and Punishment in Black America*, was awarded the Pulitzer Prize in 2018.

IMAN FREEMAN (she/her) is the Baltimore Action Legal Team's cofounder and executive director. Iman has seven years' experience as an attorney and seventeen years' experience as a management and program analyst with the federal government. Iman serves on the advisory board for Law for Black Lives (L4BL). Iman completed her undergraduate studies at Georgia Southern University, where she earned a bachelor of science (BS) in justice studies. She first entered public service after completing her master in public administration (MPA) from Rockefeller College of Public Affairs and Policy. She earned her juris doctorate (JD) from American University Washington College of Law.

RENEE CAMILLE HATCHER (she/her) is a human rights and solidarity economy lawyer. She is an assistant professor of law and the director of the Community Enterprise and Solidarity Economy Law Clinic at University of Illinois Chicago School of Law, a legal clinic that provides free legal support to grassroot organizations, community-based businesses, cooperatives, and other solidarity economy enterprises. Daughter of the late civil rights activist and first elected Black mayor of a US city, Richard Gordon Hatcher, Renee is committed to advancing the Black Freedom Movement through her work with co-ops and communities. She is a board member for the Detroit Justice Center, cofacilitator for the Black Abolitionist Solidarity Economy (BASE) Fellowship, and a member of the Law for Black Lives Movement Lawyering Squad. Renee serves as the codirector of the Solidarity Economy Research, Policy, and Law Project at the UIC Center for Urban Economic Development. Her research focuses on the solidarity economy movement and the law.

RACHEL HERZING (she/her) is an organizer and activist fighting the violence of surveillance, policing, and imprisonment. Rachel was executive director of the Center for Political Education, a resource for political organizations on the Left and progressive social movements; codirector of Critical Resistance, a national organization dedicated to abolishing the prison industrial complex; and director of research and training at Creative Interventions, a community resource that developed interventions to interpersonal harm that do not rely on policing, imprisonment, or traditional social services.

JARIBU HILL (she/her) is a civil and human rights attorney and executive director of the Mississippi Workers' Center for Human Rights (MWCHR), an organization that uses a human rights organizing framework to fight discrimination in housing, employment, and voting. In addition to founding the MWCHR, Jaribu founded several other organizations, including the Southern Human Rights Organizers Conference, Black Women's International Roundtable, CUNY Law School Mississippi Project, and the Fannie Lou Hamer Sister Roundtable. She is also a singer and composer and was lead singer with the renowned singing duo Serious Bizness for more than fifteen years.

JULIAN HILL (they/them/he/him) is an assistant professor at Georgia State University College of Law. Julian is a teacher, lifelong learner, community organizer, artist, and attorney who knows that the world we deserve, though both possible and necessary, is not inevitable. His research focuses on how lawyers can leverage corporate, local government and contract law to build a solidarity economy that prioritizes people and the planet over profits. Julian regularly advises worker cooperatives, collectives, nonprofits, and small businesses on a range of matters, including governance, leasing, and contracts. Julian is known to partner with community-based organizations to cofacilitate political education and codevelop policies and campaigns. They have facilitated workshops, both in English and Spanish, on worker cooperatives and the solidarity economy with Law for Black Lives (L4BL), the US Federation of Worker Cooperatives, Democracy at Work Institute, and the New York City Network of Worker Cooperatives, among other organizations. He has prepared and delivered testimony before both the New York State Assembly and the New York City Council on issues facing worker cooperatives and small businesses in New York.

MEENA JAGANNATH (she/they) is director of global programs at Movement Law Lab. Prior to joining the Lab, Meena codirected the Community Justice

Project, Inc., a Miami-based movement lawyering organization supporting campaigns for racial justice and human rights. She is a movement lawyer with an extensive background in activism and international human rights, including work in Haiti and Guatemala. While in Miami, Meena used her legal skills to build the power of movements locally in South Florida around workers' rights, housing, gentrification, and police brutality. She has supported delegations to the United Nations to elevate US-based human rights issues like police accountability in Ferguson, Missouri, and Stand Your Ground laws to the international level. It is this combination of local legal advocacy and an understanding of international human rights advocacy that Meena hopes to leverage as she develops the Global Network of Movement Lawyers at the Lab. Meena received her JD from the University of Washington School of Law, where she was a William H. Gates Public Service Law Scholar. She holds a master in international affairs (human rights) from the School of International and Public Affairs at Columbia University, and a bachelor in international relations and peace and justice studies from Tufts University.

BRYANNA JENKINS (she/her) is a civil rights attorney, organizer, and podcaster. She is currently the national organizing director at Lavender Rights Project. Bryanna received her BS from Morgan State University, her MA from the University of Baltimore, and her JD from DePaul University College of Law. Prior to law school, Bryanna founded and led the Baltimore Transgender Alliance and organized the city's first Baltimore Transgender Uprising March in 2015. A proud Baltimore native, Bryanna currently lives in Houston.

JOO-HYUN KANG (she/her) is a longtime organizer, trainer, and strategist. She was the director of Communities United for Police Reform (CPR) for a decade, where she worked with over two hundred local, state, and national organizations to fight abusive policing and reduce the illegitimate power, scope, and size of the largest police department in the United States. Prior to CPR, Joo-Hyun spent time as director of programs and global grantmaking at the Astraea Lesbian Foundation for Justice; was the first executive director of the Audre Lorde Project, the nation's first organizing center for trans, nonbinary, and queer communities of color; and served on numerous boards of community organizations.

DIMA KHALIDI (she/her) is the founder and director of Palestine Legal. She oversees Palestine Legal's array of legal and advocacy work to protect people speaking out for Palestinian freedom from attacks on their civil and constitutional rights. Prior to founding Palestine Legal in 2012, Dima worked with the Center for Constitutional Rights (CCR) as a cooperating attorney on the Mamilla Cemetery Campaign. She submitted a petition to United Nations officials to stop the desecration of an ancient Muslim cemetery in Jerusalem and has advocated on behalf of Palestinian descendants of individuals interred in the cemetery. As a volunteer and Ella Baker intern at CCR, she worked on CCR's Guantanamo Bay docket as well as on numerous cases that sought to hold Israeli officials and corporations accountable for Israeli violations of international law. As a law student, she interned with the People's Law Office in Chicago, assisting in the acquittal of Palestinian-American Muhammad Salah on major federal criminal charges. Dima has a JD from DePaul University College of Law, an MA in international and comparative legal studies from the University of London–SOAS, and a BA in history and Near Eastern studies from the University of Michigan.

FELIPE MESEL (he/him) is the global programs manager at Movement Law Lab. He has been working with different communities in his home country (Argentina) since he was a law student at the National University of La Plata. He has organized popular educational workshops with incarcerated law students and young victims of police repression. Prior to joining Movement Law Lab, Felipe worked in the Judiciary of the Argentine Nation, the Ombudsman's Office of the City of Buenos Aires, the National Ministry of Territorial Development and Habitat of the Nation, the National Secretariat of Social and Urban Integration, and as a human rights lawyer in the Civil Association for Equality and Justice (ACIJ), which specialized in urban and housing issues. There he worked side by side with slum-dwellers and grassroots movements. As a law professor, he taught different courses at the National University of La Plata, always trying to find non-dominant uses of law, and participated in different Latin American and international academic and activist networks.

JOEY L. MOGUL is a movement lawyer, organizer, initiator, and cofounder of Chicago Torture Justice Memorials (CTJM) and a partner at People's Law Office. Joey works with and represents organizers in their campaigns for justice and liberation. Joey has sought justice for Chicago Police torture survivors for over twenty-five years, successfully representing survivors in their criminal and civil rights litigation, and at the UN Committee Against Torture (CAT) in Geneva, Switzerland. Joey drafted the original City Council ordinance providing reparations for the Chicago Police (Burge) torture survivors. Joey has also represented several organizers and activists arrested and charged for participating in uprisings in support of Black Lives, sex workers, and those opposing the prison industrial complex, war, and militarism in criminal and civil rights cases. Joey successfully represented the No Cop Academy campaign in their FOIA litigation against the City of Chicago and the Chicago Freedom School (CFS) in securing the rescission of an illegal cease and desist order and monetary settlement. Joey is a coauthor of *Queer (In)Justice: The Criminalization of LGBT People in the U.S.* (Beacon Press, 2011).

MANDISA MOORE-O'NEAL (she/her) is a Black feminist, abolitionist, and founder of the Moore-O'Neal Law Group, LLC, a Black feminist law and policy practice. Currently she serves as the executive director of the Center for HIV Law and Policy (CHLP), a research and policy think tank and advocacy resource for people living with HIV and surrounding communities. Before joining CHLP, she was a civil rights attorney with a focus on HIV decriminalization litigation, education, and advocacy; family law litigation, education, and advocacy; employment and public accommodations discrimination litigation and education; and police accountability litigation and advocacy. Her primary organizing support work was as member of the BYP100-New Orleans chapter, SONG-New Orleans, and a founding member of the Louisiana Coalition on Criminalization and Health.

JOMARY ORTEGÓN OSORIO (she/her) is president of CAJAR (Colectivo de Abogadxs José Alvear Restrepo), a lawyer from the National University of Colombia, a specialist in constitutional law and gender studies from the National University of Colombia, a specialist in criminal law from the University Libre. She holds a master in Latin American studies from the Pontificia Universidad Javeriana, a professor of the master's degree in defense of human rights and international humanitarian law before international organizations, tribunals, and courts at the School of Law of the University Santo Tomás. A defender of human rights for twenty years, she has accompanied litigation work at the United Nations and the Inter-American Human Rights System levels on behalf of victims of serious human rights violations in the Corporación Colectivo de Abogadxs José Alvear Restrepo, including cases of Indigenous peoples, children, human rights defenders, peasants, and trade unions.

BILL QUIGLEY (he/him) is an emeritus professor of law. He served as director of the Law Clinic and the Gillis Long Poverty Law Center at Loyola University New Orleans for more than thirty years. He has been an active public interest and human rights lawyer since 1977 and has served as counsel with a wide range of public interest organizations on issues including Hurricane Katrina social justice issues, public housing, voting rights, death penalty, living wage, human rights, civil liberties, educational reform, constitutional rights, and civil disobedience. Bill has litigated numerous cases with the NAACP Legal Defense and Educational Fund, Inc., the Advancement Project, and with the ACLU of Louisiana, where he was general counsel for over fifteen years. He has been an active lawyer with School of the Americas Watch and the Institute for Justice and Democracy in Haiti. Before returning to Loyola, Bill served as legal director of the Center for Constitutional Rights (CCR) in New York City from 2009 to 2011.

TIFFANY WILLIAMS ROBERTS (she/her) is director of the Public Policy Unit at Southern Center for Human Rights. She joined the organization in April 2018 as the community engagement and movement building counsel. She has practiced criminal defense since 2008, first as a public defender with the Atlanta Judicial Circuit Public Defender and later as a solo practitioner. As a public defender, Tiffany represented hundreds of indigent clients facing felony prosecution and graduated from Gideon's Promise trial advocacy training program. She expanded her private practice to include civil rights litigation for victims of police abuse. A significant portion of Tiffany's private practice was dedicated to the pro bono representation of activists and organizers. She has been recognized by several organizations for movement lawyering and activism. A community organizer, she cofounded the police accountability organization Building Locally to Organize for Community Safety (BLOCS) in 2008 to promote a holistic approach to public safety. BLOCS successfully advocated for legislative improvements to the Atlanta Citizen Review Board along with other critical local policy changes. She is also a founding member of the Atlanta chapter of the global Black Lives Matter network.

ALEJANDRO RODRÍGUEZ PABÓN (he/him) is an anthropologist, human rights defender, and right-to-the-city defender. He has been working for three years in Temblores NGO and is currently coordinating Grita, the observatory of police violence, where Temblores investigates, coordinates, and writes human rights reports on state violence.

JEENA SHAH (she/her) is an associate professor at the CUNY School of Law. Prior to joining CUNY's faculty, Jeena was a visiting assistant clinical professor at Rutgers Law School, where she directed the International Human Rights Clinic and cotaught in the Constitutional Rights Clinic. For her work with the clinics the

Rutgers Law chapter of the National Lawyers Guild awarded her with the Arthur Kinoy Award. Before entering academia, Jeena was an attorney with the Center for Constitutional Rights (CCR). Prior to CCR, Jeena served as an international human rights attorney with community-based law offices in Port-au-Prince, Haiti, and Gujarat, India. In Haiti, with the Bureau des Avocats Internationaux, she observed the country's national elections and supported local lawyers and organizers fighting unlawful evictions of communities displaced by the 2010 earthquake and victims of the ex-dictator Duvalier's crimes against humanity. In India, with Navsarjan, Jeena supported local lawyers and organizers representing Dalit victims of hate crimes and other forms of caste-based discrimination. Jeena also practiced at Shearman & Sterling LLP, where she litigated complex commercial and civil rights matters.

PURVI SHAH (she/her) has spent her career at the intersection of law and social movements. Over the past eighteen years, Purvi has created a range of movement lawyering initiatives to politicize, organize, and deploy thousands of lawyers to work collaboratively with grassroots organizers to shift culture, systems, and power. Purvi founded Movement Law Lab in 2018 to build a new bench of legal organizations and lawyers to flank progressive/left social movements around the world. In 2015, in the aftermath of the Ferguson uprisings, Purvi cofounded Law for Black Lives (L4BL). Prior to that, Purvi was the founding director of the Bertha Justice Institute at the Center for Constitutional Rights (CCR), the first movement lawyering institute in the United States. She cofounded the Community Justice Project of Miami in 2006. While there, she represented taxi drivers, tenant unions, public housing residents, and immigrant rights groups. Before becoming a lawyer, Purvi worked as a community organizer with youth in Miami, students in India, and families of incarcerated youth in California. She has been awarded an Ashoka Fellowship, Echoing Green Fellowship, Soros Equality Fellowship, Harvard Law School Wasserstein Fellowship, Miami Foundation Fellowship, and a New Voices Fellowship. Purvi holds a BA in political science and social policy from Northwestern University and JD from the University of California–Berkeley School of Law.

OMAVI SHAKUR (he/him) is an adviser at the Little Rock Freedom Fund, a bail fund based in his hometown. He is also a lecturer and research scholar at Columbia Law School. His research interrogates state responses to resistance to law enforcement. Before entering the legal academy, Omavi represented victims of police violence and wrongful convictions in federal courts across the nation. He has also organized alongside formerly incarcerated people to expand the social safety net available to those with felony drug convictions in Arkansas. His legal career began as a public defender in New Orleans.

MONICA SIMPSON (she/her) the executive director of SisterSong Women of Color Reproductive Justice Collective, a national nonprofit headquartered in Atlanta and devoted to building the movement for Reproductive Justice (RJ), the human right to maintain personal bodily autonomy, birth if and as we wish, and parent in safety and sufficiency.

CHRISTIAN SNOW (she/her) is a longtime resident of Chicago's West Side. Christian graduated from Grinnell College with a degree in sociology and history, and obtained her JD from Northeastern University School of Law. She is currently executive director of Law for Black Lives (L4BL). Before joining L4BL, Christian worked at the Illinois Justice Project (ILJP) as a program director, where she focused on organizing policy advocates, state leaders, community-based organizations, and grassroot organizers to develop and implement a shared statewide policy agenda and strategic plan to end criminalization and incarceration and to support safe and thriving communities. In addition, Christian led the juvenile justice policy portfolio at ILJP, partnering with organizers, advocates, and stakeholders to increase community resources for young people, eliminate the use of detention centers, educate policy makers on harmful city and state policies and possible solutions, and create space for young people and their families to advocate for their own needs. Prior to ILJP, Christian worked as an associate attorney at the People's Law Office. Her work focused on assisting with civil rights cases involving police brutality and misconduct. She was first a member and then the executive director of Assata's Daughters (AD), a Chicago grassroots abolitionist organization that trains young Black people to organize in line with the Black radical tradition by providing them with a political home where they receive political education, organizing training, and revolutionary support through mutual aid.

KAYLA VINSON (she/her) is the inaugural executive director of the Law and Racial Justice Center. She coteaches Access to Law School (A2LS), a pipeline program serving people from underrepresented groups, with a focus on the greater New Haven, Connecticut, area. Before this role, she worked as an attorney in Montgomery, Alabama, where her docket included appellate and postconviction legal representation, reentry support, memory work on the legacy of racial injustice in the United States, curriculum development for middle and high schools, and research and writing about the function of white supremacy in the criminal legal system. Kayla's work investigates how the afterlife of chattel slavery mediates life, opportunity, development, and underdevelopment in the United States.

VINCE WARREN (he/him), a leading expert on racial injustice and discriminatory policing, is the executive director of the Center for Constitutional Rights (CCR) and the 2023 W. Haywood Burns Chair in Human and Civil Rights at CUNY Law School. He oversees the organization's groundbreaking litigation and advocacy work, using international and domestic law to challenge human rights abuses. Under his leadership the organization has successfully challenged the NYPD's stop-and-frisk policy and profiling of Muslims, ended long-term solitary confinement in California's Pelican Bay Prison, and established the persecution of LGBTQIA people as an international crime against humanity. The CCR is currently challenging the abuse of migrants at the US southern border, environmental injustice in the South, the torture of prisoners in Abu Ghraib, and the criminalization of transgender people, as well as providing legal and policy support to Black, Brown, and Native organizers across the country. Previously, Vince monitored South Africa's historic Truth and Reconciliation Commission hearings and was a senior staff attorney at the ACLU and a criminal defense attorney for the Legal Aid Society in Brooklyn. He is a graduate of Haverford College and Rutgers School of Law.

Organizations

THE ADVANCEMENT PROJECT is a next-generation, multiracial civil rights organization. Rooted in the great human rights struggles for equality and justice, the Advancement Project exists to fulfill America's promise of a caring, inclusive, and just democracy. We use innovative tools and strategies to strengthen social movements and achieve high-impact policy change. Advancement Project serves as critical infrastructure for the racial justice movement. Our theory of change is centered on a movement lawyering approach, community-centered racial justice lawyering, to support power building in grassroots organizations working to eliminate oppressive structures in our laws and institutions and shift narratives toward transformative change.

BALTIMORE ACTION LEGAL TEAM (BALT) is dedicated to politically conscious lawyering and to using creative, collective solutions to support the

Movement for Black Lives in Baltimore. Founded in 2015 after a community call for accountability for the police killing of Freddie Gray, BALT continues to provide legal support, advocacy, and community education for communities in Baltimore.

THE CENTER FOR CONSTITUTIONAL RIGHTS (CCR) stands with social justice movements and communities under threat—fusing litigation, advocacy, and narrative shifting to dismantle systems of oppression regardless of the risk. CCR works creatively to advance and defend the constitutional and human rights of social justice movements and communities under threat and helps them build power. CCR is committed to dismantling systems of oppression and fighting for justice.

THE COLECTIVO DE ABOGADXS JOSÉ ALVEAR RESTREPO (CAJAR) is a nongovernmental human rights organization, under the legal status of a nonprofit corporation, based in Bogotá. It was created in 1978, being one of the first human rights organizations in Colombia. Made up of legal professionals and students, supported by other areas of knowledge and the participation of different social and democratic sectors of the population at the national level, CAJAR defends and promotes human rights and the rights of people from a perspective of indivisibility and interdependence, with the aim of contributing to the construction of a just and equitable society with political, economic, social, and cultural inclusion. Its work is framed in three political lines of work: (1) fight against impunity; (2) defense of the territory and fight against the climate crisis; and (3) overcoming the armed conflict and peace building.

COMMUNITIES UNITED FOR POLICE REFORM (CPR) is an unprecedented campaign that works to end discriminatory policing in New York. CPR advances policies that protect the safety and rights of all New Yorkers to create true community safety. CPR is in the courts fighting to hold police accountable for violating New Yorkers' constitutional rights. CPR trains communities to know their rights and to observe and document police abuse. CPR engages in strategic direct action, organizing, and civic engagement to build the power of communities most impacted by abusive policing. And CPR is in Albany and at City Hall demanding law and policy changes that advance police accountability to improve safety for communities.

ESSIE JUSTICE GROUP was founded by executive director Gina Clayton-Johnson in 2014 in Oakland, California, to harness the collective power of women with incarcerated loved ones to end mass incarceration's harm to women and communities. Essie's members are the one-in-four women and the one-in-two Black women who have an incarcerated family member—mothers, daughters, grandmothers, siblings, and partners of people behind bars. Essie's signature Healing to Advocacy model has organized more than forty-eight cohorts of women spanning twenty-seven states—who are enduring a loved one's incarceration alone—together to heal, build collective power, and drive social change. Black-led and Black-centered, Essie Justice Group will ultimately organize hundreds of thousands of women from isolation and into a unified, loving, and powerful community to dismantle mass incarceration's harm and establish a bold new constituency for lasting abolitionist outcomes.

THE GLOBAL NETWORK OF MOVEMENT LAWYERS (GNML), stewarded by the Movement Law Lab, is rooted in the belief that movements confronting the present confluence of global crises need global legal strategies to accompany them. The GNML grew out of a convening held in Morocco in 2019, where lawyers and activists from over twenty-five countries came together across more than five languages to strategize about how we might work together transnationally to confront the crises unfolding before us.

THE LAVENDER RIGHTS PROJECT (LRP) elevates the power, autonomy, and leadership of the Black intersex and gender-diverse community through intersectional legal and social services. LRP utilizes the law as an organizing principle to affirm our civil rights and self-determination. LRP disrupts oppressive systems that target Black gender-diverse and intersex communities of color and lead to disproportionate levels of poverty, housing disparities, and gender-based violence, especially among Black and Indigenous people.

LAW FOR BLACK LIVES (L4BL) is a Black-led, queer, abolition-minded, multiracial, feminist, and anticapitalist movement. Made up of a network of nearly six thousand radical lawyers and legal advocates, we are building a legal network that supports Black organizing and Black movements for liberation through community action.

MOVEMENT FOR FAMILY POWER (MFP) is an abolitionist movement hub and incubator, cultivating and harnessing community power to end family policing and build a world where all families can thrive. MFP resources and supports grassroots organizers and lived experts on the frontlines of dismantling the family policing system through a three-pronged approach: connection, capacity, and care.

MOVEMENT LAW LAB brings the power of lawyers to social justice movements. It seeks to transform the legal sector, training lawyers and legal organizations to go beyond winning cases to building collective power. It builds legal infrastructure for grassroots-led progressive movements and reimagines law, cultivating new ways to democratize, decolonize, and deploy law. Together with people's movements, Movement Law Lab organizes lawyers into a force for human dignity, multiracial democracy, and ecological harmony.

PALESTINE LEGAL works to bolster the Palestine solidarity movement by challenging efforts to threaten, harass, and legally bully activists into silence and inaction. The organization provides legal advice, Know Your Rights trainings, advocacy and litigation support to college students, grassroots activists, and affected communities who stand for justice in Palestine. Palestine Legal monitors incidents of suppression to expose trends in tactics to silence Palestine activism.

For over fifty years the PEOPLE'S LAW OFFICE (PLO) in Chicago has successfully fought for the civil rights of torture survivors and survivors of police violence, wrongful convictions, and other government abuses. The office has been devoted to defending activists and organizers who have been targeted as a result of their political beliefs or organizing efforts on behalf of movements struggling for justice and liberation, including members of the Black Panther Party, the Puerto Rican independistas, ACT UP, Palestinian freedom fighters, antiwar/military/police/prison protestors, and sex workers, among others. Using lawsuits the People's Law Office has helped uncover secret abuses by police and government officials—including an FBI program to destroy the Black Panther Party (COINTELPRO) and a torture ring inside the Chicago Police Department.

SISTERSONG is a Southern-based, national membership organization; our purpose is to build an effective network of individuals and organizations to improve institutional policies and systems that impact the reproductive lives of marginalized communities. SisterSong Women of Color Reproductive Justice Collective was formed in 1997 by sixteen organizations of women of color from four mini-communities (Native American, African American, Latina, and Asian American) who recognized that we have the right and responsibility to represent ourselves and our communities, and the equally compelling need to advance the perspectives and needs of women of color.

THE SOUTHERN CENTER FOR HUMAN RIGHTS (SCHR) works for equality, dignity, and justice for people impacted by the criminal legal system in the Deep South. SCHR fights for a world free from mass incarceration, the death penalty, the criminalization of poverty, and racial injustice.

TEMBLORES NGO has actively worked to incite and mobilize community processes of transformation and social change that destabilize the hegemonic structures that have historically guaranteed practices of exclusion, denial of rights, discrimination, and violence. In their commitment to social justice they seek to promote an effective dialogue between the academic community, public opinion, state agents, and community actors, from which it is possible to make visible, denounce, and confront the forms of violence that have harmed historically marginalized citizens. They believe in a social movement that shakes the tectonic plates, that makes them tremble, that generates small local revolutions, and that allows us to build firm pillars to fight against violence, inequality, and social injustice.

Index

Page numbers followed by *n* or *nn* denote notes.

community: building, 64, 147, 167, 179; community-level infrastructure, 146–48; community-responsive legal practice, 91–96; education, 90, 93–94; engagement, 148–49; experiments, 213–14; guidance and support, 164; power, 149; power building, 64–65, 68, 133–34, 146–48; remedies, 147–48; support, 115, 167

Community Enterprise & Solidarity Economy Clinic (CESEC), 217–18

Community Justice Project, 14

community organizers/organizing: groups, 146; levels of urgency for, 199; by public defenders, 165–69; underresourcing of, 148. *See also* grassroots organizing/organizations

Community Safety Act, 143, 144, 146, 155n20

connections building, 54, 97, 100, 104, 117, 165, 191–92

Connerly, Ward, 132

contract law, 49

CopWatch alliance, 155n20

Corbitt v. Taylor, 136, 137

COVID-19 pandemic: movement lawyering during, 139–40; and state repression, 119

Crenshaw, Kimberlé, 42, 53

criminal defense attorneys, 165, 167

criminal legal system reform, 52, 194

criminal liability, 117

criminal representation and movement lawyers, 99

Critical Resistance, 36, 208–9

cultural intervention, 152

cultural signifiers, 206

culture shift, 152

Cummings, Tenisha, 158–65

Daniels v. City of NY, 155n21

Davis, Angela, 36, 38, 43, 179

Davis, Damon, 126

Davis, James, III, 216

decision-making, 46, 51, 71, 149, 185, 229, 231–32

Defender la Libertad campaign, 122–23

"Defund" demands, 194

Department of Education, 114

Department of Housing and Urban Development, 134

dependency creation and movement lawyering, 69

DeSantis, Ron, 118

Detroit Justice Center, 14

Diallo, Amadou, 155n21

Dianis, Judith Browne, 130, 131–34

discrimination in public transit, resistance against, 15–17

district attorney, 78–79

Dobbs v. Jackson Women's Health Organization, 152

doctrinal courses, 228–29, 230

documentation, 90, 98, 99, 102, 103, 122–23, 124

Donham, Carolyn Bryant, 77

double consciousness, 215–16

Douglass, Frederick, 15

drafting, 103, 136–37, 189, 218

Du Bois, W. E. B., 215–16

Duque, Iván, 121

educational inequity, 221

Educational Opportunities Project (EOP), 135

Eleventh Circuit Court of Appeals, 136

Emanuel, Rahm, 186, 187

Emergency Calls to Action, 103

emergency-related legal services, 103

Emmer, Pascal, 139

Movement Lawyering Squad, 218
movement lawyers, 1–4; in Colombia,
120–24; during COVID-19
pandemic, 138–39; in FLDC,
141–42; lessons from Ferguson case
study, 96–105; organizing lessons
from *Floyd* litigation, 144–53; and
theory of change, 12–15, 24
movement organizers/organizing:
building relationships, 202–3;
building trust and navigating
accountability, 199–201; during
COVID-19 pandemic, 138–39;
during Ferguson uprisings, 141–42;
with legal advocacy, 137–38; levels
of urgency for, 199; and policy
advocates, 191–203. *See also*
grassroots organizing/organiza-
tions; organizing
Muigwithania, 214
"multiple jeopardy," 42
murals, 155n20

NAACP, 16, 20–22; Legal Defense
Fund, 132
National Bail Out Collective, 54
national bail outs (NBOs), 54–55
National Black Political Convention,
214–15
National Conference for Black
Lawyers, 13–14
*National Congress for Puerto Rican
Rights et al. v. City of NY*, 155n21
National Lawyers Guild, 13, 125
National Voter Registration Act of
1993, 153n1
nature and capitalization, 46–47
New Afrikan Freedom, 76
No Good Prosecutors (zine), 83–84
#NoDAPL Standing Rock encamp-
ment, 14

nonprofit industrial complex, 64–65
nonreformist reforms, 75
NYC Police Foundation, 156n22
NYPD, 143–46, 155n21, 156n22

official apologies, 186
Organization for Black Struggle
(OBS), 101
organizing: to build community
power, 133–34; campaigns, 145–46;
and legal education, 225–26; and
movement lawyering, 67–68; to
secure right to return, 133–34;
spaces, value in, 200–201. *See also*
movement organizers/organizing
Osorio, Jomary Ortegón, 118–24

Palestine activism and universities,
110
Palestine Legal: countering Zionist
narrative, 114–15; cross-movement
collaboration, 116–18; defying
intentional sabotage efforts, 115–16;
forging and aligning allies, 112–14;
inception, 109–11; infrastructure
building, 111–12; narrative in the
media, 114–15; strengthening
cross-movement collaboration,
116–18
Palestine solidarity movement,
movement lawyering during:
challenges and lessons in navigating crises of repression, 109–19;
defensive legal work in crisis,
106–7; historical context as legal
strategy, 108–9; narrative warfare
and legal defense, 107–9; racist
gaslighting as systematic repression, 106–7
Palestinian refugee population, 108
Pan African Congress, 18

Parks, Rosa, 15–17
Paro Nacional (National Strike), 120–21, 123
participatory budgeting process, 226
patriarchy and capitalism, 47
Peace Accord (Columbia), 120
people power, 14, 71, 142, 200; building, 148–49; and women with incarcerated loved ones, 180–81
People's Law Office, 14, 185
People's Movement Assembly, 51
Perez, Richie, 155n21
Petro, Gustavo, 123–24
Plataforma Grita, 122
Plessy v. Ferguson, 20
police brutality, 123, 193; Coalition Against Police Brutality (CAPB), 155n21
policing, institution of, 52
policy advocacy, 168, 207–8; in support of transformative social change, 190–203
policy advocates: approaches and analyses for identifying possible policy solutions, 197–98; building trust and navigating accountability, 199–201; levels of urgency for, 199; and movement organizers, 191–203; prison industrial complex abolitionist policy, crafting, 207; root cause analysis by, 196–97
political advocacy, 123
political beliefs, 31–34, 56–57
political education, 13, 17, 32, 34, 44, 193–94, 195–96; and movement lawyering pedagogy, 227–33; of movement lawyers, 67
political persecution of activists, 117
political will, 22, 195, 197, 198
Portales de la Resistencia (Portals of the Resistance), 121

power: collective, 12, 24–25, 157; defined, 231; power broker lawyer, 79–80
power building, 6, 22, 24–25; movement lawyering and community, 64–65, 67–68, 75, 131–34; sustainable, 144–49
praxis case studies: *Floyd* litigation, 142–53; global interconnectedness of liberation struggles, 118–25; prison industrial complex abolitionist policy, crafting, 204–9; understanding law and power, 227–33
prison industrial complex, 195; abolition, 34, 36–38, 51; abolitionist policy, crafting, 204–9
"progressive" prosecutor phenomenon, 78, 83
Project NIA, 36, 186
Prop 209 (California), 132
protester hotline, 102
public defenders: abolitionist, 158–65; advocacy by, 163, 164; Black, 167–68; organizing by, 165–69; negative associations with, 174n1
public memorials, 186
public support, 37, 146
Puerto Resistencia (Resistance Port), 121
Puerto Rican Rights, 155n21
Purnell, Derecka, 36

Quigley, Bill, 63, 67, 83, 133, 233

racial hierarchy, 31, 215; and capitalism, 46, 47
racial justice, 4, 13, 14, 103, 152, 172, 218
racially biased risk assessment tools, 183

Founded in 1893,
UNIVERSITY OF CALIFORNIA PRESS
publishes bold, progressive books and journals
on topics in the arts, humanities, social sciences,
and natural sciences—with a focus on social
justice issues—that inspire thought and action
among readers worldwide.

The UC PRESS FOUNDATION
raises funds to uphold the press's vital role
as an independent, nonprofit publisher, and
receives philanthropic support from a wide
range of individuals and institutions—and from
committed readers like you. To learn more, visit
ucpress.edu/supportus.

www.ingramcontent.com/pod-product-compliance
Lightning Source LLC
La Vergne TN
LVHW090231210126
830275LV00005B/32